D0853307

THE DEATH ZONE

THE DEATH ZONE

Climbing Everest through the Killer Storm

Matt Dickinson

HUTCHINSON
LONDON

1 3 5 7 9 10 8 6 4 2

This edition first published in 1997 by Hutchinson

Random House (UK) Limited
20 Vauxhall Bridge Road, London SW1V 2SA

Random House Australia (Pty) Limited
20 Alfred Street, Milsons Point, Sydney,
New South Wales 2061, Australia

Random House New Zealand Limited
18 Poland Road, Glenfield, Auckland 10, New Zealand

Random House South Africa (Pty) Limited
Endulini, 5A Jubilee Road, Parktown 2193, South Africa

A CIP record for this book is available from the British Library

Grateful acknowledgement is made to the following for permission to print
previously published material: Stephen Venables and Hodder and Stoughton
for *Everest: Kanshung Face*; Chris Bonington and Hodder and Stoughton for
Everest the Hard Way; Peter Habeler and Sphere Books for *Everest: Impossible Victory*;
and Jon Krakauer and Macmillan for *Into Thin Air*. Further material by Richard
Cowper is courtesy of the *Financial Times*.

Papers used by Random House UK Limited are natural,
recyclable products made from wood grown in sustainable forests.
The manufacturing processes conform to the environmental
regulations of the country of origin.

ISBN 0 09 180239 3

Phototypeset in Plantin by Intype London Limited

Printed and bound in Great Britain
by Mackays of Chatham PLC

For Fiona

Illustrations

*(Unless otherwise attributed, all the photographs are © Matt Dickinson/
ITN Productions)*

Colour

Black-and-White

Maps

Acknowledgements

Firstly I wish to record my eternal thanks to my wife Fiona, and to my children Thomas, Alistair and Gregory. Their love and support was with me for every inch of the way, as was that of my parents Sheila and David.

Also I would like to thank the following people for their enthusiastic assistance both during the expedition and in the writing of the book: to Nicola Thompson for finding me a publisher; to Himalayan Kingdoms for running a faultless expedition in extremely difficult conditions; to Simon Lowe, Sundeep Dhillon and Roger Portch for making themselves and their expedition diaries available; to Kees 't Hooft and Alan Hinkes for their unstinting filming efforts on the mountain itself; to Julian Ware at ITN and Charles Furneaux at Channel 4 for believing that I could bring back the film they wanted; and to Brian Blessed, whose dream got this whole expedition rolling.

Throughout the expedition our Sherpa team, under the leadership of Nga Temba, took on the back-breaking work of setting up camps, and in particular I wish to thank Lhakpa, Mingma and Gyaltsen for their incredible efforts on summit day.

During the research for the book I have been grateful for assistance from, amongst others, Audrey Salkeld, from Rob Hall's base camp doctor Caroline Mackenzie and from IMAX Expeditions Leader David Breashears, and from Crag Jones.

My editor Tony Whittome has been – from start to finish – a constant source of encouragement, and in addition Chris Bradley and Nicholas Crane gave me valuable editorial comments just when most needed.

Finally I wish to thank Anna Gumà Martinez, without whose inspiration no mountain would have been climbed.

Introduction

Just before 4 p.m. on 10 May 1996, Audrey Salkeld, an Everest historian and researcher, was typing one of her two daily Internet reports into an Apple Mac notebook in a tent at Everest base camp when the bitter chill of the afternoon set in. Salkeld was on her second Everest expedition, hired by the American IMAX filming expedition to generate newsletters and keep the world informed of their progress.

At 5,360 metres, base camp is a cheerless place at the best of times, but once the sun has dipped beneath the surrounding ridges, it is like living in a freezer. Shivering with the cold, Salkeld left the mess tent and walked across the ice moraine of the Khumbu glacier towards her tent to find some extra clothing.

Glancing into the sky to the south, she became one of the first people, and probably *the* very first, to see what was sweeping up from the lower valleys of the Himalayas towards Everest. It was a sight which fixed her to the spot, all thoughts of seeking out a few more layers of clothing momentarily forgotten.

Sudden squalls are common in the afternoon on Everest but Salkeld had never seen anything like this before. She describes it as looking like a 'tyre dump fire, great billowing lilac clouds racing up from the south'. She called out other members of the team from their tents, and they stood watching in awe as the apocalyptic vision crept silently and swiftly towards them.

At speeds touching 80 to 100 kilometres an hour, the storm whipped into the camp just minutes later, plunging the temperature down by ten or fifteen degrees in as many seconds, ripping into the tents in a blinding fury of driving snow. The storm swept up the southern flanks of Everest engulfing the ice-clad slopes effort-lessly in a swirling mantle of hurricane-force winds. Within minutes it had the northern side in its grip, and then it rose to take the summit. The mightiest mountain in the world disappeared from view as the storm took control.

If Shiva – the Hindu god of destruction – and Nemesis – the Greek goddess of retribution – had joined forces they could not have done a better job of devastation than nature itself did that day. The timing was uncanny, as bad as it was possible to be. If the storm had struck in winter then no one would have been hurt. But as chance would have it, the tempest arrived on the busiest day of the Everest calendar, right in the middle of the pre-monsoon climbing season.

Our expedition, a British attempt on the North Face via the North-East Ridge, was at camp three (6,450 metres), poised on the edge of our own summit attempt when the storm thundered in.

We immediately knew that this was something far more dangerous that any other storm that had hit us in the eight weeks we had been there. The temperature fell to ten degrees below freezing, then twenty, then thirty degrees below. The wind became a constant, bullying force, pulling guy ropes from the glacier ice, tumbling fully-laden equipment barrels into crevasses and demolishing our canvas mess tent with frightening ease. The dome tents, built to withstand hurricane-force winds, creaked and groaned under the beating, distorted into shapes they were never designed for and straining the Kevlar poles to their limits.

In an attempt to record the event on film, we staggered out into the maelstrom, dressed in every piece of down clothing we could get our hands on.

We could have been in the Antarctic, on the Greenland ice cap, or at the North Pole, so complete was the blanket of driving snow which obscured every feature around us. Not a single landmark, not even the huge North Ridge, was visible through the raging white-out of the blizzard, and the nearby tents of the Indian expedition were likewise invisible.

Through the white wall of snow, and rising above the tempestuous roar of the wind across the glacier, was another sound: a sinister howl which told of even greater powers at play in the altitudes above us; the scream of the storm as it whirled across the North Face at 8,000 metres and above.

There, in the 'Death Zone', more than thirty climbers were fighting for their lives. On the northern side three Indian climbers were stranded, exhausted and with their oxygen supplies running out, high on the North-East Ridge. On the southern side, two commercial expeditions were strung out between the South Col and the summit – the Mountain Madness team led by Scott Fischer, and the Adventure Consultants team of Rob Hall.

The night that faced them was a night from hell. By the end of the following day, the three Indian climbers on the north side and five of the climbers on the south, were dead. The toll included, incredibly, Hall and Fischer. The total of eight fatalities made this the single greatest loss of life in any twenty-four hour period on the peak.

But that was not the end of the drama.

The storm was the blackest of many black days in a season of terror, in which one disaster followed another. There had been two other deaths prior to the storm. There were two more deaths to come. It changed the fortunes of every team on the mountain, including our own, and it ignited a flurry of sensational debate around the world as newspapers and television programmes tried to make sense out of what had gone wrong.

The storm left a mountain of questions in its wake. How could world-class mountaineers like Rob Hall and Scott Fischer lose their lives on a mountain they knew so intimately? Why were so many inexperienced climbers high on the mountain when the storm hit? Why did a team of Japanese climbers and their Sherpas pass the dying Indian climbers and yet fail to try and rescue them?

The storm lasted less than twenty hours but for those of us who decided to carry on and try to rebuild our shattered hopes of a summit bid, it never really stopped. The fatalities it caused, the doubts it raised, the powers of nature it demonstrated, were with us for every step we took. It altered the physical process of climbing the mountain, and turned our plans upside-down, but most of all it played havoc in our minds, preying on the insecurities we all shared in that most dangerous of places, and ultimately stopping in their tracks all but two members of our expedition.

For me, a total novice at this deadly game of high-altitude Russian roulette, these questions were at that moment in time as unfathomable as they were to anyone who had never stepped into the Death Zone – that beckoning, and terrifying world where there is just one third of the oxygen that exists at sea level.

I was on Everest to make a film, not to climb it. I had employed other, far more qualified people, to do that job for me. I had never climbed Ben Nevis or Snowdon, never stood on the summit of a single Alpine peak, yet, as the events of the season unfurled, my

desire to experience the Death Zone for myself became impossible
to resist.

It was an obsession which took me to the very edge of self-
destruction. But it also took me to the summit of Everest.

I

Feeling more dead than alive, I staggered the final few steps into advance base camp just as darkness swept across the Tibetan plateau and chased the last glimmer of light out of the Himalayas. It was 6.35 p.m. on 20 May 1996.

I stood alone, swaying unsteadily on my feet, trying to work out what I should do next. For a few moments I was dimly aware of the snow-covered tents around me. There was a shout from the darkness. A glowing headtorch bobbing up and down as a shadowy figure emerged from somewhere and picked a way towards me across the rocks of the glacier.

Then, with all the suddenness of a power cut, both my knees collapsed. I found myself lying on my back, staring at a sky full of stars, with a jumbo jet pilot called Roger kissing me on both cheeks and calling me a bastard. We held each other in a bear-hug for what seemed like an age as Roger's words of congratulation worked their way through the fog that shrouded my brain.

For the first time in many weeks, a half-forgotten sensation overwhelmed me to the edge of tears. The feeling of being safe. It was over. The summit of Everest was behind me.

I opened my mouth to reply to Roger but all that came out was a gabble of unintelligible words. Confused by a mixture of euphoria and shock, and scrambled by the effect that extreme altitude and dehydration had wrought on my brain, I was unable to string two words together.

It didn't even occur to me to wonder where my fellow climber Al Hinkes had disappeared, even though we had descended from the North Col together. As far as I was concerned, he had simply vanished. (In fact, as Roger later told me, he had gone to his tent to sort himself out before searching for food and drink.)

Roger pulled me to my feet, helped me out of my rucksack and unstrapped my climbing harness. Then he supported me into the unbelievable warmth of the mess tent where our Sherpa team was sitting around two steaming pots of food in a haze of kerosene fumes and cigarette smoke. Excited faces crowded round in a babble of conversation. I was guided on to a seat while Dhorze the cook prepared some sugared tea.

My three layers of gloves were pulled off by eager hands, revealing the frozen fingers within. There was a whistle as the right hand emerged to reveal the two frostbitten middle fingers. The ends of each were consumed by a growing gooseberry-sized blister of fluid, the skin marbled and cheese-like in texture.

Kippa Sherpa mimed the motion of a saw, cutting across the fingers. 'Like this!' he laughed.

'No. No.' Ang Chuldin, long experienced in judging the severity of frostbite, turned my hand in his and spoke reassuringly; 'First degree. But fingers probably survive OK. No cut!'

As I sipped the drink, the sweetness of the tea mingling with the bitter taste of blood oozing from the blisters on my lips, I felt the tent begin to spin. As the kerosene fumes seemed to engulf me, the familiar rise of nausea in my throat warned me I was about to vomit. I managed to stagger into the cleaner air of our own mess tent where I put my head between my knees and tried to ward off the fainting fit which threatened to black me out.

The cool air and the tea revived me, and it suddenly struck me as strange that Roger was here alone.

'Where is everyone?'

'They've gone down to base camp.'

'Oh.'

Roger's generosity in staying was now all the more apparent. Advance base was no place to linger and he had waited here for several days even though the rest of the team had evacuated down to the warmer and more hospitable climes of the Rongbuk valley base sixteen kilometres away. His gesture moved me greatly.

'Thanks for being here.'

'Well, I thought there had to be someone to welcome you back to the land of the living.'

I finished the tea and walked like a drunk back outside with Roger to the tents. I knew one of them was mine but in my fuddled state I couldn't remember which. Roger pointed out the correct one and I unzipped it and climbed in as he pulled the foam sleeping mat and sleeping bag from my rucksack. He pointed to my feet.

'You can't go to sleep with your boots on.'

He unlaced them and pulled them off. I could feel the frozen fabric of the inner socks ripping against the dried blood where blisters had eroded the skin. This was a moment I had been dreading. I hadn't looked at my feet since the day before our summit bid and they were feeling very odd . . . swollen and numb, just like my fingers.

Roger went to fetch more fluid for me while I plucked up the courage to shine the torch on to my toes.

They were encrusted with blood. At first I was horrified, then, looking closely, I realised the damage was superficial, the blood was from the constant chafing of the plastic boots, and the swelling was from the impact of striking my feet into the ice. There were two small areas of frostnip but nothing more. In my nightmares I had imagined the toes would already be going black and gangrenous.

Roger was back. He took a look at my feet.

'Looks like you've got away with it.'

'Yeah. Looks like I have.'

Roger gave me a big smile, 'I'll see you in the morning.' He zipped up the tent and I heard his footsteps move away.

Lacking the energy to pull off the down suit, I shoved my feet into the sleeping bag and wrapped the top end of the bag around my upper body. Then I sucked down a full litre of tea, revelling in the warming sensation as the hot fluid ran through my body.

I was desperate for sleep, but my mind had now woken from its frozen state and was scrabbling to catch up with events. Much of what I had seen and experienced had been lived through the distorting haze of altitude, and now my memory banks were trying to make some sense out of a mental filing system in total disarray. The events were there all right, in crystal definition, but their order had been shuffled, and in the case of certain nightmare images, put into a state of suspended animation from where they could not easily be retrieved.

They would flood back soon enough but for now they were under lock and key.

My overriding emotion was one of intense relief at ending the ordeal. Pathetically grateful to have got off the mountain alive, one fact played through my mind stronger than any other: that I was one of the lucky ones.

Together with Al Hinkes and the team of three climbing Sherpas, we had all survived the Death Zone and returned intact from the summit of Everest. Now I found myself running a mental check on the state of my body, ticking off the damage.

I estimated I had lost eleven kilogrammes of body weight. My legs were now so completely stripped of fat that I could easily encircle my thigh with my two hands. I had first degree frostbite on two fingers and a range of superficial injuries which are common at extreme altitude; radiation burns to the ears and lips, and pus-infected fissures on fingers and toes. Both eyes had retinal haemorrhages where blood capillaries had burst during the ascent. My kidneys were throbbing with the dull ache of days of fluid deprivation. My bowels were chucking out alarming quantities of blood every time I plucked up the courage to defecate.

The persistent racking cough, the torn muscles around my ribcage and the raging sore throat had been with me for so many weeks now that I scarcely noticed them.

But that list of minor ailments was nothing. The mountain had let me off extremely lightly and I knew it. In physical terms, the cost of my Everest summit had been negligible. If Ang Chulden was right about my fingers, then I wouldn't lose anything. In a couple of months I would be healed and no sign would remain – on my body at least – that I had ever been here at all.

For twelve other climbers in this pre-monsoon season, the attempt to climb to the summit of Everest had proved fatal. The bodies of ten of them still lay on the high slopes of the mountain. Only two of the corpses had been retrieved. The shock waves of this disaster were still reverberating around the world. The cost in human suffering, for the families, friends and loved ones of those who died, is incalculable.

Others had escaped from the Death Zone with their lives, but the price of their survival had been painfully high. One American climber and one Taiwanese had each suffered major amputations due to frostbite, losing an arm, fingers and toes, and suffering facial disfigurement.

In short, this had been a disastrous season on Everest and one which had caught the attention of the world's media in a way which hadn't happened since the blaze of publicity which heralded the first ascent in 1953.

Before I lapsed into unconsciousness, my hand moved up instinctively to check the small rectangular container which lay against my skin in the breast pocket of my thermal suit: the tiny digital video tape which contained footage from the summit of the world. My hand was still in the same position, cradling the precious roll of rushes, when I awoke fifteen hours later.

For the next forty-eight hours I lay on my back in the tent, neither moving nor speaking. Occasionally the Sherpas, Al or Roger would check that I was OK and bring in some tea or food but basically I just lay there, staring at the canvas interior of the tent.

My mind was in shock, replaying slowly through the events of the last ten days since the storm swept in. Thinking of the place we had been. Thinking of the Death Zone.

The term 'Death Zone' was first coined in 1952 by Edouard Wyss-Dunant, a Swiss physician, in a book called *The Mountain World*. Drawing on the experiences of the Swiss Everest expedition of that year (which had so nearly made the summit) he described with remarkable accuracy the effects of altitude on the human body.

Wyss-Dunant created a series of zones to help his readers understand. At the 6,000 metres zone, Wyss-Dunant concluded, it was still possible for the human body to acclimatise in the short term. At the 7,000 metres zone no acclimatisation was possible.

To the zone above 7,500 metres, he gave a special name. He called it, in German, *Todeszone*, or 'Death Zone'. Above that altitude, not only could human life not be sustained, it deteriorated with terrifying rapidity. Even using supplementary oxygen, no one can remain in the Death Zone for long.

The term he invented is a uniquely chilling one, and one which summed up the sheer horror of a place in which every breath signalled a deterioration in the human body, where the cells of vital organs are eliminated in their millions each hour and where no living creature belongs.

Like the 'Killing Fields', the 'Death Zone', in two simple words, carries with it a sense of unspeakable horror. It conjures up pictures of a place which might only have been imagined in the mind of a writer such as Tolkien; a place of quest in the medieval sense . . . a battle zone where warriors and dreamers come to fight the darkest forces of nature, and from which some men emerge so shaken by what they have experienced that they never find the strength to speak of it again.

The Death Zone is a place where the mind wanders into strange and dark corners, where insanity and illusions are ever present traps, and where the corpses, of far stronger warriors than you will ever be, lie in the screaming wind with their skulls gaping from the ripped remains of their battledress. Ghosts are there in plenty, and their warning cries echo through the night.

Death Zone visas are issued by the gods of the wind. They last just a few days at most, and expire without warning. Get caught on the wrong side of the border when the barrier comes down and you will never return.

On 10 May 1996, the barrier came down on Everest.

*

There were two very different types of expedition high on the peak making their summit attempts that day. The traditional style of national expedition which raises its funds through sponsorship, and the new-style commercial expeditions which raise their funds through paying clients.

In the case of the first, members are normally selected on merit, do not pay for the privilege of joining, and are responsible for their own safety on the mountain. In the case of the second, whilst clients have to prove they have *some* climbing experience, their primary qualification for acceptance on an Everest expedition is the ability to pay. High-altitude specialist guides are employed by the companies to assure the safety of their clients. Our own expedition was a commercial one such as this.

The two traditional-style expeditions involved in the events of the 10th were the Indian team on the northern side – organised and staffed by members of the Indo-Tibetan border police led by Mohindor Singh – and the Taiwanese national team on the south, led by 'Makalu' Gau.

The two commercial expeditions with paying clients were the Adventure Consultants team led by Rob Hall, and the Mountain Madness team led by Scott Fischer.

Compared to the Indian and Taiwanese teams, the commercial expeditions had managed to get much larger numbers of people, and correspondingly large amounts of vital oxygen equipment, into position for the summit bid on that day. The Indian team was six, with no Sherpas. The Taiwanese team was reduced to just the leader, Makalu Gau, and two Sherpas.

The Adventure Consultants group that set out at about midnight from the South Col included no fewer than fifteen people, three guides, eight clients and four Sherpas. The Mountain Madness team also had fifteen people on the South-East Ridge, of which six were clients.

For Rob Hall, leader of the Adventure Consultants team, the midnight departure from the South Col for the summit was business as usual. Hall, more than anyone, had been at the vanguard of commercial guiding on Everest since it began and, as he led his team up through the night, he would have been confident of success. He had reason to be: he had personally summitted Everest four times, and had led a total of thirty-nine clients to the top of the world in the previous five years.

As a high-altitude guide with responsibility for the lives of his clients, Hall's credentials were impeccable. On a personal level he was an inspirational leader as his 1996 base camp doctor Caroline Mackenzie recalls:

Rob was a very enthusiastic person with an open mind. He was very encouraging to everybody, very forward-thinking, a stimulating person to be around. He was always thinking of the morale of his group, and taking note of individuals' morale.

Rob Hall began his Himalayan climbing career at the age of nineteen when he climbed Ama Dablam, 6,828 metres, in Nepal, via its difficult North Ridge. Three summer seasons in Antarctica followed as a guide and rescue team leader for the American and New Zealand Antarctic programmes and he then moved on to a series of high-altitude expeditions including Denali, Annapurna, K2, Everest, Lhotse and the Vinson Massif. During 1990 he climbed the 'seven summits' – the highest points on each continent – in a record-breaking seven months.

Having established his credentials as New Zealand's most experienced expedition leader, and with an excellent track record at extreme altitude, Rob Hall set up Adventure Consultants with fellow Kiwi Gary Ball, a qualified UIAGM guide, who had shared many of Rob Hall's more ambitious ascents.

Based out of Christchurch on New Zealand's South Island, the duo specialised in challenging and expensive guided climbing expeditions. They were one of the first companies to feature Everest in their brochure. With their considerable charm, and a talent for generating publicity, the two climbers quickly established a growing list of clients keen to 'bag' the highest summit even if it did cost them $40,000 – ex-Kathmandu.

On 12 May 1992, 'Hall and Ball' pulled off an amazing coup. In near-perfect weather conditions they placed an astonishing fourteen climbers (six were clients) on the summit of Everest and got them down safely again. It was an outstanding achievement which, more than any other event, confirmed that Everest had entered a new era: this summit, like the peaks of the Alps and the volcanoes of South America, was now for sale.

By the 1993 season, Adventure Consultants was a company with a multi-million-dollar turnover and a calendar which hardly gave the two partners time to draw breath; in March they were offering Everest, in September Mera Peak. November was Carstensz pyramid in New Guinea, December the Vinson Massif in Antarctica. Hall and Ball had not only tapped into a new vogue for 'super-adventure', they had virtually created it themselves. Now they were reaping the rewards as they shuttled backwards and forwards across the globe from one adventure to the next, shepherding their high-paying clients, many of whom had built up a fierce loyalty to their charismatic guides.

But no matter how glamorous their other climbing destinations, Everest was the jewel in the Adventure Consultants' crown. That was what justified the huge amount of time and organisation it required, and that was what justified the risk. Putting clients on the summit of Everest was the very lifeblood of the company. So long as they got down again in one piece.

Yet whilst Hall and Ball had the golden touch, and the lion's share of the publicity, they did not have an exclusive on the ultimate summit. Other companies, equally ambitious, equally keen to win a slice of the Everest pie, were now competing for permits . . . and punters.

The British company Himalayan Kingdoms entered the fray in 1993 under the command of Steve Bell, a climber and ex-army officer who had made notable winter ascents of the North Faces of the Eiger and Matterhorn. Bell had trodden Everest's slopes twice before on army expeditions in 1988 and 1992 (but although he had reached 8,400 metres he had not previously summitted). Their asking price for the expedition was £21,000 per head, and as a benchmark of qualification they were unwilling to consider anyone who had not previously been to 23,000 feet. During selection Bell turned down an application from journalist Rebecca Stephens, considering her 'too inexperienced', but he did agree to take the fifty-six-year-old actor Brian Blessed, now on his second attempt. Brian's celebrity status in Britain considerably boosted the amount of publicity the expedition could generate but many doubted he was a serious candidate for the summit.

Steve Bell rose to the logistical challenge of Everest with military thoroughness. Although he didn't have the sheer charisma of Hall and Ball, his leadership was every bit as impressive. He led seven paying members of his team to the summit via the South Col route, including Ramon Blanco, a Spanish guitar-maker resident in Venezuela who became, at the age of sixty, the oldest man to reach the top. They also put Ginette Harrison on the summit, the second British woman to do so.

Rebecca Stephens, Himalayan Kingdoms' 'reject', had found her way on to another expedition and pipped Harrison to the post by five months. Bell is honest enough to admit that striking Rebecca from his list had been a mistake.

Himalayan Kingdoms had been very lucky in two respects; not only had they encountered an exceptional period of fine weather, they had narrowly avoided a total catastrophe when, by chance, they had no one at camp three (7,400 metres) on the Lhotse Face when a huge avalanche swept down and destroyed the camp. The company had not been so lucky just a couple of months before on 4 August on Khan Tengri (7,010 metres) in the Tien Shan mountains when a similar avalanche killed two Russian guides and two British clients.

By now, with papers all over the world publishing photographs of relatively inexperienced 'punters' queuing on their way to the summit, the global perception of Everest had shifted once and for all. For the media the myth had been conclusively debunked. Everest was as affordable as a Porsche or a Mercedes – and every bit as glamorous. All you had to do was reach for your cheque-book, swap your Gucci loafers for a pair of plastic boots, and the summit was as good as yours.

A new perception had emerged almost overnight: that Everest was achievable by any reasonably fit person who had the motivation – and the cash. In just a few years Everest had gone from the ultimate summit – the preserve of élite mountaineers – to a 'trophy peak', the stamping ground of a new breed of climbers who, largely ignorant of the dangers they might face, were buying their way to the top. To the Press, inevitably, they were 'social climbers', people who would pay almost any price to put a summit photograph on a mantelpiece.

Now Everest was back in the news, big time. 'Queue at the top of the world' screamed the front page headline feature in the

Observer review on 16 May 1993. Contrast this with the situation back in the late 1980s when the media had virtually run out of interest in the peak. With all its major faces climbed and oxygenless ascents of the southern and northern sides ticked off, the Press had grown weary of reporting it. In September '88 the death of a Sherpa in an Everest avalanche rated just an eighteen-word report in *The Times*. The speed climb of Marc Batard in the same month (he raced to the summit and back again in a lightning twenty-two hours and thirty minutes) was reported in the same paper with just seven words more. In May '89 the deaths of five Polish climbers in another avalanche were similarly reported in less than a column-inch.

Now, thousands of column-inches were devoted to Everest, as the new era of guided expeditions came in.

Out of the whirlwind of publicity, a new debate was spun. The increasing commercialisation of Everest was attracting criticism in powerful quarters – not least from Sir Edmund Hillary who, interviewed in a *Newsweek* article on 3 May 1993 – timed to coincide with the fortieth anniversary of Hillary's own first ascent – was quoted as saying, 'The change I dislike most is the fact that [climbing the mountain] has become a financial proposition. Everest is too important a mountain and a challenge to be able to buy your way up.'

It was by no means the first time Sir Edmund had opened Everest up to public debate. In 1990, the Associated Free Press reported his call for a five-year closure of Everest to all mountaineering activity so that nature could repair the damage caused by the hundreds of climbers who flocked to the slopes.

The ascent of Peter, Sir Edmund Hillary's own son, graphically illustrated the growing traffic in May of that same year. On the day in which he made it to the summit, sixteen other climbers also added their names to the ever-growing list.

As a fellow New Zealander, and inevitably a childhood hero of Hall and Ball, this very public criticism from Sir Edmund stung deep. And there was another twist; Peter Hillary's climbing companions on that May day in 1990 had been none other than . . . Rob Hall and Gary Ball. All the more reason perhaps for their subsequent bitterness when Sir Edmund's pronouncements put their efforts under the scrutiny of an increasingly hostile press pack. By bringing the mountain into reach for the ordinary man, Hall and Ball had been treading a delicate and dangerous line in public relations. Up until now their sheer charm and talent for generating good publicity had cocooned them from attack.

Up until now, also, their luck had held. But for how much longer? As early as 1991, editorial comment in the climbing press had raised the spectre of an imminent catastrophe. Bernard Newman, editor of *Mountain* magazine wrote, in April of that year on the subject of commercial Everest expeditions:

> It is indicative of the way that mountains are being abused. It would be terrible if the Himalayas were exploited in the same way as Zermatt or Mont Blanc. People think that, with modern technology, clothing and easy accessibility, it's less of a mountain to climb. That's not true. It's as much of a mountain as ever, and it will bite back.

There was a growing feeling amongst the climbing fraternity that guided expeditions above 8,000 metres were playing with fire and that, sooner or later, a disaster would befall one or more of the teams.

Disaster did indeed strike Adventure Consultants in 1993, but it didn't happen on a guided climb. On 6 October, six months after his fortieth birthday, Gary Ball died of pulmonary oedema at 6,500 metres on the North-East Ridge of Dhaulagiri – the eighth highest peak in the world. He was there with Rob Hall on a private expedition sandwiched into their busy schedule. It was the sixteenth major expedition the two had shared and it wasn't the first time that Ball had suffered from the onset of acute mountain sickness. A previous epic on K2 had necessitated a fast withdrawal from the highest camp of the 'savage peak' after breathing difficulties set in.

He died in Rob Hall's arms. Two days later, a devastated Hall lowered the body of his climbing partner and friend into a crevasse on the slopes of Dhaulagiri, using their best-loved climbing rope for the task. He wrote the following words in a later obituary:

> In his guiding career, which spanned twenty years, he enjoyed an unbroken safety record of which he was rightfully proud. Arguably his greatest guiding achievement was taking clients to the summit of Mount Everest. He believed that the whole Everest scene had become far too élite and he gained enormous satisfaction in being able to make this goal attainable for climbers of more modest skill.

Hall finished the obituary with this moving sentiment: 'Some people come into your life and leave footprints across your heart – and they never go away.'

Although the untimely death of Gary Ball affected Rob Hall deeply on a personal level, his determination to continue the commercial venture they had founded together never wavered. The 1994 brochure of Adventure Consultants was as full and as ambitious as ever, and '100% success on Everest!' was the headline on one of their advertisements in the mountaineering press.

On 9 May that year Rob Hall and Ed Viesturs – a legendary American high altitude climber – led a team of eleven expedition members to the summit; they broke several records in the process, becoming the first Everest expedition to get every member to the top and back down again in one piece. At the same time, Rob Hall became the first westerner to have reached the summit four times.

As Adventure Consultants' own literature concluded: 'This now brings the Adventure Consultants Everest summit tally during our last four expeditions to 39 climbers!'

In 1995, however, the successful pattern of the first few years was finally broken. The Adventure Consultants expedition of that year ground to a halt just a few hours from the summit. In conditions of deep snow, and with an exhausted team, Rob Hall decided to turn his expedition around. His decision was a wise one based on his intimate knowledge of the peak, and the dangers of being on the summit too late; but it must have rankled nonetheless, particularly with that '100% success on Everest' advertisement still fresh in the minds of his commercial rivals.

Now, in the pre-monsoon season of 1996, Adventure Consultants was back again, and so was the British company Himalayan Kingdoms, based in Sheffield, the rival which had stolen much of Rob Hall's thunder with its successful expedition of 1993. This time Himalayan Kingdoms would tackle Everest from the northern side – a much longer and more technically demanding route. Their choice of the northern side was made despite the fact that they had tried this route in 1994, and failed to get anyone to the summit.

Adventure Consultants, sticking to what they knew, would once again tackle the 'standard' tried and tested route from the south. Hall attacked the preparation with his customary thoroughness as Caroline Mackenzie revealed. 'When it came to the planning there was no complacency at all,' she told me. 'Rob was constantly thinking around what could go wrong – even down to the tiniest of details.'

Alongside them on the southern side was another commercial expedition, the Mountain Madness team led by the flamboyant American climber Scott Fischer, who – at forty – was aiming to break into the potentially lucrative Everest market.

Fischer had the type of physique and craggy good looks normally only found in Hollywood casting agencies. In many ways he was the all-round American hero, a top climbing athlete consumed with the desire to be the best . . . and to be recognised as such. Fischer had ambition oozing out of his fingertips right from the time he first began pushing himself on the rock-faces of Wyoming at the age of fifteen.

Fischer wore his blonde hair tied back in a pony-tail. Clean-shaven, with a jawline which might have been carved out of rock, he was a charismatic leader and raconteur . . . a larger-than-life character when compared to the bearded, more studious persona of Rob Hall.

'Scott led his team in a very different way to Rob Hall,' a member of a rival team told me, 'He was capable of being quite histrionic, over the top. He wasn't everyone's cup of tea but there was no doubting he could inspire his team.'

Despite the fact that this was Fischer's first attempt to lead a commercial team on Everest, there was no question of his credentials for the task. Like Rob Hall, he was an élite high-altitude climber. He had summitted K2 in 1992, and Everest without the use of supplementary oxygen in 1994.

Mountain Madness was founded in 1984 but it took more than ten years before Fischer led his first successful commercial expedition to an 8,000-metre peak. He chose Broad Peak in the Karakoram Range of Pakistan, and used the publicity surrounding the 1995 expedition to launch the prospectus for Everest the following year.

The Everest asking price was $65,000 and Fischer had two pieces of luck in the run-up to the expedition's departure. The first was to procure the services as guide of Anatoli Boukreev, indisputably one of the finest high-altitude mountaineers in the world. Boukreev was from Korkino, a small mining town in what is now the Russian Federation, just eighty kilometres from the northern border of Kazakhstan. It was in the nearby Urals that he first found his love of the mountains. Having graduated in physics, Boukreev dodged the draft for the Afghan war and found himself a place teaching cross-country skiing and climbing in the Army Sports Club in Almaty. Boukreev excelled at altitude on the 7,000-metre peaks of his homeland, but it wasn't until 1989 that he was permitted to travel to Nepal where bigger and more glamorous objectives awaited.

Scott Fischer's second piece of luck was to sign up, as one of eight paying clients, Sandy Hill Pittman, a high-profile figure on the New York social circuit. Pittman, armed with a formidable array of communications equipment from the US television channel NBC, would be filing reports from the mountain and posting Internet progress updates on a special Website. Fischer knew that getting Pittman (who had tried Everest three times before) to the summit would be a massive publicity coup for Mountain Madness and would put him in the forefront of Himalayan guiding.

Himalayan Kingdoms also had a celebrity on board, the fifty-nine-year-old British actor Brian Blessed, another big personality in every sense. Blessed's fascination – some called it an obsession – for Everest had attracted the attention of ITN Productions in London. And that was why, as the season cranked into gear on the lower slopes of the mountain, I found myself looking up at Everest and wondering how on earth I was going to make a film on a mountain I had never even dreamed I would set foot.

The offer to go to Tibet had come out of the blue in a telephone call I received on 4 January.

2

'Is that Matt? This is Alison at ITN Productions. I have Julian Ware for you . . .'

My heart missed a beat. I needed a job, badly. A pile of red 'final demands' was sitting next to the phone and it wasn't long before, that we had been so far behind on our mortgage that the company had tried to repossess the house.

'Ah, Matt. There you are. Had a good Christmas?'

Seasonal pleasantries were exchanged.

'Thing is, I've got Channel 4 interested in a film featuring Brian Blessed's new Everest expedition. Its a ten-week shoot, starts March 31st, just wondered if you might be interested?'

The question was delivered as a casual, throw-away line . . . with no more urgency than if it were an invitation to a dinner party.

'Which route?'

There was the rustling of papers at Julian's end of the telephone.

'The North Face. From Tibet,' he replied.

The *North Face*. Those words set off a spontaneous chemical reaction within me. Travelling at a mind-warping 2,250 miles an hour, a series of electrical impulses raced like hyperactive grey-hounds through my brain. Inches in front of them ran a dummy hare with 'responsibility' daubed on its backside in red paint. Thirty-five-year-old married men with three children have to think about these things. Carefully.

But I couldn't play for time; Julian Ware is not a man to keep waiting. Two milliseconds, three milliseconds . . . four . . .

The greyhounds fell on the dummy hare with manic howls, ripping it gleefully to pieces with drooling fangs.

'Yes.'

'Good. I'll set up a meeting with Brian.'

The call was terminated with a gentle click. I found myself breathing heavily.

On the floor, lying prettily amongst the twists of wrapping paper and styrofoam box inserts of Christmas, my wife Fiona was playing the high velocity flick game 'pro-action football' with Gregory, who was then five. At the television, Alistair, seven, was viciously annihilating a 16-bit rodent epidemic in the video game 'Krusty's super fun house' while Thomas, nine, lay on the sofa, trying to pretend he was reading the *Beano* when really it was *Viz*.

'I think I've just been offered a job.'

Fiona lined up a chancy, probing shot, from just outside the penalty box, her index finger hovering like a hunting kestrel above the tiny player.

'Oh yes.' She didn't look up. The finger adjusted itself by fractions of a millimetre.

'It's Everest. Ten weeks.'

The finger delivered its lightning blow, rocketing the pea-sized ball into the top of the net.

'Take a good look at your daddy, boys, he may not be around for much longer.'

The boys ignored her. Gregory lined up his players for a centre kick.

'I'm serious. That was Julian Ware.'

'Wow.'

'He's got Channel 4 interested in Brian Blessed going back for another try.'

'It won't happen.' Fiona swiftly blocked Gregory's counter attack. 'If you think anyone in their right mind is going to commission it, you're wrong. He's too fat. They've already made a film about him trying to climb that stupid mountain and I fell asleep if you remember. Forget it.'

There is no creature on God's earth as deeply cynical as the wife of a freelance television director. It goes with the job. If I came home from a trip to the Vatican and told Fiona that the Pope himself had given me a guarantee written in his own blood that he would definitely be commissioning my next documentary idea, her answer would be 'Uh-huh'.

And why is that? Eleven years ago she was a fresh-faced girl of twenty-three, tripping up the aisle of a Sussex village church with flowers in her hair. She trusted the world and its people. And me. Perhaps she saw my chosen career in television as a noble one; a mission to bring colour, entertainment, and light into people's homes. To be married to a television director . . . surely that was something to be proud of?

Oh, it was all so wonderful.

Now she knows the truth. And its not pretty. Television is a dirty business. To survive in it, you have to be part weasel, part python, and part wolf. To succeed in it, you have to be 99.9% great white shark. The capacity for barefaced lying also comes in handy, particularly if you are freelance.

The weaselling part is to get the programme proposal in front of the reluctant commissioning editor. He has a warehouse full of proposals just like yours and no time to read any of them. By stealth, by bribery, by slithering through air conditioning shafts, you get your proposal on to his desk and pray. For the telephone to ring.

It does. Oh, the tears of gratitude that greet that call. The surging upswell of joy, the euphoric, dizzy sensation that the world IS a happy place after all.

The commissioning editor is 'interested'.

That's when you become the python. You have the commissioning editor in your coils. Squeeze too hard and they pop out and escape. Relax your grip for a moment and they get interested in someone else's idea.

The months drag by, and the meetings continue. Co-production partners are sought in the far-flung corners of the globe. Camera operators are lured out of their Thameside mansions for luxurious lunches at Greek Street eateries. The momentum grows. The telephone lines are glowing red-hot. You start to use your John Lewis store card again.

Then the world collapses. The commissioning editor calls. He's 'going off' the idea.

That is when you become the wolf. You snarl, you rally the pack, you bare the fangs and fight. Through cunning, through fast-talking, through begging, whining, wheadling, pleading, cursing, bullying, bullshitting, exaggerating, and, in the end, through sheer bloody-minded stubborn refusal to give up, you force the commissioning editor to change his mind.

Suddenly he can see it all. It *was* the greatest proposal he'd ever seen. It *is* going to be a compelling documentary. Hell . . . people might even watch it, for Christ's sake. He *does* want to commission it after all.

Fireworks. Champagne. You buy yourself a new laptop.

There *is* a god. You find yourself out there, somewhere in the world, standing next to a film camera loaded with four hundred feet of celluloid. You say 'turnover'. The cameraman presses a switch. A motor turns, and a tiny rectangle of light passes through a lens and exposes a frame of film that is smaller than a postage stamp for precisely one-fiftieth of a second. The first of the millions of frames that will make your programme.

That's when you wonder if there is any crazier business on the planet. That's when you realise you love it.

Fiona finished off the game of pro-action football with a flourish. Mummy, 3 – gutted infant Gregory, 0.

I was still staring, in shock, at the telephone. 'This is it. This is the big one. I can feel it in my bones. I'm going to Everest.'

Fiona fixed me with her big brown eyes. 'I'm going to Waitrose. What do you want for supper?'

*

Two days later I took the central line to Chancery Lane and walked down the Gray's Inn Road to the Headquarters of ITN. Headquarters is definitely the right word, we are not talking about mere offices here. The awesome eight-storey atrium alone could cheerfully swallow up the combined floorspace of every other production company I have ever worked for.

A glass-walled lift whooshed me at high speed to the second floor, where the urbane Julian Ware served filter coffee from an elegant porcelain pot and briefed me on the project.

The proposed film would be a one-hour documentary for Channel 4, to be shown as part of the 'Encounters' series. Running through the budget, and the obvious difficulties the shoot would pose, we both agreed that a lightweight production team was the only option. The film would have to be shot with myself as director and no more than two camera operators, one of whom would have to possess the specialist skills to shoot on the summit if the expedition were successful. There was precious little time to prepare. The expedition was due to leave for Kathmandu in less than three months, and the film had still not received a definite go-ahead from the broadcaster.

We were moving on to the second plate of Danish pastries when, forty minutes late, Brian Blessed burst into the office with a thunderous roar, his beard bristling, his eyes backlit by some strange, demonic inner fire.

'General Bruce's ice-axe!'

In his hand he waved an ancient, deeply stained, wooden stick, topped with a rusting spike. Brian gave it an adoring look.

'I've just been given this by his family. Going to take it with me up the North Face! 1922 – you don't realise what those people *did* . . . and General Bruce was one the greats!'

Julian made the introductions. Brian was delighted. We had known each other for precisely ten seconds.

'There you are! You see, Matt, we're getting along famously already!'

Brian was nervous, and so was I. As I was the proposed director of the film, it was essential for us both that we could work together. During my time as a production manager I had seen what happens when directors and their 'stars' fall out on location. Life is too short to make films with people you don't like.

Brian was dressed like an off duty farmer on his way for an evening pint. His sweatshirt was pock-marked with the missile hits of low-flying ducks (Brian has an impressive menagerie of semi-tame animals), and beneath a rugged set of thick pantaloons lurked a scuffed pair of leather boots of a style which can only be described as clodhoppers.

'The vital thing, Matt, is to make sure you take a damn good hat with a string on it. If you take one without a string, that wind will whip down the Rongbuk glacier and you'll lose it.'

There was a long pause as I wrote in my notebook. 'Hat with string.'

Brian's eccentricity is celebrated, and so is his love for Everest. He can name every member of every pre-war expedition to Everest, and recall their trials and tribulations with astonishing clarity. He knows the routes they tried, the altitudes they reached, the fates they suffered when (as it often did) Everest beat them back with tragic results.

In 1990, after years of unpaid footwork filled with broken promises and setbacks which would surely have deterred a lesser man, Brian convinced the BBC, and the producer John Paul Davidson, to accompany him on a journey to the North Face of Everest. The result was 'Galahad of Everest', a ninety-minute film in which Brian's passion for Everest, and in particular his obsession with the climber George Mallory, were given ample room to breathe.

Dressed in the climbing clothes of the day, Brian retraced the route taken by the British expedition of 1921. Partly dramatic recon-struction, partly using archive footage and original diaries, 'Galahad of Everest' managed to evoke much of the spirit of that bygone era and addressed the mystery of Mallory and Irving's disappearance near the summit . . . a tragedy which struck a nerve with climbers and the public in the 1920s and continues to do so to this day.

But, fascinating though the historical perspective was, the real success of 'Galahad of Everest' was the opportunity to witness Brian in action on the mountain itself. Although the film was never intended to result in a serious bid for the summit, a freak spell of superb weather left the 'window' open for a foray up the North Ridge . . . and the chance really to experience what Mallory and Irving were up against.

That is when Brian surprised everyone, not least himself.

Overweight, inexperienced at altitude, seemingly hopelessly out of condition, Brian reached a high point of 7,600 metres on the North Ridge before altitude and exhaustion forced him back not far from camp five. Puffing and blowing, swearing and cursing, Brian's ordeal was so faithfully recorded by cameraman David Breashears that you almost needed an oxygen cylinder on hand just to watch it.

It did what very few Himalayan mountain films had ever done before: it made altitude, the enemy, real. The viewer could see with Brian's every faltering step, with every gulping breath, the overwhelming physical and mental battle he faced. The antithesis of the cool, experienced, professional mountaineer, Brian's perform-ance was one that the viewer could relate to.

Brian went high, higher than anyone had imagined he could. He was pushing his luck, and so was the film. By the time he turned back, he was right on the edge. Fortunately he had David Breashears by his side, an extremely strong Himalayan climber with two Everest summits to his name. Breashears' cool-headed decision-making undoubtedly saved Brian from acute altitude sickness, frostbite, or worse. Painfully slowly, Brian was escorted back to advance base camp where a highly relieved John Paul Davidson waited with the rest of the team.

Having survived the expedition, and seen for himself the sacred mountain on which his hero, Mallory, disappeared, Brian might have been expected to hang up his climbing boots and return to acting, satisfied that a lifetime's ambition had been fulfilled. But the siren call of Everest proved too strong. In 1993 Brian went back, and this time he was going for the summit.

For this new attempt he joined a commercial expedition run by the Sheffield-based company Himalayan Kingdoms. Along with ten other team members, Brian would attempt the southern side of the mountain, from Nepal, the same route that took Edmund Hillary and Sherpa Tensing to the summit in 1953. The expedition would rely heavily on Sherpa support to establish high camps, where oxygen, food, and cooking gas would be waiting. Each team member paid £22,000.

In March 1993, the expedition flew from London to Kathmandu and trekked up through the Khumbu valley to base camp where the eight-week climb began.

If Brian's performance on the 'Galahad' expedition was impressive, his effort in 1993 was truly astonishing. By far the oldest member of the team at fifty-seven, Brian made a high point of 8,300 metres, above the South Col, just 500 metres from the summit.

During the descent from the South Col, Brian and several others narrowly escaped death when an avalanche swept down the face of Lhotse and wiped out camp five, 7,500 metres, which they had occupied just hours before.

Back in Kathmandu the team had much to celebrate, and so did Brian. The expedition leader Steve Bell had put eight members on the summit, a record for a commercial Everest expedition, and Brian had proved once again that he had the endurance to perform strongly at extreme altitude. By pushing himself above the magic 8,000-metre mark without using supplementary oxygen, he had achieved a considerable feat . . . one that hinted, perhaps, of even greater things to come.

Three years later, now in his sixtieth year, Brian had signed up for his third Everest expedition, again with Himalayan Kingdoms. This time would take him back once more to the northern, Tibetan side where the 'Galahad' film had been shot six years before.

Then he had approached as an enthusiastic novice, completely unacquainted with the devastating effects of altitude and with little experience to fall back on when things got tough. Now he had the experience of two Everest expeditions to draw on, including that impressive performance above 8,000 metres on the southern side. Brian's high-altitude curriculum, for a man of his age, indicated a real talent for going high, and there was no doubting his boundless enthusiasm for the task at hand.

But would that be enough? Could Brian summit? Or had he reached his ceiling during the 1993 expedition – a personal best beyond which he could never climb?

For me, this question was a vital one to resolve. I didn't want to make a film which covered the same ground as 'Galahad of Everest', I wanted this film to go the whole way, right to the summit, and to bring back pictures of Brian on the top.

Brian had no doubts. 'This time I'm going to go for it, Matt. By God I'm going to do it!'

Brian's coffee sat completely untouched before him. In his hands, he twisted the venerable ice-axe to and fro like a cheerleader's baton, knocking the business end periodically on to his kneecap with a resounding 'clung' to reinforce a point.

'I'll get on the oxygen much earlier. That was my mistake on the southern side, I was too fucking proud to strap that mask on. But this time I'll use the gas, and I'll make it, and you'll be there with me to film it! It'll be the greatest Himalayan film there's ever been!'

General Bruce's ice-axe sliced through the air with a dramatic flourish;

'What about you, Matt? Are you a bit of a man for the mountains?'

'A bit, yes.' I gave Brian my most modest smile.

In fact for someone contemplating making a film on the North Face of Everest my mountain experience was decidedly patchy. My towering achievements so far were limited to just two summits; a Himalayan trekking peak called Pokalde, 5,700 metres, and an obscure Ecuadorean volcano of about the same height. To serious Himalayan mountaineers these are mere nodules, amusing warm-up molehills to be gobbled before breakfast.

Climbing them had been extremely difficult.

More alarming than these dubious triumphs were the ignominious failures that dotted my climbing curriculum. My track record wasn't just flawed, it was criss-crossed with vast, gaping chasms, huge, shadow-filled gorges of bumbling flops and incompetent failures.

Amongst the most astounding of these – so much so that I am almost proud of it – was a solo attempt to climb Ben Nevis in October 1981 when I was a university student at Durham.

It started encouragingly enough. Leaving on a Friday afternoon, I hitchhiked up to Edinburgh and then across to Glasgow. As night fell, a rainstorm began, and progress ground to a halt. By 2.30 a.m., I was stuck just north of Dumbarton, soaked to the skin, and feeling very sorry for myself. Very few cars were about, and those that were showed no sign of stopping.

Remembering a motorway service station a few miles back down the road, I decided to beat a tactical retreat south and wait there until dawn. As I walked, I put out my thumb, just on the off chance of a lift.

To my astonishment, a vehicle stopped. It was a motorhome converted from an old fish-and-chip van. A family welcomed me inside, and commiserated on my plight. When the driver heard I was heading for Ben Nevis, he proposed a different plan. Climb Snowdon instead.

The family were heading home to Flint, on the North Welsh coast. They could drop me there at first light, leaving an easy hitch along the A5151 towards Bangor, and then a quick raid down into Snowdonia from where the mighty peak itself could be swiftly and triumphantly conquered.

It was warm inside the van and, subject to my taking off my dripping outer raingear, a bunkbed was on offer. Snowdon it was. Ben Nevis could wait. (In fact it still does. I haven't climbed it to this day.)

When I woke up in Flint, I found the couple's daughter – she must have been about eight or nine – had covered me with a blanket as I slept; 'I thought you looked cold,' she said and then gave me a Mars bar for breakfast.

The 'easy' hitch along to Snowdonia proved a lot more elusive than anticipated, and it was almost midday by the time I was dropped off at Betys-y-Coed. A low blanket of cloud shrouded the national park, reducing visibility to less than a few hundred metres. The mountain itself was sulking, nowhere to be seen, and I had no maps and no money to buy any.

Having consulted a national park map in a car park, I set off into a fine mist of drizzle in the direction of Snowdon. For two hours I battled my way along a boggy path which stayed stubbornly in the valley floor. I kept telling myself it would surely start to rise soon. The path then degenerated further as it entered more marshy terrain. I found myself hopping from one tussock of bogweed to another. Glutinous wallow-holes of black slime lurked on either side.

The cloud thickened as I lost the trail completely. I began fighting my way upwards through fields of sour-faced sheep, crossing stone walls and getting snagged on barbed-wire fences. Eventually, with just an hour of murky daylight left, I collapsed against the rusting carcass of a derelict tractor and conceded defeat. Snowdon can wait, I thought.

In my pack was a quarter-bottle of Southern Comfort. I drank it

in less than half an hour, then ate a packet of Jaffa cakes and a
Scotch egg. Feeling distinctly queasy, I then beat a retreat off the
mountain . . . if indeed I was on the mountain at all . . . reaching
the safety of tarmac as night fell.

Having hitchhiked through the night, I arrived red-eyed and
exhausted in Durham on the Monday morning just minutes before
lectures began. Strangely, despite the stinging shame of having failed
to climb anything, I considered it an excellent weekend.

The one part of my mountain history which did give a glimmer
of hope, and the one about which I now told Brian and Julian was
my time as a trekking guide. In the summer of 1984 I ran a series
of mountain treks through the High Atlas mountains in Morocco
for the adventure holiday company Explore Worldwide.

Every two weeks a new group flew into Marrakech via Paris. I
would sit in the airport café drinking pastis with Philippe, a French
guide for a rival trekking company, and watch the new arrivals walk
off the plane. Philippe had a talent for spotting members of his own
group and delighted in a running commentary as they emerged;
'That's one of mine,' he would state confidently, each time a pretty
girl emerged.

Elderly women, or those who did not meet Philippe's demanding
standards got a:'That's one of yours'.

Most infuriatingly, Philippe was almost always right. '*Le Trekking*'
was chic in France at that time, and his groups did indeed seem to
include unusually high percentages of gorgeous girls. Mine had
unusually high percentages of whiskery old matrons and bearded
librarians from Solihull. Seen on the trail, Philippe's groups were a
glittering fashion parade of skin-tight cycling shorts and wrap-
around reflector sunglasses. Mine wore moleskin britches and hairy
army surplus shirts from Millets.

At the airport Philippe would deliver a parting shot: 'As usual,
Mathieu, I have ze gazelles . . . and you have ze goats! See you in
two weeks.'

Then, having effortlessly manoeuvred the pick of the crop into
his turbocharged Toyota, Philippe would roar off into the night
with his gazelles, leaving a vapour trail of diesel fumes and Chanel
behind him.

These irritations aside, my time as a trek leader in the High Atlas
was time well-spent. I learned that strange things happen when
people and mountains meet. The treks were not so hard, rarely
more than six hours of walking each day, but in the heat of a

Moroccan summer they could be demanding enough. In the High Atlas I watched personalities change, just as the mood of the mountains changes from one valley to the next.

Mountains peel layers away like a car being dismantled at a scrapper's yard. They strip off veneers and shells, leaving just the distilled essence of a person behind . . . the chassis on which the body panels are bolted. Seemingly placid group members could burst into sudden, violent, rages. Hard-talking Glaswegian hit-men could be reduced to tears. Mousey matrons could become mountain lions, thundering up peaks and down valleysides at superhuman speeds.

In the middle of this dynamic, shifting entity, is the trek leader, encouraging, cajoling, informing, and trying to prevent one member from ripping another's head off when personalities clash. It was psychologically demanding, physically exhausting, and filled with the gentle, ironic humour which seems to be an inevitable consequence of the British once they find themselves in a group. I loved it, especially when a lone, and particularly lovely gazelle did finally walk off the Marrakech plane with an 'Explore' baggage tag on her rucksack.

'Mine,' I told Philippe. He was spitting with rage.

But trekking is not climbing, and Toubkal, 4,165 metres – the greatest peak in the High Atlas – would be a mere ink dot on a map of the Himalayas.

In short, I was seriously underqualified to join an Everest expedition of any description, let alone one to the technically difficult, vast North Face. As previously mentioned, I had never climbed the highest mountains in Britain, nor had I reached the summit of any peak in the Alps. I had never taken a formal climbing course or even properly learned the rudiments of ropework.

Worse again, was my tendency to make mistakes. Unfolded maps fly from my hands in the gentlest of breezes, carabiners mysteriously drop off harnesses, water bottles leap out of rucksack pockets and hurtle down ice slopes without warning. I have set fire to tents, dropped sleeping bags into freezing rivers, and lost enough pairs of sunglasses to stock a medium-sized store. Such clumsiness is inconvenient at lower altitudes but above 8,000 metres it can kill you.

'I'll just set my sights on base camp,' I told Brian, 'and leave the high-altitude shooting to a specialist cameraman.'

'Nonsense.' Brian was adamant. 'You'll be with me the whole

way. Once you get out there and see that great shining pyramid sitting at the top of the Rongbuk glacier, she'll have you in her spell.'

So saying, Brian delivered a knuckle-crunching farewell handshake and left for a voice-over session in a Soho studio.

*

'You think it can work?' Julian poured out the dregs of the coffee.

I had liked Brian tremendously but, looking at it as a film-maker, the project still had some major question marks hanging over it.

'I think I need to do some research. There's no point in going ahead unless we're absolutely sure Brian can make a summit attempt. If he does, and we can find a way to shoot it, it'll be really something. If he doesn't make a summit attempt, we'll be left with a remake of "Galahad" and I don't want to do that.'

Julian gave me a week to make up my mind.

I began to canvas opinion on Brian's chances. I spoke to some of Britain's top high-altitude specialists and they all said the same thing. Based on Brian's impressive altitude record, he *could* make a summit attempt if all went well with weather and logistics.

On a professional level I was now inclined to take the offer, and there were other, more personal reasons why ten weeks in Tibet was an attractive idea at that particular time.

My marriage, eleven years old, was cracking at the edges, in the middle of a crisis which I desperately needed to resolve. Everest, I began to realise, could give me the space I needed to sort out the mess.

3

I met Fiona in 1981, my first year at Durham university but it took me a while to realise how much I fancied her. I was studying Archaeology and Anthropology, she did General Arts, so our paths didn't cross that often in the lecture halls . . . in fact neither of us went to many lectures anyway.

Fiona had a cheeky smile, a cascade of unruly black ringlets and a penchant for ambitiously short skirts. She smoked Benson and Hedges cigarettes, bit her nails to the quick and drank so much gin and tonic that a friend once bought her five shares in United Distillers as a birthday present. On the tennis court, even after half a bottle of Pimms, she was still capable of smashing the best players in the university. She never joined any of the college teams, probably because she couldn't be bothered. I thought that was very cool.

Every time I caught a glimpse of Fiona she always seemed to be floating past on a punt polled by a brilliantined Old Etonian, or drinking champagne in the late summer sun on the university green with a bunch of people wearing velveteen cummerbunds.

Occasionally we met at parties, and we knew each other well enough to say hello in the street, but I was very wary of Fiona's 'Ra' friends and that was a problem no matter how much she made me laugh. My social world revolved around the exploration society which, in the second year at Durham, I was now running. My friends were travellers and wanderers and dreamers who spent every last waking moment of the day poring over maps depicting places they could not possibly afford to visit. Fiona's world revolved around the college drama scene and the laddish beer-swilling fringes of the university rugby team – a social set which I absolutely went out of my way to avoid. We didn't have a single mutual friend.

There was another barrier between us at the time we first met. Fiona was involved with someone else, and I was involved with several someone elses. My personal life was going through one of its periodic entanglements in which a long-term relationship, a medium-term relationship and a couple of extremely short-term relationships were variously, and simultaneously, collapsing, re-igniting, climaxing, imploding, or simply grinding to an ignominious halt.

Given all the above, the chances of a relationship with Fiona were looking shaky to say the least, but all that was to change unexpectedly with a three-minute conversation we had after a chance meeting in the street. I think it was the only time I ever saw her carrying a book. We walked together across one of the city's many bridges and, on a sudden impulse, I asked her if she wanted to come to the Lake District for a weekend camping in the mountains with some friends. To my surprise she said yes immediately.

And that was how it began.

I fell for her in a big way. Some weeks later, on Midsummer's Eve, we shared our first kiss halfway through a bottle of Theakston's cider on a hilltop overlooking the soot-encrusted spires of Durham. The sun was setting and the air was filled with pollen and dandelion fluff. I was suffering from a violent attack of hay fever. Midway through the kiss I had a sneezing attack.

By the time September and a new term came around, we were back together and spending increasing amounts of time in each other's company. By about Christmas I realised with a shock that I was most definitely in love. Over the winter break I got a commission from the *Traveller* magazine to write an article on the Trans-Siberian railway. Fiona came with me on the journey. To while away the days as the train trundled slowly across the vast wastelands of the former Soviet Union, we drank spectacularly cheap Russian champagne and made love in our cabin between stations.

In Siberia the stations are a very long way apart.

By the normal course of events, given my previous failures with steady girlfriends, my relationship with Fiona was due to grind to a halt. But it didn't. In fact it got stronger and stronger. By the time we realised that we had better do something about our exams, we were virtually living together. At the last minute, with the crunch just days away, panic set in and I managed to revise enough to give me a second-class degree. Fiona also scraped through after a couple of weeks of all-night revision.

Somehow, somewhere, I had come to the notice of the Foreign Office – or to be more precise MI6, the Secret Intelligence Service. After a series of interviews conducted in central London, they offered me the chance to apply for a career which would have plunged me into the world of covert intelligence-gathering. After some very serious thought I declined their offer. I didn't want to be a spy, I had already decided on a career in television.

I had to start somewhere so I wrote to the BBC, asking to join one of their trainee schemes. They wrote back an extremely brief letter informing me that 38 million people had applied for six vacancies and anyway I had missed the deadline for applications.

In a fit of rage of the 'I'll show the BB Bloody C what fools they are' variety, I applied for the first cash-paying job I saw in the local paper and got it. Cleaning out chicken sheds was not exactly the high-profile media career I'd envisaged but it was a start. I lasted three disgusting days then went on to other equally soul-destroying jobs doing construction work, assembling double-glazing units and travelling the country putting up marquees at fêtes and fairs.

Fiona worked at a travel agency and we pooled all our money. The idea, when we had saved enough, was to go on a long journey across the Sahara in the old Landrover which I had recently purchased for £500. On the day we departed, Fiona's bewildered parents had the tearful look of a couple that weren't at all sure they would ever see their daughter again.

They nearly didn't.

The Landrover broke down. Bang smack in the middle of the Sahara desert on the piste from Tamanrasset to Djanet in the deep south of Algeria. And when I say broke down, I mean it really did break; the rusty old chassis snapped in two just above the rear axle with the dramatic result that the poor old Landrover dragged its arse along the ground like a dog with no rear legs. If it hadn't been for some Italians who happened upon us by chance we could have been in serious trouble.

Using an ingenious collection of bits of broken leaf spring (I had quite a collection of these by this stage in the journey) and by drilling fixing points into the broken chassis we managed to jack the vehicle more or less back into shape and bolt the pieces of metal across the broken section. Then, after a dodgy welding job in the nearest oasis, we limped back to England at about fifteen miles an hour.

Restless for more travelling, I applied for the job of trek leader with adventure holiday company Explore Worldwide and was accepted. During my first season in the High Atlas mountains of Morocco I had plenty of time to think and it was Fiona who was foremost on my mind. The journey across the Sahara had brought us closer together and now I realised that I desperately didn't want to lose her. After the High Atlas I was already pencilled in for a season running felucca sailing boats down the Nile for the same company; that would take me away from Fiona for another extended period – perhaps six months – and I wasn't at all sure she would hang around waiting for me much longer without some sort of longer-term commitment.

In the closing days of my Moroccan contract, after a few beers in the Foucauld hotel in Marrakech I found myself thinking about what the chances were of a long-term relationship – a really long-term one – succeeding. Would I ever stop travelling? Could I kill off the restlessness that run through me as thick as my own blood? Could I ever – and the very words struck a chill deep inside me – 'settle down'?

The answer to all of those was an emphatic 'no'. A cosy domestic life was absolutely the last priority on my personal list. It threatened every freedom I had and seemed to me to be tantamount to giving up. A few beers later I was still wrestling with the problem and I decided that flipping a bottle top might give me a hand in the decision-making process. Logo side up would mean 'yes', crinkle side up would mean 'no'.

I balanced the metal disc on my thumbnail for a second then spun it into the air . . .

When I got back to England I asked Fiona to marry me.

We set the date for September and then I left to guide drunken Australians down the Nile, leaving Fiona and her mother to make all of the arrangements for the wedding.

The first few years were manic: Fiona ran a Tuscan villa company from a back room of our small house in St. Albans and had Thomas, Alistair and Gregory in rapid succession. I concentrated on establishing my career in television. By a series of lucky breaks, the BBC offered me a researcher contract on 'Wogan', the early evening chat show. The show was live, which added a certain adrenaline to the job. It was also intensely competitive amongst the eight researchers, who had to come up with a constant flow of high-profile guests if we were to get our contracts renewed.

It was an extremely exciting and glamorous show to work on. With guests like Arnold Schwarzenegger, Princess Anne, Mel Gibson and Zsa Zsa Gabor, our average working week was filled with extremely interesting lunch appointments. There were moments of real drama too; on the night before Live Aid, the 'Wogan' producer Jon Plowman decided late that he wanted Bob Geldof on that night's line-up. We tracked Geldof down to Wembley where he was putting the finishing touches to the biggest live concert ever, but we couldn't get a message to him.

'Go and get him,' Plowman told me.

'How?'

'I don't know. Just get him on the show.'

I left the television centre at about 5.50 p.m., in a souped-up BBC limousine. 'Wogan' went live at 7 p.m. Having blagged my way into Wembley stadium past some pretty determined security I found that Geldof was on-stage rehearsing with the Boomtown Rats. Between numbers I walked on to the middle of the stage, told him who I was and told him the BBC wanted him for that night's 'Wogan'. Geldof told me, in his usual earthy style, that he was busy and couldn't come. I pointed out that if he made it on to the show he would be able to persuade an extra eight million people to watch Live Aid the following day. Geldof walked with me off the stage there and then and after a high-speed chase through west London we made it to the studio just as the opening titles to the show were running.

It was that kind of programme.

By 1988 I was in a good position at the BBC with the prospect of producing and directing jobs just a few years away. But the constraints of working within a big institution were eating away at me. I was already restless to move on. When I looked at the staff producers above me, with their safe salaries and secure careers I realised that I did not want to be one of 'Aunties' men.

I resigned from the BBC and went freelance, a move which most of my colleagues thought was crazy. Fiona supported me completely, even though the move would inevitably mean less financial security.

John Gau Productions offered me my first freelance job, as Associate Producer on the ITV series 'Voyager', which featured expeditions and adventures in the wild corners of the planet. That run of thirteen half-hour programmes changed the direction of my career, and took me increasingly out on to location. In my first year on the job I shot in countries such as China, Egypt and Morocco. The whole process of producing 'Voyager' was a fascinating one, but more than anything I loved being in the field, filming people who were the best in the world in their chosen fields of adventure.

The films were highly visual and got a prime time early evening slot on ITV where they won good audience figures. But for me, their real success was in the way we portrayed the adventurers. We tried, as far as we could, to get the protagonists to reveal more about *why* they chose to risk their lives for a goal that most people would regard as crazy. Getting under the skin of our heroes was the key.

By 1990 I was producing and directing for the second series of 'Voyager', filming (among other projects) a record-breaking hang-glider flight from the world's highest live volcano in Ecuador, and following a world powerboat champion as he attempted to regain his title in one of the world's most dangerous sports.

Then things got really busy. Together with 'Voyager' series editor Colin Luke I created the BBC1 series 'Classic Adventure', which we filmed on location in India, Kenya, Brazil and Greenland. We pushed the limits a little further on this new series and the expeditions we filmed were sometimes extreme. In India we shot a very hazardous whitewater descent of the Brahmaputra river, in Kenya we filmed a team of hang-glider and microlight pilots flying through the wilderness terrain of the Rift Valley.

Life as a freelancer in television is always precarious but, special-ising as I did in overseas expedition work, there were other inevitable pressures which built steadily as the years went by. The sheer amount of time I spent away was definitely making life more difficult for Fiona as she was left to manage all our financial affairs. We had always walked a tightrope financially and the responsibility of staving off mortgage companies and banks was often down to her.

For me the travel was part of the drug, part of the kick of the films I made, but being on the road so much was sometimes difficult for me too. Having established my career I couldn't possibly afford to turn work down, and the relentless months of location work meant I missed many important events which I really should have been there for. My brother's wedding. Numerous of my own wedding anniversaries. New Year's Eves. Half of the time I wasn't even in the country to see my own films being broadcast.

But there is a limit to how many 'Happy Birthday' telephone calls you can make to your children from hotel rooms in Chiang Mai or Mombasa before it starts to get you down. Then in 1992, while I was away in Nepal filming an expedition of disabled climbers attempting a trekking peak, Fiona's sister Stephanie suffered an unexpected tragedy. Her husband Howard, who was thirty-one, collapsed on a rugby pitch from heart failure and later died. Completely unaware of this, and totally out of touch in the Himalayas, I got back to Kathmandu to hear this tragic news (four weeks old) from Fiona. I had missed the funeral, that was bad enough, but more importantly to me, I had missed the chance to help Fiona and her family through an incredibly difficult time. Fiona really needed me during those days and weeks and I wasn't there to support her. It had always been a standing joke between us (albeit a bitter-sweet one) that I was the 'invisible man', but on that occasion being the invisible man wasn't a joke at all. I felt I had failed Fiona in a very fundamental way, and that wasn't easy to live with for either of us.

The list of companies I worked for grew through the early 1990s as the projects rolled on: Mentorn Films, Pioneer Productions, Antelope Films, Mosaic Pictures, Goldhawk Films, Diverse Productions, they all wanted adventure and I was one of the very few directors specialising in that field.

Somewhere in the recesses of my brain, and in Fiona's too, a few red warning lights were beginning to flash. Many of the projects I was directing contained elements of danger, or featured people who were taking risks. Broadcasters want drama, and as the years go by, they have come to expect 'extreme' expeditions almost as a matter of course. As the person in charge of the content of the film it was my job to push – sometimes quite hard – for the best possible pictures. How many times, I began to ask myself, could I ask people to raft perilous rapids 'one more time', or film climbers working on extreme cliffs without ropes before someone was going to get seriously hurt? No film is worth even the smallest injury, let alone fatality, but I had heard of many instances where filming had led to this.

The possibility of something going badly wrong increasingly haunted me and there were risks for the crew as well. If there's a river to be run, we run it too. If there's a cave system to be explored, someone from the crew has to be there shooting it. In China, making a film about a surfer trying to ride the biggest tidal wave in the world, our crew boat was caught in the maelstrom and flipped over. The revolving propellor of the outboard missed the cameraman's head by a matter of inches. I can think of plenty of other near misses, most of which I never told Fiona about.

Then, in January 1994, I stared death in the face.

We were filming on Mt. William, a peak in Antarctica which has on its upper slopes a number of enormous hanging glaciers and seracs. As we descended from the summit, on the final stages of the climb, the seven of us (five climbers and two of us filming) entered a steep ice gulley. It was four o'clock in the morning and the scene was lit by the gloomy half-light of the Antarctic summer.

Suddenly, several hundred metres above us, the sky was filled with a terrifying sight. The billowing cloud of a massive avalanche descending upon us from the North-East Face of the mountain. It moved incredibly fast, and there was barely time for a screamed warning before it engulfed us.

In the few seconds before we were hit, my brain was able to calculate where the avalanche must have come from and to conclude that the whole of the North-East Face had ripped away. All day we had known full well that the snow was in prime avalanche condition but we had waited six weeks for a weather opportunity to climb the peak and this was our last chance. Now, millions of tons of snow and ice were about to smash us to pulp.

There was absolutely no doubt whatsoever in my mind that we were all going to be killed. It was the same for the other six, they too saw no way we could survive. We pushed ourselves into the ice and waited to be crushed or ripped off the Face and dashed on to the rocks hundreds of metres below us. It is a very curious sensation to be utterly sure that your life is about to end. My life didn't exactly flash before me but I do remember feeling an extraordinary experience of calm and a sense of wonder at the power that was unleashed upon us.

It didn't happen. The shock wave engulfed us at more than one hundred kilometres an hour but the debris of the ice avalanche shot right over our heads. The gulley was steep enough to have thrown the force of the avalanche away from us. Some smaller blocks hit us, and one of the climbers nearly lost an eye from an impact, but apart from the bruising, we were fine. Somehow we had all managed to hang on to our positions. Ten minutes earlier we had been standing right at the top of the gulley where death would have been inevitable.

It took me a while to tell Fiona about that incident.

After the avalanche I was increasingly aware that I had to move on from adventure if I was to develop my film-making career . . . and stand a reasonable chance of staying alive. Apart from the risks, there are only so many expeditions that you can film in a world in which all the major challenges of exploration have been ticked off. I was exploiting a very tiny niche, and with each film I made that niche was diminishing.

But, pressed by the need to earn money, I had no choice but to continue to put my energies into developing new adventure projects in an attempt to keep the cash coming in while at the same time doubling my efforts in another field, movie scriptwriting. Increasingly, I found it hard to summon any real enthusiasm for the adventure films I was making and my movie ideas were an escape . . . a way of dreaming, a way of letting my imagination run wild.

As far as my relationship with Fiona went, this too was entering a dangerously rocky phase by the end of 1994. The pressures of trying to hold the family together when I was so often away, combined with my perpetual restlessness, was adding up to a diminishing return for Fiona. She was putting a great deal more into the relationship than I was, and getting less out of it year by year. Trying to keep tabs on an absent and increasingly wayward husband was no joke and our relationship seemed to teeter from one crisis to another.

Fiona had never tried to own me. That was the beauty of our relationship, but it was also its flaw. We were two very different people united by a bond of real love, by a family, and by the tendons of loyalty which we both felt. But we had always known that, in essence, we were not similar people at all. There were a lot of dreams we shared, but there were a hell of a lot more that we didn't. Those fundamental differences had now reared up and were prising us painfully apart.

The horrible realisation was beginning to dawn that Fiona might actually be better off without me, and I found that very difficult to deal with. But to resolve it, to become the husband she actually wanted, would mean giving up freedoms which selfishly I had come to take as a matter of course. I had always been a traveller, in fact I had always seen myself as a free spirit (whatever that is), but I loved Fiona far too much to keep hurting her as much as I seemed to be doing. A body clock inside me was tick-tock-ticking away, telling me, whispering in my ear like it first did when I found myself lured off at the age of seventeen on journey after journey into the Sahara desert, that it was time to go. But an equally strong set of pressures was telling me to grow up and meet my responsibilities.

Now, the Everest expedition gave me the opportunity to sort myself out and make a decision about which direction my life was going. Ten weeks in Tibet would give me plenty of time to think, and away from the problem perhaps I could find a new perspective and work it all out.

I called Julian Ware at ITN Productions and told him I would take the Everest job. Then I loaded twenty volumes of the *Children's Britannica* into a rucksack and went out into the footpaths and fields of rural Hertfordshire for a five-hour walk.

*

I chose my camera team with a great deal of care. Very few camera operators have filmed above 8,000 metres but if our project was to be a success I had virtually to guarantee that one member of my team could be there to record a summit attempt.

Alan Hinkes was my first choice, and I put the proposal to him on the telephone with just six weeks remaining before we were due to leave. As Britain's most successful high-altitude climber, Al has an Everest-sized profile in the world of mountaineering and had filmed on the summit of K2. He was one of only two British climbers to have reached the summit of the second highest mountain in the world (K2 is 8,611 metres) and returned alive. In addition, he had summitted four other 8,000-metre peaks.

Al had twice been on Everest but the summit had eluded him. I knew he was looking for another opportunity to go back, and my offer to pay him would be hard to resist. He wasn't trained as a cameraman but I was confident he could turn in a workable result in extreme conditions.

A plain-speaking northerner, Al has a reputation for bluntness and has his fair share of enemies in the climbing world amongst those who resent his highly commercial approach and his talent for self-publicity. He is a hard person physically, capable of remarkable endurance, and at first meeting he seems a hard case psychologically too.

With a tightly cropped military haircut and a set of glacial blue eyes, Hinkes looks every inch the high-altitude hero that he undoubtedly is. He has a pugnacious undercurrent which rubs some people up the wrong way. Very much an individual, I was told that he had not always made a good team player on previous expeditions but from my point of view that was not so important. I wasn't hiring him for his diplomatic skills. What I needed was someone who could operate a camera in the Death Zone and there are few people better qualified than Al to do that.

Al listened carefully to my proposal, successfully managed to bump up the fee I was offering, and accepted the contract.

As principal cameraman for the lower altitudes I chose Kees 't Hooft, (his name is pronounced 'Case') a Dutch film-maker based in London who I had worked with before on several films. Kees has the vague look of a slightly dotty professor, with a thinning sweep of gingery hair and the refined features of an intellectual. He spends his weekends attending Jungian philosophy classes and has an unexplainable fascination for the English aristocracy. He is never happier than when rubbing shoulders with dukes, duchesses and lady dowagers and presumably they like rubbing shoulders with him too because he does seem to meet a lot of them.

Essentially a gentle person, Kees has the type of excessive good manners normally found only in butlers and wine waiters, but underneath the mild exterior lurks a very strong climber. He had been to almost 7,000 metres on Makalu (8,481 metres) filming for a Channel 4 documentary, and had operated camera for me on Pokalde Peak in Nepal. I called to check if he was interested;

'Certainly, but what date does the expedition finish?'

'The sixth of June. Why?'

'Oh nothing really, just that I'm getting married on the eighth.'

My heart sank. This news would obviously rule Kees out of the expedition, leaving me with a difficult gap to fill. Surely he couldn't abandon his fiancée for ten weeks just before the wedding? Could he?

Yes he could.

'I think I had better have a little chat with my fiancée,' Kees told me, sounding numb.

Kees asked me for a twenty-four-hour 'cool off' period to talk things through with Katie Isbester, his betrothed. A professor of political science at the University of Toronto, Katie didn't hesitate. 'I would be most upset if you didn't go on my account,' she told him.

Kees called me back and told me he was on for the expedition.

The third member of my team was Ned Johnston, an American film-maker of high repute. He would join us to shoot on 16mm film for the first three weeks of the expedition, coming with us as far as advance base camp and then returning with the film footage to the UK, leaving the rest of us to continue on digital video camera.

The remaining weeks passed in a blur of equipment-gathering, physical training to get myself fit, and the one thousand and one other details that precede any major shoot.

*

On 31 March, at Gatwick, the expedition members came together for the first time. Only Roger Portch and Richard Cowper were missing, as they had both travelled independently to Kathmandu. We looked and felt oddly out of place queuing up at the Royal Air Nepal check-in with our piles of flight cases and blue expedition barrels amongst holiday-makers heading for Tenerife and Mahon.

The expedition leader Simon Lowe was there, looking harrassed and hot in a massive down jacket. Simon wore his hair long, scraped back and tied in a pony-tail, which certainly wouldn't have won him any brownie points in his former life as an Army officer. He had been with Himalayan Kingdoms as operations manager since leaving the Army under the 'options for change' clear out of 1993. He had been to Everest twice before, in 1988 to the West Ridge from the north side and in 1992 to the same ridge from the south side. On both occasions he had climbed higher than 8,000 metres. Behind his bespectacled, slightly hippyish air, Simon was a tough negotiator, as he immediately proved by persuading Royal Air Nepal to cut several thousand pounds off our excess baggage bill.

Simon's second in command, Martin Barnicott – known as 'Barney', was also there, shod in a weathered pair of fur-lined mukluks. Softly spoken, Barney had the shifting gaze of someone who has spent a lifetime in the mountains. Reluctant to make eye contact, he looked like he was scanning corners of the departures hall for an incoming avalanche. Naturally shy and self-effacing, I knew from his reputation that he is one of the best high-altitude guides in the business. He had guided (and summitted) Everest with Himalayan Kingdoms in 1993, and would now have a crucial role to play in Brian's attempt. He seemed anxious to get the introductions out of the way and get on with the flight.

If Barney was successful during our expedition, he would be the only British climber to have summitted Everest from the north and the south . . . a potential first which he shrugged off with a non-chalant 'We'll see.'

Sundeep Dhillon, the expedition doctor, was busy doing some last-minute packing, stuffing sterile swabs and sinister-looking inspection devices into a huge barrel. Sundeep, a Captain with 23-Parachute field ambulance based in Aldershot, had obtained army leave to join our expedition at his own cost. He was on the final leg of a personal quest which had taken three years of his life, to become the youngest person ever to have climbed the 'seven summits' the highest points on the continental landmasses. Kilimanjaro, McKinley, Aconcagua, Elbrus, Carstenz Pyramid, Mt. Vinson – it was a project which had taken him to the furthest corners of the world and to the brink of financial disaster.

Now, 'only' Everest remained on Sundeep's list . . . a mountain which he was unlikely to be able to afford to attempt more than once in his lifetime. He had taken out a bank loan of £20,000 to join the expedition and would be paying it off for years to come. This, coupled with the high expectations of his commanding officers, meant that Sundeep was under considerable pressure to succeed.

Tore Rasmussen, the Norwegian member of the expedition, had flown into the airport from Oslo earlier in the day and had the jaded look of someone who has already spent too many hours in a waiting lounge. A black belt karate expert, he had hard, slate-coloured eyes set beneath impressively bushy eyebrows. Tore had the compact body and high muscle definition of a top-class athlete. His hand-shake could crush avocado stones. Simon had climbed Aconcagua with him and had a high regard for his strength at altitude.

Kees's pretty Canadian fiancée Katie was there too, looking slightly bemused to be wishing her husband-to-be goodbye when their wedding was just a couple of months away. Realising that last-minute planning would be too late by the time Kees returned, they were plotting the finer details of the wedding ceremony and the travel arrangements of family members (large numbers of Kees's family would be flying to Toronto from Holland) right up to the departure gate.

Brian arrived with his family, bearing with him a single bag which looked suspiciously light. The rest of us had numerous bulging packs, zips strained to breaking point, into which the thousands of essential items had painfully been squeezed. Just one of my kitbags – the one containing extra food – was bigger and heavier than Brian's entire load. He looked as if he was leaving for a weekend break in a country hotel.

'Where's all your gear?' I asked him.

'That's it.' Brian patted the bag, looking shifty.

'It can't be.'

'Well I can buy any extra bits and pieces in Kathmandu. You can get everything there.'

I was about to pick up on this when Brian moved on, noticing that Kees had the camera out and was preparing to film. A consummate performer, Brian cannot resist the opportunity for fun when a camera is waved in his direction:

'The main piece of advice, Kees, is never camp below the French. They will shit on you from a great height.'

As soon as he saw the cameras were out, Al Hinkes also leaped into action. Armed with a handful of brightly-coloured stickers, he moved from one barrel to the next, sticking on logos from some of his various sponsors.

'Oy!' Simon shouted at him, laughing, 'have you ever thought I might not want those stickers on my barrels?'

'Nope.' Al kept sticking.

We filmed Brian's farewell to his wife Hildegard and daughter Rosalind and then bid our own goodbyes.

I walked with Fiona to the car park and made sure she had the right change for the ticket machine. Over the past twelve years we had been through these airport partings many, too many, times before but this time we held each other tighter than ever.

'Don't worry. It's only a film . . . just like any other shoot.'

'Just come back in one piece or I'll be seriously pissed off.'

With that, she smiled, wiped away the tears and drove away, pausing only to blow a kiss through the back window.

Fifteen hours later, after a stop in Frankfurt, we arrived in Kathmandu, minus the huge barrel of medical equipment and drugs which Sundeep had so painstakingly, and expensively prepared. A volley of faxes and telexes was sent out to London and Frankfurt in the attempt to track it down.

An eager gang of porters loaded our equipment on to the back of a pick-up truck which promptly shot off in a plume of black smoke. We followed it at speed through the backstreets of Kathmandu in a rickety old bus, dodging trucks and swerving to avoid the odd cow sitting impassively in the middle of the road.

Squinting in the early morning light, feeling dazed after the sleepless night flight, I thought back to the first time I had arrived in Kathmandu as a traveller of eighteen on my first big solo journey. My recollection was of a tranquil, gentle place, in which the ringing of bicycle rickshaw bells was the loudest form of noise pollution. Since 1978, a lot had changed. Now, the streets were filled with the choking fumes of badly-tuned engines as trucks filled with building materials hurried to their construction sites and taxis touted for fares.

At our hotel, an embarrassingly grand banner was stretched across the entrance. Daubed on it in huge red lettering was: 'The Summit

Hotel welcomes the 1996 Himalayan Kingdoms' Mt. Everest Expedition (North Face).'

'We like to keep a low profile,' Simon said.

Garlands of flowers were placed around our necks by smiling hotel staff and a small ceremony was held in which we were annointed with red paste on our foreheads and provided with an egg and a clay bowl of raki.

'Firewater!' exclaimed Brian, and downed it in one.

Waiting for our arrival were the remaining two team members, Roger Portch, a British Airways pilot, and Richard Cowper, the *Financial Times* journalist who would be reporting on our progress.

Roger struck me immediately as a calm and self-confident personality, exactly the type of person you'd want to have at the controls of a jumbo jet while bumping around in a tropical storm. A talented climber, he had an impressive Alpine climbing history and was another of the team to have climbed Aconcagua, 6,860 metres, the Argentinian volcano which is highly regarded as a 'warm up' for the greater altitude of Everest. To afford his place on the team, Roger had sold his BA shares. When he spoke of the expedition to come, his total enthusiasm for the task was transparently, and charmingly clear; to climb Everest would be the greatest moment of Roger's life.

Richard was harder to read. An expert on the politics and economics of Asia, he looked like he would be more at home at a political briefing than in the rough and tumble of an expedition. His mission was to send back a series of articles including a profile of Al Hinkes and a piece on the pros and cons of oxygen-assisted climbs. He had brought his own dome tent out from the UK, a 'Himalayan hotel' of gigantic proportions with an intricate double pole system to resist even the fiercest of storms. The rest of us, with our inferior expedition-issue, Nepalese-constructed ridge tents, were green with envy.

The Summit is a pretty hotel with an immaculately-tended garden, positioned on a small hill overlooking Kathmandu. Normally it is a haven of peace but our arrival soon changed that. Within a few hours the first-floor balcony was crowded with a jumble of expedition equipment as new gear was tried out for the first time. Most of us had only managed to pull together the final pieces on the list in the dying moments before departing for Nepal. This was our first and last chance to make sure it all fitted together.

Problems immediately became evident. My plastic high-altitude

boots were so huge that the neoprene overboots Al Hinkes had
brought out from the UK, would only fit after considerable effort.
They were so stretched that the slightest tear would cause dramatic
damage. I made a mental note to take extra care with them. My
crampons too, were stretched right to the outer limits and looked
like they would snap in two from metal fatigue after a few hours of
use. There was nothing to do about that other than carry the spare
parts which might enable a repair.

Kitting up was strenuous work. Putting on the footgear, particularly when clad in the down suit, left me short of breath, even
though Kathmandu sits less than 10,000 feet above sea level.

Brian's equipment problems were more critical. His crampons
didn't fit at all, confirming my fears that he was not very well-
prepared or equipped. He went to the Tamel tourist market area
with Barney to track down a better pair, which provided one of the
first sequences we shot for the film.

Tamel is one of the joys of Kathmandu. It is a series of winding
streets flanked by hundreds of enterprises offering everything from
embroidered waistcoats with marijuana motifs, to bootleg CD's of
Simply Red and U2. In the wood-carved interiors of Tamel cafés,
chocolate cake and banana fritters are served up now just as they
were in the heyday of the hippy era. In fact, alongside the crowds
of trekkers – easily recognisable from their Gore-tex boots – the
sandaled feet of second-generation hippies still pad Tamel's dusty
alleys.

Passing a photographic shop, I decided on impulse to buy an
eight-dollar-plastic camera. This single-use Kodak 'fun' camera, I
thought, might be useful if my other two stills cameras had problems. I stored it in a barrel and promptly forgot all about it.

In contrast to Brian, Al had a virtual mountain of gear, spewing
out from an impressive array of barrels and kitbags, many of which
bore the names of previous expeditions to other fearsome peaks. As
a 'regular' on the Kathmandu scene, Al kept a permanent stash of
equipment in the town, to avoid air freighting it backwards and
forwards several times a year: a mark of the true professional
and another way in which Al was a different mountain creature to
the rest of us. His passport also told the same story, with page after
page of Nepalese, Pakistan and Chinese visas.

Our Sherpa crew came to the hotel the next day to help check
out the general expedition equipment. They looked a young, but
extremely strong team. Led by the experienced sirdar, Nga Temba,

who had summitted Everest himself in 1993, the nine high-altitude Sherpas and two cooks would be an essential part of the summit bid.

Working with the Sherpas in the hotel garden, where we were serenaded by a persistent cuckoo, the two-man tents were erected and surveyed for damage. The heavyweight mess tent proved more of a problem. Its complicated metal poles beat us until Sundeep, who knew the design from his army training, patiently showed us how to piece it together. The cooking equipment, food stores and oxygen were counted and packed ready for the journey to base camp.

That night, our last in Kathmandu, we ate together with the Sherpas, where free-flowing beers quickly broke the ice.

We pulled out of the Summit hotel on 3 April and began the eight-hour drive towards the town of Tatopani and the Chinese border. Al was in good form, regailing us with dubious stories and even more dubious jokes. One of these mystified Richard, and prompted his question, 'Al, what exactly *is* a "fudgepacker"?'

Even Al couldn't bring himself to answer that one.

We drove up into the foothills of the Himalayas, passing through villages which became progressively more picturesque as we gained altitude and distance from Kathmandu. After centuries of cultivation, the mountain slopes of Nepal are etched with millions of terraces and in these opening weeks of spring each terrace was carpeted with a blaze of green shoots.

After a pause to fix a puncture we arrived at the Nepalese border town of Kodari two hours after nightfall. The 'Friendship' Bridge, the narrow span which forms a fragile border link between Nepal and China, was closed for the night so we booked into a simple resthouse perched above the turbulent Bhut Kosi river. High above us, on the Chinese side, the lights of Zangmu glittered enticingly beneath a full moon.

That night, whilst unloading the supplies from the truck into a storeroom, I misjudged the height of a door and smashed my head hard against the frame. Mistake, I told myself, seeing stars. I had got into the habit of analysing such clumsiness in a futile attempt to try and discipline myself to avoid it. I still had a very real fear that my biggest enemy on the mountain might be myself and my lack of co-ordination. I sat on a barrel, feeling sick, swearing at myself and trying pathetically to work out how I'd failed to see how low the frame was.

The route from Kathmandu
through Tibet to Everest Base Camp

After a cold omelette and chips we bedded down for the night in our sleeping bags. I found it difficult to sleep; the thought that tomorrow we would be in Tibet gave me a delicious shiver. I had wanted to travel through that mysterious high land, ever since a tentative and ultimately disastrous journey through Nepal in 1978 which ended with me running out of money and collapsing with amoebic dysentery on to a Kathmandu rubbish heap.

Just after midnight Kees was violently sick, having, like Sundeep, picked up something in Kathmandu. He spent the rest of the night running to the fetid toilet with acute spasms. In the morning I asked him how he was feeling.

'Oh, fine,' he said, 'but a slightly restless night.' He went on to eat a large breakfast.

While the border formalities were being completed, we went to some lengths to get some surreptitious shots of the expedition trucks crossing the politically sensitive bridge. We felt rather foolish when we walked across; a group of Italian tourists went in front of us, openly filming the scene with their video cameras and getting no reaction at all from the guards. On the bridge a sign announced that we were 1,770 metres above sea level.

'Seven thousand and seventy-eight metres to go,' Al said.

4

Between the Friendship Bridge and the town of Khasha – or Zangmu, as it is now more commonly known, is a steeply rising three-mile track which constitutes a no man's-land. Halfway up, a team of shabby convicts were engaged in forced labour, under the watchful eye of an acne-faced guard. One of the prisoners was chipping at a huge boulder of stone, producing chips for road-building. His pile of gravel was about a metre high. As we passed, he looked up and waved. He had an intelligent, refined face. I wondered who he was and what crime against the people he had committed to deserve such a punishment.

At the top end of this stateless zone we were met by smiling representatives of the Tibetan Mountaineering Association – the 'host' organisation responsible for our transportation and official paperwork. At the border itself we unloaded the equipment from the truck and waited, sleeping on the kitbags, for most of the day while customs and immigration were sorted out in a glass-fronted office building which wouldn't have looked out of place in Milton Keynes.

Brian entertained himself by bellowing a few choice encouragements from his perch in the back of the lorry. Luckily, the border guards failed to decipher the true nature of these utterances and the paperwork continued.

Just before nightfall, the border barrier was lifted and our small convoy drove through into Tibet.

Roughly the size of Western Europe, Tibet has been occupied by China since the invasion of 1950. Prior to our journey, I had sought out some literature from the Tibet Society of the UK and their publication made for harrowing reading; since 1950, the Tibet Society contends, over 1.2 million Tibetans have died in a wide-spread programme of imprisonment, torture and executions. Tibet's unique culture and Buddhist religion have been systematically suppressed, with the destruction of over 6,000 monasteries and public buildings. More than 120,000 Tibetans have fled to become refugees in India, Nepal and elsewhere.

Just sixteen at the time of the invasion, the Dalai Lama, Tibet's head of state and religious leader, has for the last forty years pursued a non-violent path towards a solution, but despite his winning the sympathy of the many millions who have listened to his campaign, the Chinese have so far shown little sign that they will leave Tibet.

We were entering a country which had been occupied by an aggressive neighbour for more than forty-five years and for which no liberation was in sight. The town we now found ourselves in was a perfect example of how uneasy day-to-day life in Tibet has become.

Zangmu consists of one long street which zigzags up the valleyside in a series of switchbacks. Lined with wooden-built dwellings and shops, it feels every inch the frontier town. Rain had turned the unpaved surface into a muddy quagmire through which pedestrians waded ankle deep, dodging the brightly-coloured trucks and army Jeeps which raced up and down at reckless speeds. Pigs, chickens and dogs, rooted successfully amongst piles of rubbish, and as night fell, rats too came for their share of the spoils.

The ethnic mix of Zangmu's residents gave the town, like every other Tibetan place we stayed in, a split personality. The ethnic Tibetans were the most striking – their handsome faces tanned and creased from exposure to the constant winds of the plateau, their felt clothing stained with woodsmoke and yak grease. The men wore their hair in long pigtails, tied with vivid scarlet cloth, the women wore embroidered shawls and beads of glass around their necks. They watched us with glittering black eyes as we waded past in the mud, whispering and laughing at our stumbling progress and bizarre puffed-up mountain clothes.

The soldiers of the People's Army did not smile at us. In fact they scarcely looked our way as we passed them in the street. Dressed in their characteristic green uniforms with the shiny row of buttons and the comically oversized peaked cap, they seemed well-scrubbed and, for the most part, extremely young. They had the bewildered air of those who find themselves inexplicably far from home – as indeed they were if they came from Beijing thousands of miles away.

For them, Zangmu was the end of the earth. They stood in front of the shops, gazing at the goods on display with bored expressions, and sat watching poor quality television pictures in the eating houses where stale Chinese beer and noodles were the daily and only fare.

The merchants and traders of Zangmu were also predominantly ethnic Han Chinese, lured to the town by the newly flourishing trade with Nepal. They too had the far-away look of people who are trying to put down roots in an alien land. The men, with brilliantined hair and striped business shirts, looked smarter than the town deserved. They could be seen and heard in their offices above the street, talking urgently into crackling telephones, making deals. Their wives and daughters ran the shops below – often little more than cubicles – selling plastic kitchenware, batteries, canned foods and imported western goods like Head and Shoulders shampoo and Coke.

I watched one of the shopkeepers padlock her doors for the night. Dressed in an elegant silk blouse and pinstriped-pencil skirt, she tiptoed home across the horribly muddy street in a pair of four-inch stiletto heels, hopping nimbly from one dry patch to another to avoid soiling her shoes. Three indescribably scruffy Tibetan youths watched her too, fascinated by the dainty way she skipped across. One of them made a joke which had them all laughing; to them she must have seemed from another world.

In Zangmu we were only a few miles from Nepal but this was unmistakably China; one of the first things we did was to change our watches to Beijing time, four hours ahead of Nepalese time. Here, liaison officers decided which hotel we would stay in and announced a time for the set evening meal. The hotel was a cold, eerie place, with echoing corridors and missing windows through which the evening raincloud drifted. Flooded spittoons and over-flowing ashtrays lurked in the stairwells. The rooms were filled with an odd assortment of Day-Glo green and orange nylon furniture with a swirling psychedelic carpet design guaranteed to induce nightmares.

The restaurant was in the basement, next to a deserted bar which was barricaded by a padlock and chain. We sat in a depressed huddle around a circular table, eating green vegetables and rice with pork, washed down with beer which was so flat it contained not a single bubble of gas. Back in the room, I battled against a wave of nausea for two hours trying to get to sleep, and then succumbed to a violent bout of vomiting and diarrhoea which kept me in the freezing bathroom for much of the night. Kees, now recovered from his own illness, was kind enough not to complain even though my retching kept him awake for hours.

Feeling very shaky, I managed to drag myself down to breakfast for a cup of green tea, trying not to notice the nearby Chinese diners who were wolfing down great platefuls of garlic pork with lip-smacking relish. That I could survive. But when the waiter opened a dirty-looking fridge next to me, the smell of rotting meat was so intense I had to escape to the street where I was sick once more on to a pile of rubbish.

Most of the morning was devoted to finishing the immigration paperwork. As expedition leader, Simon was entrusted with this and, lacking anything else to do, I went along with him. At the immigration office tempers were seriously frayed. Frustrated by the complicated procedure, and believing (mistakenly) that Simon had jumped the queue, a tour leader with a group of frazzled French clients offered to punch his face in. A shouting match ensued, with much jostling and jabbing of elbows to get to the bewildered immigration officer's desk. Simon, impressively calm, won the day, and got our paperwork seen to first: a victory which earned him the tour leader's rebuke, 'Pah! You English! I see it is not only your cows which are mad!'

We left Zangmu at 11.30 a.m. in a convoy of three Toyota landcruisers and a truck. This was our 'official' transportation, provided by the Tibetan Mountaineering Association at an exorbitant cost to be paid only in US dollars.

After a military checkpoint, we crossed the dangerous landslip zone above the town. In heavy rains, the mountain has been known to avalanche lethal rock and mud down on to the inhabitants. Hundreds of lives had been lost before building was banned in the danger zone. Even in the light drizzle we experienced that morning, small rocks were on the move. The driver looked carefully above him before picking his way carefully across the slender track which was dotted with loose boulders.

For four hours we followed the precipitous road along the Bhut Kosi valley, rising steeply in low gear through forests of mountain pine, and crossing the fast-flowing river several times by decrepit concrete bridges. Next to me, Tore referred constantly to his wrist altimeter, noting with satisfaction every fifty-metre gain. 'Two thousand three hundred metres,' he told me, his eyes glued to the dial.

After thirty kilometres or so, less than an hour from the village of Nyalam, the road began a more serious climb up a mountainside which was scarred with old landslides and avalanche debris. Giant bulldozers were rebuilding sections which had recently been swept away and on one or two of the more fragile 'squeezes' we got out of the landcruisers and walked to avoid overloading the delicate track. In fact, the whole mountainside was completely waterlogged from the melt water of the previous winter snow. With virtually no vegetation to bond the shaley earth together, the result was like soggy porridge sliding down the side of a saucepan. The entire mountain was on the move and we were happy to get off it on to firmer, rockier ground as we rolled into Nyalam.

Strategically placed on the very edge of the Tibetan plateau, Nyalam sits at the head of the Bhut Kosi valley and at the foot of Shishapangma, the broad-backed 8,012-metre peak. Like Zangmu, the town is modestly arranged around one erratic high street which is flanked by lodges and tea houses. Some boasted ambitious Christmas light displays which brightened and dimmed according to the power of the town's generator. Most of the residents were Han Chinese – engineers and roadworkers whose thankless task was the constant rebuilding of the valley link to Nepal.

Here there was some confusion; our liaison officers wanted us to stay in one of the Nyalam lodges for the night, but Simon wanted to drive on for another hour and find a camping place where we could spend a few days acclimatising to the altitude of the plateau. In the end a compromise was reached; the expedition would be planted in a suitable camping place with one of the TMA representatives to keep an eye on us. The rest of the TMA team, and the drivers, would return to Nyalam where they could stay in relative comfort.

Thirty kilometres from Nyalam, with just half an hour of daylight remaining, we found the perfect camping spot in a scruffy village: a tiny patch of grass ringed by willowy trees. A ragged band of children watched us with open mouths as we clumsily pitched our tents. In the deeper shadows beyond a low wall, the wild-looking adults of the village were also gathered, chatting excitedly as we unloaded the mountain of equipment from the truck. Every few minutes, the children's curiosity would get the better of them, drawing them right up to us as we fought with canvas and pegs; at this, one of the Sherpas would wave a huge stick in the air and chase them away with a mighty roar. This rapidly turned into a hysterical game of cat and mouse, with the laughing children running for their lives through the glade with manic Sherpas on their tails. It ended, inevitably, in tears, when one of the infants ran headlong into a tree.

As if by some unseen signal, the villagers all slipped silently away into the night as we finished preparing the camp. We ate in the mess tent for the first time, forcing down rice, cabbage and dumplings even though the altitude – 4,600 metres – had reduced our appetites to a shadow. My stomach had still not recovered from the sickness of Zangmu, so I concentrated on getting fluids inside me, drinking several pint mugs of tea and hot chocolate. We fell asleep to the sound of dogs fighting in the village street.

For the next four days this tiny glade was our home as our bodies adapted to the thin air of the plateau. The process of acclimatisation is one which cannot be hurried; this was just the first stage in a carefully-designed programme which would enable us to live for two months above 5,000 metres, and eventually to go very much higher. Even here, at 4,600 metres, the gentlest movement betrayed the thinness of the air. Bending down to lace up a pair of trekking boots could result in an attack of breathlessness, moving a twenty-kilogramme barrel a few metres demanded a sit-down recovery period and unpacking a rucksack entailed a wearying effort.

Headaches and mild nausea were experienced by all of us during the first twenty-four hours and two of the team had other health problems; Ned succumbed to the stomach illness which had struck many of us in Nepal and at Zangmu. He feared it was giardia – a form of dysentery – and ate raw garlic to try and kill the amoebae. Tore was suffering from the return of a recurring back problem brought on by an old karate injury in which an opponent kicked one of his kidneys so hard that it was dislodged from its anchoring tissue. After an emergency operation, the kidney was repositioned (more or less) back in its proper location but Tore still worried when back pain struck. It could mean the onset of a dangerous infection.

On the second day we began our training walks up into the snowcapped mountains that overlooked the village. The first few treks were simple and brief, one- or two-hour scrambles up rocky slopes to not more than 5,000 metres. Most of us paired up in twos or threes for these sorties but Al and Brian both chose to set out alone. The psychology of this intrigued me and I pondered why these two outwardly very different characters would share the desire to train alone. Perhaps they were not so different after all?

By the third and fourth day, with our bodies better adjusted to the altitude, we pushed a little harder, above the snowline, reaching a minor windswept summit at 5,600 metres after a four-hour climb. From this vantage point we had an inspiring view back towards the borderlands of Nepal, where row upon row of 6,000- and 7,000-metre sentinels stood guard. The valley we had climbed up from seemed, from this new viewpoint, to be even more barren than it looked at close quarters, with the mighty river reduced to a slender silver strand, no bigger than a gossamer thread.

From the top, I spotted a tiny dot moving halfway up a neighbouring peak. At first I thought it was a bear, but when it paused and turned in profile for a moment I realised it was Brian on one of his solo training sessions. A short while later, far off in the opposite direction, I saw another dot. Al was picking his way along a snow-covered ridge on his way to a peak at roughly the same elevation as the one we were standing on. He paused for a second and I waved an arm in the air to see if he had spotted us. He waved back, then continued his lonely climb, lost, presumably like Brian, in a world of his own.

That night, Al failed to get back to the camp by nightfall, leading some of us to wonder what had become of him. Simon was not the least bit concerned:

'Don't worry about Al. He'll be fine.'

Half an hour later Al's headtorch bobbed out of the black night, just as the evening gong was sounded for supper.

Camping so close to the village and its fields, we had the perfect opportunity to witness at first hand the daily battle of the villagers to scrape a living from the arid land. It was spring, planting time, carried out under skies of deepest blue, and accompanied by the biting, frigid westerly wind. Each morning at sunrise, the villagers left their stone-built houses for the fields. Old women, mothers with newborn babies wrapped tightly on their backs, men whose faces were stained as black as ebony by the burning effects of sun and wind, the fields absorbed their labours as effortlessly as the desert soaks up water.

They worked with the hoe and the plough. The first was wielded by hand, blow after blow, hour after hour into the stony soil, with backs bent double and legs astride. The ploughshares were ruggedly simple, fashioned from heavy iron and with weathered wooden shanks, much as they were one hundred years ago in Europe. They ran behind teams of yaks – animals who obviously have all the right strength and all the wrong temperament for the task. The plough drivers beat them with long sticks, and threw stones at their hairy rumps with unerring accuracy, but the yaks still frequently ran amok, fighting, clashing their great heads together, and dragging the plough into neighbouring fields with the driver following on, shouting abuse.

The fields were small, irregularly-shaped, and bordered by raised channels through which irrigation water was allowed to flow at key times of the day. Every possible scrap of cultivatable land was terraced and prepared for seeding, with piles of yak and goat dung ready to enrich the ploughed furrows when the time was right.

Taking a handful of the yellow soil, it was hard for me to imagine that any crop could ever find nourishment within it. It was little more than dust: as desiccated and parched as sand. With each new onslaught of wind, the top surface became airborne in a driving cloud, filling the eyes and noses of the fieldworkers and rendering the land even more infertile.

Only two crops are hardy enough to survive this inhospitable terrain: barley and millet. Along with the milk and meat of the yak, they have become the staple for all human life on the Tibetan plateau, and without them no permanent habitation would be possible. I watched an elderly man scattering barley seed from a leather sack, his throwing arm moving to and fro in an elegant arc, shooting the tiny white seeds into the air like water droplets from a sprinkler. His actions seemed those of a supreme optimist . . . or of a madman. But he had seen the same fields sprout and grow every summer season of his life, so why should this year be any different?

It occurred to me then that when we next passed through the village, on our way back to Nepal when the expedition was over, these dry, dust-shrouded fields would be a blaze of green life. That made our own precarious venture seem a very long one indeed.

We packed up the camp on 9 April and set off in convoy, east across the plateau on the next stage of our journey through Tibet. The dirt road stuck faithfully to the valley floor for the first two hours, passing villages every five or ten kilometres. That morning, it was not just the fieldworkers who were busy at their labours; roadworking gangs were also hard at work. Every hundred metres along the road, a pile of gravel had been carefully placed on the verge. These piles stretched all the way back to Zangmu, so a major refurbishment was obviously under way. The road gangs task was to fill the many potholes and corrugations that peppered the track. This they did with the most basic of tools – a spade and rake. They wore face masks against the dust, and thick woollen coats against the cold but it was still the bleakest of jobs – not helped probably by the sight of wealthy foreigners like us racing past in our nice warm Toyotas.

By late morning the road left the river and began an abrupt climb up towards the Lalung La pass, one of the highest roadcrossings in Tibet at 5,300 metres. The final few hundred metres made for dramatic driving, with the Toyota lurching along a heavily-rutted track flanked on both sides by a metre of wind-hardened snow. The col itself was festooned with prayer flags tied to the telegraph poles like bunting at a jolly country fair. We stopped at the pass to take photographs and to admire views of both Xixapangma and Cho Oyu – two 8,000-metre giants which effortlessly dominated the horizon. Al had climbed them both and he pointed out the routes to us as we shivered in the freezing wind. He made it sound very easy, condensing what had been months of struggle into a few paraphrased highlights, so that both peaks seemed little more than weekend jaunts.

Just after the col we passed a traveller on foot, an Indian or Nepalese holy man wrapped in a brown blanket, with bare legs and no protection on his head.

'Pilgrim,' our liaison officer told us, 'maybe going to Lhasa. Maybe tomorrow dead. Many of them die.'

The pilgrim carried no food or water, yet made no gesture to try and stop us. Our driver raced past, leaving him in a cloud of dust. I was astonished that anyone could survive such cold with so little protection, and how he endured the nights was beyond my imagination. Maybe, as the liaison officer warned, he would be dead before his pilgrimage was complete.

Descending to the plateau once more, the road began to follow a new river, this time flowing east. The valley opened out into a wider plain, dotted by the ruins of ancient caravanserai and forts. This was greener, lusher land than the valley we had stayed in, and herds of goats – sometimes many hundreds – were grazing on new shoots.

Suddenly, rounding a corner, we came upon our first view of Everest. Our convoy pulled to a halt and for several minutes there was no sound other than the clicking of cameras and the ever-present rush of the wind.

Even though it was more than eighty kilometres away, Everest felt close enough to be touched. The fine details of the North Face, more perfectly triangular than I had imagined, were easily visible to the naked eye even at this long distance. Now I could understand why to the Tibetans Everest was 'Chomolungma', the goddess mother of the earth, long before western surveyors determined its status scientifically as the highest summit in the world.

Seen from the Tibetan plateau, Everest's greatness does not need theodolites for confirmation, it is, indisputably, head and shoulders above everything else on earth with a grandeur, a presence, that far outweighs that of other Himalayan giants.

I had seen the summit of Everest before, from Namche Bazar in Nepal, but that view was nothing compared to the vision now revealed to us. From the south, Everest is shy and elusive. I had seen just a glimpse of its very peak, the last 10% of the South-West Face. Crowded as it is, by Nuptse and Lhotse, you have to climb right into the western cwm, above base camp, before the South-West Face is truly revealed. Even from Kala Pattar, the famous Everest viewpoint for trekkers, only a frustrating portion of the mountain is visible.

From the north, Everest does not hide behind any veil, it reveals itself in all its glory with no preamble or guile. It just sits there alone, proud and magnificent, a pyramid of rock, sculpted by the most powerful forces on earth over millions of years. No other peak encroaches on it: none would dare. It effortlessly fills what seems to be half of the horizon. Seen from where we stood, there was no room for any doubt at all: this was the ultimate mountain.

Today, as on most days, the famous 'plume' was trailing impressively from the North-East Ridge. Simon estimated it was about thirty miles long. This white mane of Everest is evidence of the ferocious winds which scour the higher reaches of the mountain, a visible manifestation of the invisible jet stream which runs from west to east across southern Tibet. When these winds hit Everest at anything up to 150 kilometres an hour, ice crystals are clawed from the rock and spirited into the air where they fly, held horizontally in the grip of the air flow, until they fall to earth far to the east.

The plume has a compelling, hypnotic quality, like the Northern Lights, or ocean waves breaking on a shore. Once you start watching it, it becomes hard to tear the eyes away, so seductively does it shift and reshape with the passing of time. Seen from the plateau, the plume is silent, but, like watching someone scream behind sound-proof glass, the mind has no trouble in imagining the sound that must be accompanying it.

Awestruck, we climbed back into the Toyotas, each wrapped up in his own thoughts. Brian, Al, Barney and Simon had seen this

view of Everest before; they, undoubtedly, were already under its
spell – that was why they had come back. The rest of us were
experiencing new emotions. The mountain, which during the run-
up to the expedition had existed only in our dreams, was now a
tangible and frighteningly real presence. The North Face had looked
utterly forbidding and steep, even at this great distance. For the first
time, the hard realisation hit me that one or more of us, could die
on those slopes in the coming months. It all went very quiet inside
the vehicle as we drove onward along the bumpy track.

By mid-afternoon we reached the town of Tingri, home to a
sizeable army camp and several basic eating houses which cater for
conscripts and passing tourists. We ate a filling mutton stew in a
smoke-filled lodge and washed it down with cups of bitter Tibetan
tea. On the walls, flashy posters advertised Sektor Italian watches
and Gore-tex alpine clothing brands – goods which mean as much
to the average Tibetan as spacesuits and bulletproof vests do to the
average westerner.

Tingri is built on the edge of a swamp, with several shallow lakes
surrounding it. Al had stayed here many times and he demonstrated
how in certain places the ground behaved like jelly when it was
jumped upon. We spent an entertaining few minutes jumping up
and down in our heavy mountain boots, feeling the earth wobble
beneath our feet, and causing some watching children to crease up
with laughter.

Leaving Tingri, we passed through a military checkpoint and
arrived at Shekar Dzong, our nightstop, by 5 in the afternoon. The
town itself is uninspiring but behind it sits one of the most wondrous
monasteries in Tibet. Built many centuries ago, this marvel of construction sits on a knife-edge ridge, regally overlooking the
surrounding plains. At its height, the monastery was home to
hundreds of monks. In 1950, during the Chinese occupation of
Tibet, it became a seat of resistance and the scene of fierce fighting.
Finally, the Chinese sent in Mig jets and the monastery was bombed
into submission. Today it is still in ruins, a poignant monument to
the savagery of that event and the many hundreds of other acts of
destruction that were characteristic of the Chinese invasion.

Our 'hotel' in Shekar was chosen by the liaison officers and it
immediately made us wish we were back in the tents. The hallway
was so cold that a dripping samovar had created stalagmites of ice
on the concrete floor. The rooms were like prison cells, with sagging
metal beds and a single hairy blanket. The communal toilets had

evidently never been cleaned since the days of Mao. We gathered in the restaurant to pick at some food with the Sherpas. It was a meal which not even Brian's jokes could lift.

The biggest joke of all – somehow the Chinese always seem to have the last laugh – was that this travesty of a 'hotel' was costing us sixty US dollars a head for the night, the official, Beijing-set rate for foreigners. Rip-offs are always annoying, doubly so when they are official ones.

We put the 16mm film gear together the next morning and filmed the expedition convoy leaving Shekar on the final stage of the journey to base camp. The Chinese drivers, perhaps not surprisingly, got very irritated by my requests for them to stop and start as we leapfrogged ahead several times to shoot a selection of travelling shots, but we got the sequence we needed, and finished as the vehicles crossed the Pang La pass, 5,750 metres, our clearest view yet of Everest.

On the southern side of the Pang La, the track descended and deteriorated sharply, the large potholes giving us a bumpy ride. Reaching the valley floor, we turned west for the first time since leaving Kathmandu, taking the stony trail that leads to the Rongbuk monastery and base camp. Here, the villages were richer and better-built than the others we had seen, with elegant painted houses, and well-fed horses in the fields. The valleysides, by contrast, were rocky and almost devoid of vegetation except for one or two splashes of vivid green where a hamlet lay tucked with a few precious fields and one or two hardy trees.

Although Everest was now obscured by intervening hills, the milky-coloured river we now followed was fed by its snows. Here it is known as the Rongbuk, draining the northern slopes of Everest and Makalu and flowing in a great loop across the Tibetan plateau before cutting boldly in a series of deep gorges through the Himalayas at Tsanga to enter Nepal as the Arun. In the south of Nepal it is joined by the Sun Khosi, and then flows on across the Indian plains to merge with the Ganges at Katihar.

The mystery of how the Arun performed its miraculous crossing of the Himalayan watershed was one which perplexed early geographers. The problem was solved in 1937 by L.R. Wager, a geographer and explorer who mounted an expedition into the then unknown gorges of the Arun. His conclusion was that the river had formed long before the Himalayas began to rise, and that it had maintained its course by cutting progressively deeper gorges as the mountains uplifted. Wager published his theory of antecedal drainage in the *Geographical Journal* of June 1937, establishing beyond doubt that the Arun river predated the greatest mountains on earth.

With winter barely over, the Rongbuk river was little more than a stream, fed by a trickle of silt-laden melt water from Everest's glaciers. Within a few months, with the rising temperatures of summer, the river would change character completely, becoming a raging torrent of melt water. We passed the remains of numerous destroyed bridges – testimony to the power of this seasonal flood.

Crossing the river on an impressive newly built bridge, we continued west on the southern bank, passing teams of strong-looking yaks on their way to base camp. Laden with fodder and the supplies of their herders, the yaks are driven up each spring to coincide with the arrival of the pre-monsoon expeditions. They have plodded along the same trail for centuries, bringing supplies to the monastery which has existed at the foot of the Rongbuk glacier for at least four hundred years.

The track gradually turned south, rounding the valley spur until we were looking right down the Rongbuk glacier, with the North Face of Everest looming massively ahead. Fresh snow had fallen on the face in the hours since we had last seen it from the Pang La, and many of the dark areas of rock were now a dirty white colour. Once more we stopped the vehicle and assembled the film equipment, shooting half a roll before clouds blew in and obscured the view.

Much to the frustration of our drivers, who were by now jumping up and down with impatience, we filmed again at the Rongbuk monastery, interviewing Brian in front of one of the gold-capped stupas. He was in pensive mood, and talked openly about his fears for the months ahead:

Sometimes I feel full of confidence, and then I just die with fear. It's such an awesome mountain. I'll have to take it one step at a time . . . one day at a time. And if she'll allow us, we'll make it to the top. But by God it's not going to be easy.

Finally, with a freezing wind at our tail, we drove the last axle-twisting twenty minutes along the glacial moraine, and arrived at base camp, 5,500 metres, with just enough daylight left to clear platforms and pitch our tents. As we struggled with the canvas, the cloud momentarily cleared on Everest, revealing the summit bathed in fiery red light. It was 11 April, nine days since we had left Kathmandu, twelve days since leaving the UK. The travelling was over; now the expedition could begin.

*

As a child I had often wondered what a 'base camp' really was; like a 'snowhole' or a 'bivouac', it sounded exciting – but what was it exactly? The best mental picture I could achieve was a collection of pretty alpine-style huts filled with jolly climbers enjoying mugs of steaming cocoa. Lit by roaring hurricane lamps and warmed by an open fire, it was a reassuringly cosy place, a world apart from the blizzards which raged outside.

A short visit to base camp on the northern side of Everest would have quickly put me right, and shattered a few childhood fantasies. A more hostile, less heartening, spot would be hard to imagine outside of the polar regions. Arriving expeditions scatter themselves far and wide across the glacial valley, seeking out shallow dips and hollows which they imagine will protect them from the wind. They are wrong. The wind of Tibet is inescapable ... it is part of the fabric of the place, like the stones, and the dust. And the smell of stale yak shit.

This was no fleeting visit. Our camp here would be home for the next ten weeks, a place to return to each time we came back from the higher camps on the mountain. The process of acclimatisation is a slow one and it is usual for even experienced teams to spend at least six or eight weeks letting their bodies adjust to the paucity of oxygen prior to a summit attempt.

Every tiny feature of the Rongbuk valley conspires to make life more difficult. The ground is frozen, and cannot be penetrated by even the sturdiest tent peg. The rivers are frozen too, or where they run they are filled with silt and cannot be drunk. Sleeping bags, put out to air, are picked up by the wind and whipped away. Washed clothes freeze as stiff as boards. The air is dry, adding to the draining effects of altitude. Throats become sore. Lips become cracked. Fingers split and get infected. Minds start to wander, thinking of home ... thinking of anything but the terrifying mountain which sits above the valley.

I was excited to be at Everest base camp, but I can't say I liked it.

The old hands, Barney and Al, built substantial stone walls around their tents to prevent the wind from destroying them. Others, lazier like Kees and myself, made a half-hearted attempt to copy them and had to rebuild our tent several times after bad storms.

Base camp is an easy place to get very depressed, as several members of our team were to find out in the coming months. 'Glacier lassitude' – the disease so brilliantly introduced to the world in the book, *The Ascent of Rum Doodle*, is pervasive and all-consuming once it has you in its grasp.

One team member whom I thought unlikely to become a victim of depression was Brian; he had been here before and had his own ways of dealing with it.

'Take care here, Matt,' he advised, 'or you'll go fucking crazy. Just get your tent as comfortable as you can and make sure you read plenty of books.'

I took his advice. In the first five days at base camp I read the eight-hundred-page *Scramble for Africa*; a biography of Sherpa Tenzing, a biography of Paul Getty, *Trainspotting*; two Patrick O'Brian novels; *Our Man in Havana*; and Paul Theroux's *Jungle Lovers*. Kees was less prolific, or perhaps a more diligent reader. In the same period he read fewer than one hundred pages of the German war epic, *The House of Krupp*, lingering over each page like a connoisseur relishing a fine cigar.

A new fear began to grip me, almost as powerful as the fear of what could befall us on the mountain: the fear of running out of reading material.

Simon chose a prominent site for our camp, not far from the place chosen by the British expedition of 1922. Nearby was the small moraine hillock picked by the Chinese as the location for the TMA base . . . an ugly stone-built construction with an overflowing toilet block nearby. In this cheerless place, unsmiling liaison officers ticked off the days, resentful of this 'hardship' posting, and entertained only by a fuzzy television set fed by a satellite dish which would not look out of place at Jodrell Bank.

We were one of the early arrivals, beaten only by the Norwegians and the Japanese. On each of the four days it took us to establish our camp, the rumble of trucks announced newcomers. Soon there were German, Catalan, Slovenian and Indian expeditions scattered around the glacier. Some, like the Catalan expedition, consisted of just five or six team members with very little Sherpa support. Others, like the Indians, had more than forty members, and substantial Sherpa teams.

In total, more than 180 climbers (only a handful of which were women) would be attempting the North Face of Everest during this pre-monsoon season; a sign of the growing popularity of the northern side, and a dramatic increase from the early 1980s when getting permission from the Chinese at all was extremely difficult.

Al, a member of the high-altitude élite, was in his element, catching up with old friends. He knew climbers from many of the other expeditions and spent long hours swapping news of who had climbed what, by which route, and who had died since they last met. On the occasions I could listen in on these conversations, they always fascinated me; serious high-altitude mountaineers discuss avalanches, falls and ferocious storms in the same matter-of-fact way that normal mortals discuss the football results. A death here. A camp obliterated there. Fatalities are reported with the same sense of inevitability that casualties are reported from the front-line of a war; the news digested with the barest nod of the head, or a raised eyebrow.

Inside they must be wondering when their turn will come.

The rest of us made contacts at our own pace, lured into rival camps by the gravitational pull of freshly ground coffee and the aroma of newly baked bread . . . or in Sundeep's case perhaps by the discovery that the Indian expedition had two pretty girls on board. Each camp had its own idiosyncrasies, as we quickly discovered. In the Norwegian camp, an ingenious diesel-powered heater warmed the team members while they tinkered endlessly with their satellite fax, munching on dried fish and strips of reindeer meat.

In the camp of the Indian expedition, the tents were like Mongolian yurts, the members sitting cross-legged on exotic carpets imported from Delhi. Visiting it, you felt as if you had stumbled into the domain of a wandering Moghul king. The Indian leader was Mohindor Singh, a high-ranking official in the Indo-Tibetan border police, from which ranks he had formed his team. With thirty-nine members, Singh was in charge of a huge expedition and his logistics (and therefore his logistical problems) were on a far grander scale than ours. Nevertheless he attacked them with military efficiency and within days he had his members setting out up the glacier to establish advance base camp.

My favourite 'other home' belonged to the Catalans, six climbers from Girona in the north of Spain. What their mess tent lacked in structure (it was constructed mostly from plastic sheeting), it more than compensated for in the warmth of the welcome and the excellence of its coffee. They had thought carefully about their food; a large ham was hanging from the roof, and a deliciously pungent cheese stood in pride of place on the table.

The Catalans were, like the Russians, attempting a more difficult and more avalanche-threatened route than our own proposed line. Instead of turning left up the East Rongbuk glacier, they planned to carry on to the eastern side of the North Col where they would establish advance base near 'Tilman's camp'. Assisted by just three Sherpas, they hoped to ascend the difficult ice face from there to the Col and then continue up the North Ridge. With so little support it was an ambitious proposal even though several of their team had considerable 8,000-metre experience.

'I think we need more Sherpas,' one of the Catalan climbers confided in me. I could only agree. They left base camp before us, taking everything with them as they had neither the resources nor the manpower to keep a permanent camp at the foot of the Rongbuk.

The deficiencies of our own mess tent became clear as each day passed. With no heater and just a single flimsy layer of canvas, it was extremely cold, particularly at night. Dressing for dinner meant putting on thermal gloves and outer gloves, along with (as a minimum) a down jacket or down suit.

Roger quickly became the focus of our early conversations in the mess tent; we were endlessly fascinated by his job.

'How safe are those jumbos?'

'What's the nearest you've got to crashing?'

'Any babies born on board?'

'Can you loop the loop in a 747?'

Roger patiently answered these and more for hours on end, his supper often untouched and congealing in front of him. From that point on, Brian took the mickey out of our aviation obsession ruthlessly. Whenever there was a lull in the conversation he would fire a question at our resident pilot:

'The Messerschmit 109, Roger, is it true what they say about the stall rate?' or 'Ever shot down a Junkers, Rog?'

At the end of each meal I would retreat to the comparative warmth of our two-man tent and massage my frozen feet back to life.

Next door to our own mess tent was the Sherpa canteen. If ours was the 'officer's mess', theirs was very much a working men's club, sensibly annexed to the cook tent so that the maximum heat was retained. Much has been written about the 'us' and 'them' of eating arrangements such as this, but Sherpas are far too wise to be done over in matters of comfort. Their mess tent was warmer and far more sociable than our own, with an occasional barrel of alcoholic 'chang' on hand to keep out the cold.

Our two base camp cooks were Dhorze and Dawa, ever smiling, ever busy, ever chopping onions with the chipped blades of machetes in the dark smoky confines of their kitchen. Like all cooks they had their good days and their bad days, but somehow their bad days seemed to outnumber the good. They were far better company than they were *chefs de cuisine*, but no one had the heart to tell them, we liked them far too much.

'I'll have you know that Dhorze spent a week in the kitchen of a major Kathmandu hotel,' Simon said grandly one night, alarmed by the rising tide of complaints after just a few days at base camp.

'Cleaning out the bins?' was someone's cruel response.

On soups they were at least consistent, producing cauldrons of steaming broth pepped up with ginger and the prolific use of garlic. Their main courses were geared for bulk intakes of carbohydrate with huge mounds of rice, pasta and dumplings, garnished with boiled cabbage and strangely scented lentils. It always looked all right. It just didn't taste very good.

Sometimes what the eye beheld was not backed up by what the taste bud revealed. Strips of cabbage could taste like boiled soap, mild-looking lentils could attack the tongue in a searing rage of chili pepper, and even the humble baked bean could leave the victim with a lingering aftertaste of cheap aftershave, like gargling with Brut 33. Inevitably, the craving for more familiar fare was hard to resist, and the bottles of HP sauce and tomato ketchup were soon in strong demand.

'Got any spam fritters?' was Al's daily request.

'Eggs! Give me eggs, God damn you!' was Brian's.

Still, we cheered heartily every time the food was brought into the mess tent, unwilling to disappoint our cooks. Later, back in our own tent and feeling faintly traitorous, Kees and I dined on Emmenthal cheese and oatcakes, rounded off with Bendicks Bittermints and a splash of Courvoisier brandy from my personal food supply. Others, like Tore and Brian, who had no supplies of their own, found they could not stomach much of the food and so ate badly. They said little at the time, but the complaints would become a lot more vocal before the expedition was over.

Occasionally, when mutterings reached a fever pitch, Simon would graciously declare the next meal a 'Wayfarer' meal, and let us loose on the prepacked foil sachets of ready-cooked western food. He timed these announcements perfectly, basking in the tidal wave of gratitude like a headmaster who has just announced an unexpected school holiday, and cunningly diverting attention from the other minor grievances which fester away on all expeditions. 'Wayfarer' days were eagerly awaited by all, and were the only times I saw Brian eat anything like a substantial meal.

While we bickered about the food in the 'officer's mess', the Sherpas were consulting with the Lamas of the nearby Rongbuk monastery to determine an auspicious date for the puja ceremony. This was fixed for the morning of 14 April; we would leave for the trek to advance base camp the following day.

The preparations for the puja ceremony had begun in Kathmandu with the purchase of strings of prayer flags paid for with a 200-rupee donation from each team member. At base camp, the Sherpas built a two-metre-high stone cairn just outside the camp and collected the food and drink which would be consumed at the ceremony. Kees, Ned and myself would not be able to participate in the main part of the event, because we intended to film it, so I donated my precious litre of Paddy's Irish whiskey in the hope that the gods would excuse our absence.

After breakfast, the entire expedition gathered by the cairn, dressed in full high-altitude regalia complete with the heavy down suits and wind layer. Crampons, ice-axes and harnesses were also brought along and placed against the cairn to be blessed along with canned foods, biscuits, and bowls of rice. It was a colourful scene, played out beneath a perfect azure sky; one of the clearest days we had seen, with no more than the lightest of winds.

I had expected the Lama to be a venerable old man in an orange robe, but in fact the ceremony was led by a young Nepali dressed in a brightly-coloured fleece and a pair of expensive sunglasses. He sat reading from a prayer-book as incense was burned, lifting the prayers to the gods.

Just as we were preparing to film, our DAT sound recorder started to misbehave, affected perhaps by the sub-freezing temperatures in which it was kept. Kees spent several frustrating minutes trying to reanimate it but it stubbornly refused to transport the tape. He changed the battery and tried again. Still nothing. I was starting to sweat inside my down suit: the puja ceremony was one of the film sequences we could not afford to miss.

Ned started to shoot mute pictures with the 16mm Aaton and I ran to the tent to get the standby digital camera, forgetting that my short sprint would leave me gasping for air at this altitude.

When I returned, we recorded the sound on the back-up camera, keeping fingers crossed that the result would still be in sync. It was the first serious equipment failure, and it did nothing for my peace of mind. I was already haunted by the fear that we would have a camera failure high on the mountain, but the possibility of our gear giving up at base camp had foolishly never occurred to me.

Despite the problems, Ned managed to shoot the puja ceremony through to the climax when the prayer flags were unfurled and attached to the specially-built cairns. The group stood together for the final chants, throwing handfuls of rice and Tsampa towards the flagpole with a rousing cry. Then the whiskey and beers were broken out, and toasts drunk to the success of the expedition.

It was an auspicious start to the expedition, unlike the puja for Simon's previous attempt at Everest, where the central flagpole had broken in the wind just seconds after it was raised (an ill omen, understandably greeted with horror by Sherpas and members alike).

'To Everest!' Brian raised his glass, 'We come not to conquer you but to befriend you! Chomolungma!'

Then we retired to our tents. At 5,000 metres, a single glass of whiskey was enough to wipe us out for the day. I dozed fitfully, visited by nightmares in which our cameras suffered horrible fates; spontaneously jumping out of packs and sliding into crevasses, tumbling down seracs and getting crunched under the feet of stampeding yaks.

When I woke up, I found a real nightmare in progress: mad professor Kees with a voltmeter and screwdriver in hand, and with one of the back-up cameras and the DAT sound recorder in pieces around the tent. Odd screws, tightly-coiled springs and other crucial-looking components were strewn around him in the most alarming fashion.

'Kees! What the hell are you doing?'

'Oh just tinkering.'

'Tinkering? If you screw those machines up, Kees, we've got no bloody film! What the hell's that, for example?'

I pointed to a printed circuit board from the DAT which seemed to have fallen into one of Kees's climbing boots. Kees looked wounded.

'Oh. Not quite sure. But I think it has a problem.'

Kees has always been the master of the vague response and under

pressure he sometimes clams up completely. He gave me one of his
'trust me' looks, and resumed his tinkering, pushing the metal
probes deep into the guts of the DAT machine like a back-street
surgeon performing a dodgy transplant operation.

'And what's wrong with the camera?'

'The microphone is falling off. I'm just removing the plastic casing
and reassembling it.'

'I think I'd better go for a walk.'

Unable to watch, I left Kees muttering over his voltmeter and
went to the Catalan camp to see if their ham was finished. When I
returned, he had both pieces of equipment working perfectly. 'Oh
ye of little faith' was his final word on the subject before wandering
across the moraine to celebrate with a bath in the freezing cold river.

It was the last chance for a wash; our trek to advance base camp
would begin the following morning.

5

At dawn on 15 April the yaks were herded reluctantly into huddles as we took down our tents and packed up the equipment ready to leave. From their depressed air and collective bad temper, it was pretty clear the yaks knew what was coming: the trek to advance base camp is 'hard drill', as Simon described it, particularly if you are a yak carrying a fifty-kilogramme load.

In theory the yak herders and their beasts work on a price structure laid out by the Tibetan Mountaineering Association. To read their literature, the hiring and organisation of yaks sounds no more difficult than, say, hiring a 'redcap' baggage porter at Heathrow. In practice, the scene at base camp on the morning of our departure was gloriously chaotic, with chief sirdar Nga Temba besieged from all sides by yak herders objecting to the size of the loads, and haggling for bonuses.

Tibetan yak herders are not coy; they do not find it awkward to express their displeasure like many westerners do. Negotiations are carried out with a dazzling array of scowls, ugly pouts, and murderous glances. Nga Temba remained calm, which seemed to infuriate them more. Soon, he was besieged by a jostling, yelling mob, with no sign of a single pack being loaded.

Just as it seemed violence was inevitable, a Tibetan negotiator in a brightly-coloured silk hat emerged from the TMA building and tried to pacify the yak herders. None of us had any idea what he said, but his words whipped them into an even bigger frenzy. Individual loads were now under discussion as the mob moved from one pile of equipment to another. Boxes were lifted and rejected as too heavy, packs were tested and thrown contemptuously aside.

Then, bewilderingly, the mood abruptly changed. The arguments finished and the yak herders split into groups to load their animals. Agreement had been reached and everyone was happy, with not the slightest indication that they had been close to a riot just minutes before.

We ate an early lunch, and then left ahead of the main body of the expedition, to film the team members and yaks together as they came towards us up the Rongbuk glacier. We had three or four false starts, with a film jam in the 16mm camera, but Ned pulled out his spare magazine in the nick of time and got a wonderful series of telephoto shots, through the shimmer of radiation haze. I operated the DAT sound, recording the eerie whistling of the yak herders echoing off the walls of the valley.

After leaving the broad moraine plateau the track takes the left hand, eastern side of the valley, and funnels into a constricted gulley between the glacier and the crumbling slopes. These shed a continuous fusillade of runaway stones and boulders whose clattering approach sets the nerves on edge. In the gulley there was ample evidence of big rock slides, where football-pitch-sized sections of the valley walls had given way and slumped down to the glacier ice.

Because we were one of the first teams to leave base camp, the trail was barely broken through the snow. The yaks had a hard time of it, frequently stumbling to their knees or getting stuck in the compacted narrow path through the ice. The herders had to maintain an almost constant barrage of shouts and yells to encourage them to go ahead.

'Huioy!' was one of the mildly threatening shouts, but the one to clear a really bad yak jam was 'Irriaaaargh!' – a terrifying roar which almost always shifted the blockage. Where words failed, a substantial rock was lobbed at the yak's rump. That never failed.

The Rongbuk glacier is a huge mass of ice but so much rubble lies on it that the ice itself is barely visible on the lower stretches. Only after an hour of trekking does it start to reveal crevasses and distant ice pinnacles, but they too are stained dark grey from the glacial dust.

Three hours after leaving base camp, we began the steep climb up the spur which marks the beginning of the East Rongbuk glacier. Brian pointed out to me how easy it had been for Shipton to miss the significance of the narrow valley on the survey expedition of 1922.

At a casual glance the valley gives no clue that a huge glacier system lies behind it, so cunningly does it conceal its true significance. The mouth is little more than an innocent cleft in the valley wall, when seen in scale with the rest of the landscape. A pathetic trickle of water (it is more a brook than a stream) runs out of the defile down towards the Rongbuk glacier. There is no sign of any ice, and anyone looking up the valley from the Rongbuk sees nothing more than an unpromising stony ravine.

No wonder Shipton got it wrong; he dismissed exploring the valley in favour of continuing down the Rongbuk proper on the 'direct' route which leads straight to Everest. Now I could see the situation for myself, I was not at all surprised by his decision – the direct route doesn't seem just the obvious option, it seems the only one.

The orientation of the East Rongbuk valley is another confusion. It looks as if it leads away from Everest. Trekking into it, there are thus two surprises, firstly that the glacier system contained within it is every bit as significant as the Rongbuk itself. The second is that the East Rongbuk valley and its glacier curve unexpectedly in an elegant southerly arc, right to the foot of the North Col. The mystery of why so little water apparently escapes from the mouth of the valley is thought to indicate that a huge underwater river runs unseen beneath the rock.

Shipton couldn't know it. How sad it is that he had no air support, for one aerial pass would have unlocked the secrets of the East Rongbuk in a matter of minutes. But the East Rongbuk was the hidden key which would ultimately unlock Everest's North Face. It would take a further expedition, and another two years, before this vital geographic twist would be surveyed, after the 'obvious' route proved to be too technically daunting and rebuffed all attempts.

For a further two hours we made our slow plod up the spur and into the valley where a boulder-strewn path snaked along the northern side of the milky stream. The yaks picked up speed once we started to climb, and they soon overtook us. The yak herders followed them with astonishing ease, sure-footed and fast in their plastic shoes and old canvas army boots, even when crossing treacherous ice patches. They were endlessly singing and whistling, finding spare breath in their lungs where we had none.

With an hour of daylight remaining, we established camp on a small cliff above the river, beneath a slope which showed signs of massive instability. It was our first attempt at putting up the Mountain Quasar tents, and Kees and I had to enlist Al's help to work out which poles went where.

We ate together in a makeshift cook tent and then crashed out exhausted by 8 p.m. As I tried to get to sleep, boulders popped

out of the nearby cliff and crashed down into the river with horren-
dous bangs and splashes. A horrific thought occurred to me: Kees
and I were in the most vulnerable of the tent positions – just a
couple of metres from the cliff edge, which was obviously in the
process of falling to pieces. If our section of cliff suddenly gave way,
we would be dumped twenty metres down into the river in the midst
of hundreds of tons of rock.

With every new stonefall my heart leapt and my breathing rate
increased. For an hour or more I lay in a state of terror and then
fell into an uneasy sleep, filled with dreams of falling and the rumble
of landslides.

I am sure that at sea level I would scarcely have thought about
the risk; or would have reduced it to a logical assessment based
on the knowledge of how many millions of years that piece of cliff
had been in position. But, here at 5,800 metres, my brain seemed
more prone to fear and paranoia – another of the insidious effects
of altitude.

Kees had his own problems. For the last three or four days he
had been developing a raging sore throat which had now evolved
into a racking cough. The nights were particularly bad.

'You'd better see Sundeep about that throat, Kees.'

'Oh, I don't think I'll worry him about it yet,' he replied, then
collapsed in another coughing fit.

Typical Kees. He'd have to be in the final stages of acute mountain
sickness before he would voluntarily seek a doctor's help. In the end
I bullied him into seeing the doc, but most of Sundeep's medicines
had gone missing with the barrel that vanished *en route* from London
to Kathmandu. Sundeep could only offer cough sweets and lozenges
– or antibiotics. Kees decided to see how the condition developed
and continued to cough through the nights.

The weather deteriorated the next morning, with grey clouds
threatening from the west. The wind was bitter, forcing us to put
on every thermal layer beneath the windproof Gore-tex clothing. I
protected my face with a scarf and a silk balaclava, preserving precious warmth by breathing into the woollen fabric of the scarf.
Occasional snow flurries whipped down the valley as we rounded a
rocky pass, crossed the small glacial river and began the trek up the
East Rongbuk glacier.

Conversation tailed off as we began to pick our way up through
the dirty mounds of ice. We were all struggling to force enough air
into our lungs to cope with the erratic trail. The path was

inconsistent, sometimes rising, sometimes falling, and defying any attempt to get into a rhythm. Splashes of red blood marked the snow at regular intervals, for many of the yaks had cut their feet on the sharp terrain.

I felt exhausted and irritable after the restless night, and found that the muscles in my legs were devoid of power. Every time the path began to climb, my pace slowed to a crawl, with impatient yaks and their herders shouting behind to get past. The rucksack, which had felt fairly light back at base camp, now pulled down on my shoulders as if it were loaded with ballast.

I wanted to get a film sequence of the team climbing up the East Rongbuk glacier – and ideally in bad weather conditions. For obvious reasons, the tendency with mountain films is to shoot predominantly in good weather conditions when the light is strong and the risk of damaging equipment is at a minimum. Melting snow and spindrift can penetrate even the best-protected film camera with disastrous results. But a large proportion of Himalayan climbing is carried out in conditions which are anything but good. I wanted to capture that, to avoid going back with a film that made it all look too 'nice'.

But as the morning went on, my energy was gradually seeping away. To film, we would have to open the packs and assemble all the equipment and that meant fifteen to twenty minutes standing still in the freezing conditions with fingers and toes going numb and the rest of the team waiting for us. The prospect of the physical effort of shooting the seven or eight shots was a depressing one. With my brain and body running well below their normal levels, raising any enthusiasm at all was extremely difficult.

The more I thought about it, the more attractive it became to forget about the filming for the moment and just concentrate on putting one foot in front of the other and completing the day stage. That was all the other team members had to do, wasn't it? I found myself experiencing, for the first time in ten years of filming expeditions, an irrational anger at the enormity of the task we were facing. How could anyone expect us to shoot a film on Everest? The day-to-day realities of climbing are hard enough. But to film as well, and carry all the film equipment?

I was swearing and cursing under my breath, getting myself into a real state at the injustice of it all and feeling distinctly sorry for myself. What the hell was I doing here? All this pain for a few television pictures? Shit, we could shoot this sequence and it could easily never appear in the final cut. All that work for nothing. What could be more pointless?

I was not having a good day and my physical strength was fading fast. The thought that we would have to do this trek up the East Rongbuk at least twice more before the end of the expedition only added to my malaise. I seriously doubted now that I would have the strength.

Two hours later, we paused by a frozen melt water lake to drink from our bottles. I had filled mine with sweet black tea back at the camp and, having wrapped the bottle inside my sleeping bag in the pack, the liquid still retained a hint of warmth. The effect of the tea was immediate, diffusing a warm glow through my body. I was like a frozen cartoon character who turns from blue to pink in a matter of seconds.

With the liquid came an almost instantaneous change of mood. The anger melted away and was replaced by a sense of shame that I could have lapsed into such a negative frame of mind.

What was going on? With a shock, I realised. I had let myself become dehydrated during the first hours of the day and lost the critical balance of fluids in my body. The depression and anger had been the result. It was the first time I had experienced such a mood swing from dehydration but I had no doubt that water loss was the cause. Why else, after half a litre of tea, would my state of mind have swung back so dramatically the other way?

It was an exciting moment of discovery. Every piece of acquired knowledge was another step up the learning curve . . . and another step up the mountain. I drank the rest of the tea and carried on, determined that I would not let anger take me over again.

Another hour of hard work brought us to a small flat platform where the Indian expedition had erected an intermediate camp. Our yak herders were having a break, crouched in the falling snow cooking tea. They greeted us with gap-toothed smiles as we struggled up the slope, cracking jokes between themselves and coughing loudly in the smoke. The smell of burning wood and cheap Chinese cigarettes filled the air.

Neat piles of plastic expedition boxes were stacked against the green Indian army tent, each one bearing the stencil 'Indo-Tibetan border police'. Large sacks of yak fodder were dumped alongside, guarded by a ferocious-looking dog. It would have been good to rest and eat here but we had no means to cook and so continued down a steep incline, across a frozen river and up on to the next feature of the East Rongbuk, the straight three-kilometre ridge of moraine which would lead to our next camp.

The depressing rubble-strewn hillocks of the lower glacier were now replaced with a vision of extraordinary beauty. To our left, were the pinnacles described by Mallory as the 'fairy kingdom', the sail-shaped towers of ice which sprout miraculously from the glacier like the sawtooth scales on a dragon's back. Shaped by the wind, the pinnacles range in colour from purest white to deepest blue.

This was a place where we *had* to film.

Ned was carrying the Aaton, I had the DAT and the microphone, and Kippa Sherpa was carrying the tripod, the heaviest and most awkward load. On the crest of the ridge, we unloaded the equipment, taking great care to shield the camera from the blowing snow. For the next hour we filmed a series of shots with the climbers and the caravan of yaks framed against the highly visual backdrop of the ice towers. The climbers were happy to comply with our requests to pause while we got into positions ahead of them, it gave them an extra rest. Stopping a line of yaks, however, is impossible once they are on the move, but we got whatever shots we could as stragglers came up behind the group.

Then, with the snowfall thickening, and the wind rising, we hastily packed the film gear away and continued up the moraine 'highway'. The ice pinnacles had all but disappeared in the white-out, becoming a series of half seen ghostly shapes. Our filming had been just at the right time, with the weather bad enough to 'read' on film, but the pinnacles still visible. Ned was pleased, and so was I.

We reached the next camp at about 4 in the afternoon after seven hours on the move. Our average progress, I calculated, was just one kilometre per hour at this altitude, compared to the usual two or three kilometres an hour which might be expected by a fit group on mixed terrain at sea level. We kicked clear platforms and erected the tents as a fresh flurry of freezing snowfall began, backed by a consistent northerly wind running directly off the ice. Our fingers froze in seconds when we took off the thick overmitts to thread the fiddly tent-poles into their sleeves.

This second intermediate camp occupied a spectacular location at the junction of the East Rongbuk and Beifeng glaciers. Everest was obscured behind the massive flank of Changtse, but other views now opened up towards the outlying peaks of Changzheng 6,977 metres, and Lixin 7,113 metres.

Our water supply was from a frozen glacial pond, held fast

between two crumbling ice pinnacles. While Kees got the gas cooker going, I climbed down the short snow step to fill the water bottles and the biggest of our saucepans. Setting up a mess tent was not practical here so each tent was responsible for its own food and drink.

A hole had been smashed through the six-inch-thick ice to gain access to the unfrozen water beneath. In the couple of minutes since the last visitor filled his pans, a layer of fresh ice had already formed, thick enough to need a blow from my ice-axe to smash it. I managed to get my gloves wet in the process of collecting the water and by the time I got back to the tent, the fabric had frozen as hard as iron. I had to prise my fingers apart with my other hand to remove them from the saucepan handle.

We put on the water for tea, and talked lazily through the day's filming for half an hour while we waited for the pot to boil. Simon had warned us to boil the water well here as the source was almost certainly polluted. Clearing the platform of snow for our tent had backed his theory up; the ground at this camp was littered with toilet paper and human waste from previous expeditions.

Kees's cough had worsened in the past twenty-four hours and my own throat was now feeling none too good. The first of a string of throat infections was setting in and swallowing food was becoming difficult. Neither of us felt like eating but we forced down a pre-packed meal of bacon and beans and then collapsed into sleep. As had been the pattern of previous days, I woke several times to use the pee bottle, passing more than a litre of fluid. Kees, better groomed in matters of social etiquette perhaps, chose to exit into the freezing night air to answer his own calls of nature.

The shouts of the herders gathering up their yaks woke us at first light.

Leaving the second intermediate camp, we now entered the 'trough' – the final stage of the East Rongbuk trek which would lead us to advance base camp. The 'trough' – so called by the early expeditions of the 1920s, is a natural depression which sits between two parallel lines of ice pinnacles. Filled with moraine rubble, it is, compared to picking a way through the ice maze of the glacier itself, a relatively simple path which runs directly to the flat basin at the foot of the North Col. We climbed in silence through a murky white layer of cloud, oblivious to the views of Everest's North Ridge which now lay above us.

Now the altitude was really beginning to make itself felt. Not since an asthma attack as a child had I struggled to breathe as I did on that last day's journey into advance base camp. The soreness in my throat had flared up overnight into an infection which was now getting hard to ignore. Each breath of super-dry air merely antagonised the inflamed tissue and a sharp digging pain began to throb away like a pin being pushed in and out a few inches behind my tonsils. Pausing to spit out some bloody mucus which had oozed from my throat, I reflected that this was probably the least enjoyable day's trekking I had ever known.

I resolved to try and get medical attention for my throat once we got to the camp, knowing that this was just the early stages of what could get a lot more serious . . . and even prevent me going higher. I had read an account of the 1924 British expedition in which Howard Somervell (who had climbed over 28,000 feet in his attempt on the summit) found himself choking to death after a piece of infected flesh came loose and blocked his windpipe. Somervell wrote:

I made one or two attempts to breathe but nothing happened. Finally, I pressed my chest with both hands, gave one last almighty push – and the obstruction came up. What a relief! Coughing up a little blood, I once more breathed really freely – more freely than I had done for some days.

The 'obstruction' Somervell wrote of was the entire mucus lining of his larynx.

We were now one thousand metres above base camp – higher than all but a handful of peaks outside of the Asian continent, including giants like Kilimanjaro and Mt. McKinley – yet we still hadn't reached the foot of the mountain.

The tents of advance base camp came into view just after 2 p.m. 'Almost there,' I told Kees. But the distance was deceptive. The tiny flecks of red and green canvas were much further away than they seemed; I had been deceived by the foreshortening effect of the thin air. We trudged on for another two hours before we made it, taking care to overtake Brian so we could film him coming into the camp which would be our home for the next two days.

At 6,450 metres, camp three, or Advance Base Camp, makes base camp seem like a Caribbean resort. Squeezed into a narrow rocky strip of rubble between the dirty ice of the glacier and the decaying rock wall of Changtse's South-East Face, it is not a location in which relaxation comes easily. The terrain is unrelentingly brutal; walking from one tent to another is an obstacle course of lurking crevasses and ankle-twisting rocks.

Eating, sleeping, every human function, has to compete against the tidal wave of exhaustion and apathy that goes hand in hand with altitude. Every single action, whether it is tying a bootlace or summoning the energy to answer a call of nature, is carried out in slow motion – partly because the mind can't bear the thought of doing anything anyway and partly because the body is operating on oxygen levels which are simply not enough to run the engine at full power.

At the evening meal on our first night I stared miserably for nearly thirty minutes at a plateful of greasy packet noodles before I could finally summon the enthusiasm to try a mouthful. Try as I might, I couldn't swallow it. Without saying a word, I walked out of the mess tent and spat the mouthful on to the glacier. Then I vomited the semi-digested remains of lunch on top of it and retired, shuddering with the cold, to the tent.

The next morning, after a night plagued with nightmares and claustrophobia, I felt like I was coming round from the effects of a general anaesthetic. My brain felt like someone was trying to cleave it into two chunks with a blunt hacksaw and it took me over an hour to generate the will-power to get out of the sleeping bag and walk to the mess tent for some tea.

Later in the afternoon Simon called us together for an announcement.

'There's a bit of bad news come up from base camp,' he told us, pausing to catch his breath. 'We just got a message to say that a couple of thieves broke into the equipment tent last night and got away with a kitbag.'

'Whose was it?'

'No way of telling until we get back down there.'

The news was something to chew over in the long hours of tedium. Who had been the unlucky member of the expedition who had lost a bag? And what had been in it? On an expedition such as this, every piece of equipment has a specific purpose . . . whichever bag it was, it would almost certainly, contain items which, once lost, could affect someone's chances of success. All our high-altitude clothing was down there, waiting to be brought up on the next run to ABC (Advance Base Camp) – if plastic boots or down suits had gone then there was little chance of a replacement being shipped out in time.

'Who do you think did it?' I asked

'Yak herders,' Al volunteered.

Sad to tell, he was probably right. It was hard to see how anyone else could have been the culprits – base camp was seething with the temporary camps of the yak herders and the knowledge that our equipment tent was virtually unprotected must have made it a tempting target. Having stolen the bag, the booty could easily be stashed in one of the thousands of crevices and small caves which surround the Rongbuk base.

Concerned with this lapse of security, Simon descended to base camp one day early. The rest of us sat it out for forty-eight hours at advance base, listlessly letting our bodies acclimatise to the paucity of oxygen and feeling pretty rough. Only Sundeep the doctor could generate a sense of wonder in the mysterious process of acclimatisation taking place silently within us.

'Just think of all those red blood cells changing and acclimatising. Incredible, really, isn't it?' he said in a burst of enthusiasm as we sat in the gloomy half-light of the mess tent.

The only reply was the sinister slurping of soup. For the rest of us, acclimatisation was a grisly affair which had to be endured rather than enjoyed.

On 19 April, when the time came to leave, we packed and headed down the glacier as fast as we could for base camp. The sixteen-kilometre trek, which had taken us three days to complete on the upward journey, now took most of us just eight hours.

But for two members of the team, the descent of the East Rongbuk was not so straightforward. Brian and Richard, the *Financial Times* journalist, debilitated perhaps after the gruelling rigours of the first trip to Advance Base Camp (or camp three), both found their strength waning as the day went on.

Most of us reached base camp just before nightfall, and as it got dark, we scanned the glacier anxiously for any sign of headtorches. There was no sign of approaching beams of light even though we could see for miles. By 7 p.m. we realised that Brian and Richard must be having a problem and, taking a Thermos flask of tea, a sleeping bag, and some extra survival clothing, Roger, Sundeep and I headed back to try and locate them.

We had to retrace our steps for several hours, almost to the point where the East Rongbuk joins the Rongbuk, before we found Brian and Richard being ushered through the night by the ever-patient Barney, Simon and Al. They were both exhausted and close to collapse. Simon was mightily pleased to see us.

Brian was slumped against a rock mumbling apologies: 'It's this bloody glacier. Just ran out of steam. Can't seem to get the legs going at all.'

Richard was in a stranger state, almost euphoric in his advanced state of fatigue. Perhaps through dehydration, half of what he was saying didn't make any sense. He asked us if we had any beer then burst into hysterical giggles.

'Richard certainly seemed to have the initial symptoms of acute mountain sickness,' Sundeep later told me, 'and for a while I thought it could be the onset of cerebral oedema. When we had a chance to examine him at the Norwegian camp we realised he was badly dehydrated.'

After sipping some tea, both recovered enough to continue towards base camp, albeit at a painfully slow pace and leaning heavily on the Sherpas for balance and support.

At base camp, which he reached at 3 a.m., Richard continued to behave irrationally, showing reluctance to drink. In the end Sundeep had to insist that Richard drank the liquids he was being offered, for his own good.

The episode reinforced the dangers of altitude and shook my confidence in Brian's physical condition. He had performed so strongly on the way up to advance base that I had not even considered the possibility of a problem on the way down.

'Don't worry, Matt,' he reassured me the next day, 'just a momentary blip. I've had it before, it's always the same on the first trip up to ABC. I'll be better on the second one.'

It was typical of Brian's generous personality that he sought to reassure me after his problem descending the glacier. He had gone through a very painful day, but showed not a shred of self-pity. After a couple of days' rest he did indeed make a remarkable recovery and did not 'hit the wall' again in such a dramatic way.

For Richard the episode had a less happy ending. On arriving at base camp he received the bad news that the bag stolen from the mess tent during our absence had been his. In it was his portable computer, and a quantity of money. To lose the cash was bad news but to lose the computer was worse. Richard's reports for the *Financial Times* were to have been written on it.

Understandably depressed by this, and perhaps still in shock from the sudden deterioration he had experienced on the glacier, Richard made a snap decision the next day. Hearing that a Jeep was leaving for Kathmandu with Ned Johnston, Richard decided to quit the expedition.

He packed his remaining bags, shook hands with the bewildered team, and left, announcing that he would spend a few days in Kathmandu and then fly back to Europe.

As a parting gesture Richard did agree to leave his luxurious tent behind. Brian and Barney moved in with impressive alacrity, ousting rival claims by the simple expedient of throwing all their gear into it approximately thirty seconds after the Toyota bearing Richard disappeared down the glacier track.

*

'The reading of the list.' Simon was standing in front of us, notebook in hand, on the morning of 27 April, four weeks into the expedition. We were back at camp three – advance base camp – for the second time, and, as part of our acclimatisation programme, the whole team was primed for our first foray to camp four on the North Col.

'Mug, spoon, jumar, harness, sleeping bag, water bottle, pee bottle. . . .'

It was a perfectly clear day, with every detail of the North and North-East Ridges sharply defined in the brilliant light. The summit triangle of Everest, seen through a rippling haze of heat radiating off the ice, looked enticingly and deceptively close.

Of the acclimatisation stages, the climb to camp four on the North Col was the most important and most committing test to date. For the first time we would be moving on steep ice, using crampon spikes on our boots and following the fixed ropes which had been placed by the Norwegians some weeks before. We knew it would be physically demanding and the psychological pressure was also high; the route is avalanche-threatened and the altitude is severe enough to reduce progress to a crawl.

The Col had been the setting for one of the greatest single tragedies ever to occur on Everest's slopes. In 1922, an avalanche had swept seven Sherpas to their deaths during the British expedition led by the Hon. C.G. Bruce. Mallory wrote about the horror of the event and the rescue that followed in which two Sherpas were pulled miraculously alive from the crevasse into which they had been carried.

In more recent years the North Col had continued to prove its

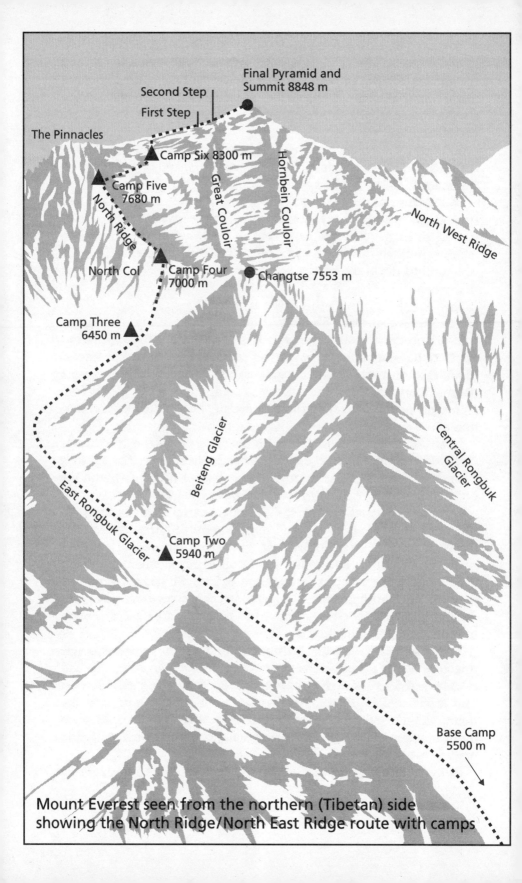

Final Pyramid and Summit 8848 m

Second Step

First Step

The Pinnacles

Camp Six 8300 m

Camp Five 7680 m

North Ridge

Great Couloir

Hornbein Couloir

North West Ridge

North Col

Camp Four 7000 m

Changtse 7553 m

Camp Three 6450 m

Beiteng Glacier

Central Rongbuk Glacier

East Rongbuk Glacier

Camp Two 5940 m

Base Camp 5500 m

Mount Everest seen from the northern (Tibetan) side showing the North Ridge/North East Ridge route with camps deadly reputation. In 1990 three climbers had been killed on the ice slope when disaster struck a Spanish team led by C.P. de Tudela.

That knowledge, and the intimidating presence of the ice cliff itself, had worked predictably on our nerves. Few things focus the mind quite so effectively for the climber as the thought that millions of tons of ice might avalanche catastrophically from above at any moment.

Al Hinkes was preparing for his first significant shooting day using the Digital video camera. The climbing of the Col was a key sequence in the film and the first time Al's climbing cameraman skills would be put to good use on the shoot. I had high hopes that the lightweight cameras would now come into their own and we had spent several hours familiarising Al with the workings of the Sony.

Kees and I would have plenty to occupy us simply to complete the physical challenge of the climb and I was not anticipating we would be able to give Al much help. I was acutely aware that the day's climb would take me higher – several thousand feet higher in fact – than my previous altitude 'best'. Without a comparable climbing experience to draw on, there was the sharp stab of fear in the pit of my stomach; the fear that ultimately, I would 'hit the wall' and fail to reach camp four. That would be embarrassing to say the least, and would leave Al and Kees with a huge burden of responsibility for the critical high-altitude stages of the shoot.

I dabbed glacier cream on to a finger and smeared the greasy solution liberally on to my face and hands, taking care not to miss the underside of my nose and my ears, both vulnerable to the intense radiated light bouncing off the ice.

We filmed the team assembling the final pieces of equipment and leaving advance base camp in a straggling line. The Sherpas had gone ahead earlier and were already visible as a series of black dots at the base of the Col as we filed off the rocky moraine on to the permanent ice of the glacier. We kept to the right, beneath the North-East Ridge of Changtse on the line first established by the early British expeditions.

As was his custom, Al did not leave with the rest of the group but stayed behind pottering with a pile of equipment outside his tent. When I looked back towards base camp after more than an hour of progress, I saw his lone figure leaving at a fast pace to catch us up.

Why Al chose to do this was something which Kees and I had

often discussed. There was no doubt that Al was faster than the rest of us, in fact considerably faster under most conditions; but surely he could have modified his pace and slowed down to join the rest of us? We all knew that Al was a 'loner', but sometimes it was difficult to interpret his behaviour as anything other than anti-social. I thought there was some sort of psychology at play – a subconscious statement perhaps to accentuate his superclass mountain reputation. If that was true, that Al was, as some members of the expedition believed, 'showing off', then it was unnecessary: we all knew that he was in a different league from the rest of us.

Before the Col, the terrain evens off on to a gently sloping ice plateau which fills the rounded valley end marking the southernmost extension of the East Rongbuk glacier. As a natural amphitheatre, sound bounces back and forth from wall to wall and even a kilometre away from the Col I could hear the calls of the Sherpas as they climbed. The clattering fall of rock from Changtse was another accompaniment, each sharp impact of stone creating a bang which echoed across the ice.

With no clouds to filter the effect of the sunlight, the heat radiating off the ice was intense. By midday I could already feel my skin beginning to burn as the effect of the glacier cream wore off. I applied another layer and advised Kees to do the same. Being fairer in complexion, he had already worked his way through several layers of burned skin and his nose was permanently raw red from sunburn.

Three hours after leaving advance base camp we reached the foot of the Col. My nerves, already stretched by the prospect of the climb to come, were not calmed by the vision above us. From a distance the ice wall is impressive; seen from its base it is little short of terrifying. The wall stretches up to the sky in a series of gravity-defying seracs (massive free-standing ice towers) and hanging glacial ice, a waiting mass of energy held together by nothing more than the adhesion of one tiny frozen ice crystal to the next.

Half of the ice wall is smooth and rounded off like confectioner's cream, shaped by the Tibetan wind and the eroding effects of sunlight and frost. The remainder consists of shattered pinnacles and gaping scars where avalanches have ripped uneven portions of the face away and dumped the remains on the valley floor below. Fresh avalanche debris was lying not far from the spot where I now stood with Roger.

'Psyched?' I asked him.

'Definitely. The sooner we get up this thing the happier I'll be.'

Expedition base camp on the Rongbuk Glacier. Everest, seen centre frame, dominates the horizon with its famous 'plume' of blowing ice crystals.

Left: Brian Blessed decked with a garland at the Summit Hotel in Kathmandu. The expedition was Brian's third attempt at Everest.

Below: Team members trekking up the Rongbuk Glacier with Everest's North Face behind. The three-day walk up the glacier is the first of the challenges when coming from the north.

Left: The yak herders set out for advance base camp with Everest in midframe. Several tons of equipment were portaged up the East Rongbuk in this way.

Right: Members of the Sherpa team en route for base camp.

Below: The North Face of Mount Everest 8,848 metres (29,029 feet).

Right: The camp on the North Col showing the North Ridge behind.

Below: Matt Dickinson with Changtse seen behind.

The Himalayan Kingdoms team climbing up the North Col. This avalanche-prone wall of ice has been the scene of many tragedies. In the distance is the North Ridge.

Alan Hinkes at camp five with oxygen bottles.

Left: Camp six on the North Face of Everest at 8,300 metres, the highest mountain camp in the world. The remains of the previous storm-destroyed tents, and abandoned oxygen cylinders, can be seen.

Right: Matt Dickinson on the summit of Mount Everest at approximately 10 a.m. on 19 May 1996.

Left: The famous 'Second Step' of Everest's North East Ridge with Matt Dickinson shown half-way up. The 'Second Step' is one of the most difficult of the challenges on summit day when ascending from the north.

Right: Alan Hinkes pictured on the summit of Mount Everest with a photograph of his grandmother and daughter. In the background are Mingma and Gyaltsen.

Left: Matt Dickinson on the cluttered summit of Mount Everest, striking a 'Hillary' pose!

Below: First degree frostbite on two middle fingers of Matt Dickinson's hand, as sustained during his ascent. The blisters later healed completely.

Bottom: Matt Dickinson (left) and Alan Hinkes (right) at the Summit Hotel in Kathmandu having returned from Tibet.

We spent a further half an hour putting on our crampons and harnesses (the first time in 'anger'), and I was surprised at how tiring this simple act was. Then, as I stood, I snagged a spike of one foot into the nylon snow gaiter of the other. Unbalanced for a split second, I fell on to the ice. My knee took the full impact. I unsnagged the spike from the ripped gaiter and lay for a few moments while the pain subsided. Glancing round, I saw that Simon and Barney were busy with their own gear and had not noticed my mistake. It only took a few minutes for the pain to disappear, but my anger with myself for the error burned away for a lot longer.

Al had caught us up a short while before and the two of us left ahead of the main body of the team to film Brian and the others as they began the ascent. The first stage was one of the steepest, a physically demanding pitch up a rotten ice section into which deep steps had been cut. It was the first time I had ever climbed on fixed ropes, and to begin with I made the error of hauling myself up using the strength of my arms. Within a few minutes I was exhausted and completely out of breath.

By trial and error I gradually got the hang of it, depending more on my legs for upward movement, and using my arms less.

Compared with my inefficient and stumbling progress, Al was smooth and fast, looking completely at home on the ice. He was the only member of the team who ignored the fixed ropes, climbing free alongside them, utterly confident that his snow and ice skills would prevent a fall. But I was glad of the extra security the ropes gave. We made steady progress, quickly putting about one hundred metres of vertical ascent between us and the main group of climbers.

'How do you want to play this?' Al called back to me from ahead. He was already preparing the camera to shoot.

'See if you can move away to the side and get a wide shot as they come up.' I had to pause several times during this reply to get my breath.

'OK.' Al tied his rucksack on to one of the snow anchors which held the fixed lines and moved away easily across the steeply angled slope, his crampon points leaving no mark in the iron-hard polished ice. He found a position about fifty metres across the face and deftly cut a standing platform with his ice-axe.

Al filmed the team members coming painfully up the steep first section on to the easier angled ice, calling across every few minutes to ask advice on the shots and tell me what pictures he was getting. Brian was making slow progress, pausing frequently for breath and,

at one point, dramatically collapsing on to his knees. Behind him
the others waited patiently, glad perhaps of the chance to rest.

'Get a close up on Brian,' I shouted over to Al.

'It's right on the end of the lens. It'll be a bit wobbly.' Al was
hand-holding the camera and had no tripod to stabilise the images
once on the end of the zoom.

'Try it anyway.'

'OK.'

Twenty minutes later Brian and the rest of the group arrived at
my snow anchor, Brian apologising for his slow progress.

'So sorry, loves,' he gasped, 'just feeling a bit knackered, that's
all. But I'll get up it, the bastard!'

He looked dreadful. A frozen stream of spittle had congealed in
his beard, and his face was ghostly-white from the glacier cream. I
stood aside while Barney clipped him on to the anchor point for
some rest. There was no doubt that Brian was having a harder time
of it than the rest of us. His age alone was enough to give him a
disadvantage, and although he had lost weight consistently since the
expedition began, he was still carrying more than any other team
member.

Al and I put on our rucksacks and went ahead once more to find
another vantage point for filming. The rhythm of the climb soon
established itself again; step up, slide the jumar tight up the rope,
pause, breathe, step up . . . and so on. With a determined effort I
could manage ten to fifteen steps before I had to take a longer rest,
but any more than that was unthinkable. I was shocked by how
slowly I was moving but no amount of will-power could have
speeded my progress. Climbing at this altitude – just a little under
7,000 metres – was like trying to drive with the brakes full on.

Al, the powerhouse, was moving as strongly as ever and only
stopped to let me catch up.

The fixed ropes stretched on interminably, snaking up between
two bulging flanks of ice and then disappearing to the left underneath a steep wall about 300 metres above us. From advance base
camp we had often watched through binoculars as other teams made
their way up this part of the route, and we had even wondered why
they seemed to be moving so slowly; one group I watched took
almost an hour to move up one fifty-metre rope pitch. Now,
experiencing the full impact of altitude for the first time, I too was
moving in slow motion, my target number of continuous steps falling
from fifteen to ten . . . to five.

Three hours into our climb up the ice wall I was down to a single step at a time, with a two- or three-minute pause between. I found myself leaning increasingly on the ice-axe for support, longing for rest. Frequent bites of chocolate kept my sugar levels up, but in the heat I had already almost finished my two litres of orange juice.

About halfway up the face, the route crossed a snow-filled crevasse and then evened off on to a flat area large enough for ten or fifteen people to rest. I slumped in a heap on to this platform and drank the last few mouthfuls of fluid. From this vantage point the full splendour of the East Rongbuk glacier was laid out, the ice flowing as elegantly as any river away from the embrace of Everest and off towards the North. To the left, under Changtse's North-East Ridge, I could just see the dots of coloured canvas which was advance base camp.

By the time Brian reached the platform he was suffering badly. He collapsed on to his side, coughing and retching in a series of violent spasms. Barney helped relieve him of the rucksack, and handed him a water bottle.

'Got to get someone to carry my bag.' Brian's voice was little more than a plaintive croak.

Barney and Simon talked through the options and agreed that the only way Brian was likely to reach the top of the Col was if his rucksack was carried. But by who? They decided to call back one of the Sherpas from camp four to help Brian out. Shortly after, Kippa Sherpa arrived on his way back down and was given the task. As he had climbed to the Col already that day, I was staggered by the good grace with which he accepted this decision, which committed him to hours' more work than he had been expecting. He shouldered the pack and struck off up the fixed ropes at a phenomenal rate.

Brian rested for a while to catch his breath, then continued upwards, noticeably faster and happier without the weight on his back.

Before reaching camp four, there was one further sequence to be filmed, a fifteen-metre-high ice pitch which was undoubtedly the hardest section of the climb. I knew that we would get excellent footage if we could get in position at the top of the ice stage, looking down on the climbers with the valley dropping away sheer beneath them. I also suspected that some of the team members would find the section physically very demanding; wrapped up in the struggle of the climb, I hoped, they would forget the presence of the camera and enable us to get some compelling footage.

Four hours into the climb, we reached the steep pitch. It was now mid-afternoon and the full heat of the day had worked on the compacted ice, turning the entire route into soft, granular snow of a type that makes progress doubly hard. We traversed the face beneath a threatening serac. I moved as quickly as I could, not trusting the snow conditions which, as far as I could judge, were now ripe for avalanche. Every foot jammed into the snow created a mini-slide, some of which continued down the face for ten to fifteen metres before coming to a stop.

The snow had the consistency of semi-thawed ice-cream, and the useful cut 'steps' which we had relied on earlier were now eroded and melted away. On two or three occasions my foot pushed down on to what I presumed was solid ice, only to slip down the face in the slush. I pushed the ice-axe deep in to provide extra stability, moving continuously to get the section over with as fast as possible.

Beneath the steep section I had to rest for five minutes to regain my breath. The muscles around my ribs were just beginning to ache from the continuous heavy load they were put under to suck down sufficient oxygen.

Al was already halfway up the steep pitch and I followed him, using my jumar clamps on the fixed ropes. With no option but to rely heavily on the pulling power of our arms and shoulders, this was the most strenuous work we had encountered. Here too the 'steps' had been destroyed by the heat of the day, forcing us to kick hard into the still frozen stuff underneath.

'We're up here a bit late, really. We should have set out a lot earlier,' Al called back. I didn't have the breath to reply.

Feeling slightly dazed, I reached the top and clipped on to the snow anchor for support. Al was already cutting himself a small platform to film from. His capacity for work at this extreme altitude was very impressive, and, by the time the rest of the team were approaching the bottom of the steep pitch, Al was ready and waiting with the camera poised to shoot.

Interestingly, Brian put in one of the stronger performances on this difficult stage, more so than Roger, Sundeep and Tore who were all struggling as I had done. His frame was built for this heavy upper-torso muscle work, and he hauled up with powerful thrusts, gasping huge intakes of air between clenched teeth.

'Trekkers! You look like a line of bloody trekkers!' Al yelled down.

It was true, the team did look like a complete shambles from our vantage point, a tightly bunched line of grunting, panting figures, faces screwed up against the glare of radiation, shoulders hunched in exhaustion.

'We're heading for the Khumbu Lodge,' Simon yelled back. 'Is this the right way?'

Roger reached the top of the steep ice, panting very hard and leaning heavily on his ice-axe.

'The worst thing,' he said, once he had regained a bit of puff, 'is that I'm paying for this.' He managed a smile and then moved on up the slope, the final pitch before the more gentle traverse which would bring us on to the Col itself and the welcome sanctuary of camp four.

Sundeep and Tore both came up without a word, every ounce of breath devoted to the serious business of supplying the lungs with air.

I was very happy with the way the day's filming had gone so far, but to complete the sequence we still needed to film the team's arrival at camp four. I went on ahead up the final rope length to recce the camp and find a good location to shoot from.

Reaching the Col I was surprised by how little space there was available compared with the southern side. Pictures of the South Col reveal a vast, flat area with acres of room. The suitable places for camps are far more restricted on the North Col, and the teams have to tuck themselves into a narrow strip on the lee side of the ridge crest itself, thereby gaining a little precious protection against the prevailing westerly winds.

The cramped situation is further complicated by the presence of the large crevasse which runs right beneath the crest. This, ever-widening each month, is an unwelcome reminder of the unsettling fact that the entire North Col camp is sited on the top of a vast piece of ice which will one day collapse. I reassured myself that the combined weight of the expeditions could not hasten this process one iota when compared to the millions of tons of ice involved.

I worked my way up through the tents belonging to other expeditions, greeting a few familiar faces which we had got to know at advance base camp. As it was late afternoon, many of the tents were occupied by exhausted-looking climbers and Sherpas who had come down from load carries up to camp five.

The early arrivals had naturally taken the prime spots on the Col, leaving us with the furthest and least protected end of the ridge.

Swirling plumes of spindrift were rotoring off the ridge on to our tents as I arrived.

From our site I could see, for the first time, the route ahead up the North Ridge and across the North Face to the summit pyramid. The Ridge was bathed in the last few rays of sunlight, and as I watched, these died away, leaving the ice steely grey and forbidding. The route looked absolutely huge, and our day's toil up to the Col suddenly felt puny and insignificant. I couldn't even see camps five or six, as they were too far off to be visible to the naked eye.

There is an irresistible temptation to overplay the importance of the climb to the Col, and the inexperienced members of our expedition (including me) had fallen right into this trap. Make it up the Col, went the common wisdom, and you've as good as made it to the summit.

What bullshit.

As my eyes took in the immensity of the North Face, I recognised the fallacy of this assumption. Climbing the Col doesn't magically qualify the climber for the summit. Far from it. Climbing to the Col is merely a warm-up stage, a qualifying round which admits the climber into an arena where far greater challenges begin.

I was humbled and frightened by what I saw, now realising that the struggle I had experienced on the Col was just a tiny taste of things to come. It was difficult to tear my eyes away from the summit and I watched it in a trance until thick cloud blew in and obscured the view.

When Al joined me, we set up the camera for the final time that day and filmed as the weary climbers came in. The Col was in shadow, and the temperature was already dropping rapidly as the wind rose.

I did a brief interview with Brian, who, whilst he was extremely tired, still had the energy to give us a few words.

'I hate the Col!' he coughed, 'but we made it.' Then he collapsed on the snow, worn-out. I admired Brian's strength of character, all of us were aware that he had had a tough day, yet he had not been at all irritable or depressed, the normal signs of a climber who is out of his depth. He seemed to take the pain in his stride without letting it get to him psychologically. I was beginning to understand why Brian did so well at altitude.

The Sherpas had already erected most of the tents, and the only work left for us was to cut ice blocks to anchor them down. This type of Sherpa back up was a massive help, and a key part of the strategy for commercial operators like Himalayan Kingdoms who seek to save every ounce of their clients' energy wherever they can. Our arrival at the Col would have been a lot colder, and a lot more exhausting, if we had had to erect the tents ourselves. When I saw Nga Temba I thanked him for doing such a great job. He looked faintly shocked, as if the very idea of praise was an alien one!

Kees and I finished bedding the tent down with the ice blocks and then cut several more to melt for drinking water. Choosing the source for these was a delicate task, because much of the easiest ice to cut was soiled with urine or other waste. By the time all the chores were finished, the last few moments of daylight were slipping away.

Inside the tent, illuminated by our headtorches, the scene was one of complete confusion. There is not much space to spare in a mountain Quasar at the best of times and the sides of ours were bulging inwards dramatically from the weight of snow we had just shovelled on.

We were using the high-altitude sleeping bags – the really thick ones – for the first time, and, taken out of their stuff sacks, they now swelled like giant slugs. Add to that the profusion of other clothing, the Thermarest inflatable mattresses and the duvet jackets which we would undoubtedly need for warmth, and there was little room for either of us to move.

Kees, with his neat sense of logic, quickly organised his own side of the tent into some semblance of order, banishing his rucksack to the back and magically tidying the cooking area at the front so that the gas stove could be lit. I fumbled around inefficiently, cursing the lack of space, until I too forced my ever-expanding equipment into a more or less manageable heap.

A voice shouted through the dark, raised against the increasing volume of the wind; it was Simon, checking up on us.

'Matt and Kees. You got your brew on yet?'

'Yeah!'

He was right to make sure. Drinking was a paramount need after our hard day's work, and yet preparing that drink was the last thing we wanted to do. Lying back on the soft sleeping bag, I knew I would be asleep in seconds if I closed my eyes. Every tired fibre, every stretched muscle was calling out for sleep, yet to succumb would be a direct route to acute mountain sickness and could even lead to a possible coma. Many of the saddest and fastest fatalities from altitude sickness have occurred when climbers have fallen asleep without replenishing their vital body fluids.

The hissing noise of the gas had its own soporific effect and the ice seemed to take forever to melt. We chatted aimlessly about the highlights of the day while we watched the pot slowly begin to steam.

The evening was spent brewing, drinking and eating as much as we could, a tedious process given the long wait time for each pan of ice to melt. Tea, coffee, Bournvita and soup all went down – a measured intake which gave us about two litres of fluid each. We were doing the right things but I could not shake off a rising feeling of nausea which had been with me since mid-afternoon. Lying completely still and concentrating my mind on other things, I tried every trick to rid myself of the sickness. But, by nine o'clock in the evening, I couldn't fight it any more. In a sudden violent spasm which barely gave me time to unzip the front tent flaps, I vomited the entire evening's fluid up in a retching attack which left me gulping for breath. For several minutes I lay half in, half out of the tent, while the attack subsided.

'Shit!' I collapsed back into the tent, my head pulsating with a throbbing pain.

The sickness was bearable, but the real implications were really depressing. Having lost all the fluid we had so painstakingly melted and drunk, I was now faced with a simple decision: go to sleep and take a chance that I had ingested enough of the fluid to get me safely through the night, or go outside to cut more ice and start melting all over again.

The temptation to forget it all and go to sleep was almost overwhelming. But I knew I couldn't do that. I spent fifteen minutes putting on my boots and jacket and went out into the freezing night to cut the ice, cursing my bad luck and feeling more angry than I can remember. Back in the tent I assembled the gas cooker once more, coaxed it back into life and watched as the first pan of ice slowly – impossibly slowly – began to melt. Kees, not surprisingly, crashed out to sleep.

To save weight I had not packed a book. Now I regretted that decision as I stared into the darkness of the tent and fought the urge to sleep.

Two interminable hours later I hit the target of two litres of fluid, packed away the cooking gear and tidied up the front of the tent as best I could. I was not even aware of lying down on the sleeping bag in the fraction of a second it took me to fall asleep.

Next morning we had a leisurely start. Simon's original plan had been to continue for a short way up the North Ridge to increase our acclimatisation, but that idea had been abandoned somewhere along the way. Now we prepared to descend the Col and commence the trek all the way back to base camp.

The descent was fast and relatively straightforward, a question of clipping on to the fixed ropes for security on the easy sections, and abseiling the steeper stages.

Halfway down, I made a clumsy mistake. Standing on a snow step, I unthreaded my figure-of-eight descendeur (the alloy metal device used to control an abseil) from the rope to transfer it to the next section. Working with frozen fingers, I fumbled the figure-of-eight and dropped it. At the same instant, the snow step I was standing on gave way a little, jerking my body down awkwardly. I clutched at the rope with my free hand to stop the fall, cursing my stupidity.

By a stroke of luck, the figure of eight lodged against my boot and I was able to retrieve it. If it had dropped down the ice slope it would have fallen right amongst the climbers below me, which would have been embarrassing at the least, and potentially dangerous if it had hit anyone on the head. I glanced up at Simon, who was climbing down just above me, to see if he had noticed my blunder. But he was busy sorting out a tangle in his own harness and had not seen it.

I was grateful for that. Making cock-ups in front of the expedition leader was something I could do without. How could he trust me to abseil down the first and second steps, the difficult rock stages above 8,000 metres which are the highest rock-climbing pitches in the world, when I had fumbled a vital piece of equipment here in the relatively easy terrain of the Col? I regained my composure, and secured the descendeur back on to the rope.

I had got away with it, just, but the incident opened the door on a flood of old doubts and that flash of anger at myself. My capacity for making stupid mistakes was likely to increase with altitude as the mind-numbing effects of oxygen depletion set in. I continued the climb down the Col in subdued mood, concentrating extra hard at the rope change-overs and taking care to defrost my fingers before handling the descendeur.

Two days later we descended the Rongbuk glacier for the second time back to base camp, relishing the warmer temperatures and thicker air, and regaining at least a vestige of appetite. To an outside observer we were a relaxed party, taking the rare moments when the wind dropped to lie in the sun by our tents. But internally the stresses were grinding away at us all. This period of waiting at base camp would be the last. The next time we shouldered our rucksacks for the trek up the Rongbuk would be on our way for the summit attempt.

6

I was shaving in a bucket of ice-cold water in the mess tent at base camp when Kees swaggered back from the Indian tent. The Indians had had a problem with their satellite phone and boffin Kees had been called in with his magic soldering iron to work it out. By some miracle he had managed to breathe life into the defunct machine and the Indians had offered him a free call by way of thanks.

'I managed to get through to Katie in Canada.'

'Great.'

'And there's some news.'

'Oh yeah?'

'I'm going to be a daddy.'

'Jesus. That *is* great!'

That night we celebrated Kees's news with some disturbingly evil Tibetan brandy, accompanied by a raft of predictably smutty comments at Kees's expense. Looking smug, the father-to-be brought out a slender tin of Cuban cheroots and offered them around. Failing to find a single taker, and rethinking the wisdom of lighting up at this lofty altitude, Kees contented himself with the occasional sniff at the unlit cheroots.

'The aroma alone is enough,' he pronounced, grandly.

Next morning, slightly hungover, I was lying in my tent reading when I heard the rumble of a diesel truck rolling up the Rongbuk glacier. Shortly after, there was a shout from Simon:

'Monty!'

I poked my head out of the tent and saw Simon greeting someone by the mess tent. Sundeep called over.

'Looks like the pussy wagon's arrived!' he said.

The 'pussy wagon' was the dubious name which had somehow evolved for the incoming trekking truck which we knew would be visiting us any day. On board was a team of ramblers on a tour of Tibet with the trekking arm of Himalayan Kingdoms' operations.

As the weeks had gone by, the combined imaginations of our (all male) expedition had conjured up a vision, fired up no doubt by our enforced period of sexual abstinence, of the lithesome beauties this group would surely contain. In fact, over recent days we had talked about little else over our evening meals, proving (as if it needed to be proved) that men behave badly regardless of the altitude.

'Let's say there's twenty in the group, at least five or six have to be girls,' someone would speculate.

'More like ten or fifteen, I reckon.'

'They'll be gasping for some men . . .'

'Definitely.'

'Bound to be some Scandinavian girls on it.'

'Several probably.'

'Historically, Tibet always has attracted nymphomaniacs . . .'

But when the 'pussy wagon' did finally disgorge its occupants, we realised how far off the mark we had been. Along with Monty, the tour leader, there were just four paying clients: an anxious looking couple in their sixties and two nobbly-kneed men with beards.

In one respect we had been right. The trekkers *were* gasping – but from the effects of the altitude rather than anything else. It was all rather a blow.

But there was one good side to the truck's arrival – it carried with it a bundle of post from friends and family in the UK. We grabbed our letters and retreated to the tents to read the precious missives.

Fiona's letter was full of family news about a short holiday to CenterParcs and a round-up of new plantings in the garden. Sitting in the bleak stone environment of the Rongbuk, where scarcely any plants grow at all, it sounded incredibly lush. It was all cheery enough, but the darker undercurrent to the letter was not difficult to decipher – Fiona knew very well how hazardous this expedition might be, and the stress of that was obviously turning the ten weeks into something which felt closer to ten years.

It wasn't an unusual situation for us to be in, with me on one side of the world, and she on the other, but it was different this time and not only because it was a dangerous shoot. Fiona knew that Everest would be a watershed for me in many ways: that I wanted it to be my last adventure film, that I was trying to find a way to break the destructive pattern that our relationship had got into.

It wasn't that the relationship itself was a bad one – far from it;

in fact many of the good things in our relationship remained surprisingly intact. We had always been essentially happy together when we had *been* together, in fact in all the years we had never once raised our voices at each other in anger and somehow we still found the ability to laugh.

But that didn't alter a fundamental problem: after two or three days back with my family I invariably found myself pacing the floor wondering how the hell I was going to tell Fiona about the latest attack of itchy feet. It wasn't that I was bored with being there, it was more a permanent dissatisfaction with myself – a feeling that I could be doing *better* in the films I was making, *better* in the scripts I was writing, in fact pushing myself a darn sight harder all round. Perhaps that was the driving force that pushed me out of the door?

Whatever it was, Fiona was pretty fed up with it.

So what to do? There was still a massive amount of affection, and love, between us and I didn't want to throw that away. And I certainly didn't want to alter the chemistry of what was basically an extremely happy family. But I had pushed Fiona to the point where living with me was a lot harder than living without me. The tension of never knowing when I was going to sling on my rucksack and go had turned her into a bag of nerves.

I lay in the tent all afternoon, staring into space.

That night, at the evening meal, I found myself in a quieter than usual mood.

'You look a bit down,' Roger said, 'What's up?'

'Thinking of home.'

'Ah.'

It needed no more explanation – every single one of us suffered from homesickness at one time or another and we all knew it was inescapable.

'Better not to get letters from home,' Brian said, 'It's too much to bear.'

And in a way, he was right.

*

With so much time on our hands, the subject of how and when the team would be split was, not surprisingly, a well-worn topic of conversation. With nine climbers still in the running for a summit bid, splitting the group was a logistical necessity on two fronts: there were simply not enough tents available at the higher camps to support us all in one push – and a summit team of nine would be dangerously unwieldy. We would leave in two teams, three or four days apart.

The split was not a difficult decision for Simon. As Kees, Al and myself were on board to film Brian, we would have to be in his summit team, as would Barney in his role as guide. That made us a self-defining team of five.

The four-man team was Simon, Tore, Sundeep and Roger.

But which team would go first? That was the question which obsessed us during this extended wait at base camp. We discussed the pros and cons endlessly while we waited for Simon's decision. Going first was a psychological advantage mainly because it meant less time spent stagnating at base camp. We had reached a peak of fitness, a peak of acclimatisation, and our minds and bodies were poised on a hair-trigger ready for the attempt.

Days spent at base camp were wasted days, depressing days, days when a virus picked up from a visiting team of trekkers could wipe out any chance of success. Then there were the mental pressures of the waiting period. Doubts multiplied inside us like bacteria, the corrosive fears building as each of us contemplated in our own way the known and unknown risks to come.

We were all desperate to leave for the mountain.

There were other factors which gave the first team a perceived advantage. The oxygen and food supplies were all in place at camps five and six and had been carefully calculated on a 'man-day' basis. What if the first group had a one- or two-day weather delay and were forced to use up those supplies which had been allocated to the second group? Simon had assured everyone that he would simply restock the camps if this happened but, given the huge task of portaging the heavy cylinders up to the high camps, there was always the nagging doubt whether the precious oxygen would be in the right place at the right time.

Al pointed out another drawback for the second team if the first team were delayed. Tent space was extremely limited at camps five and six – just two mountain Quasars would be available, space for four, or five at a pinch. The second group could be on their way up, only to find that the descending climbers were unexpectedly occupying camp five, creating a bottleneck and thereby forcing the upcoming team to abort their attempt. Al had experienced this very scenario on his second Everest expedition. In fact, a logjam at camp five had wiped out his chances of the summit.

A medical emergency or accident might also scupper the chances of the second group if it were forced into a rescue mission for members of the first. The odds seemed to be stacking up against the second team, but one factor above all others could wipe out every one of those advantages at a stroke: the weather.

'It doesn't make a blind bit of difference which team goes first or second.' Al was, as ever, the voice of wisdom on this subject. 'If the weather socks in then neither group will make the summit. The second team have got just as much chance of hitting the right weather window as the first. It's down to luck.'

The weather window. That precious, fragile, elusive moment of opportunity. That, more than oxygen, food and tent space, would decide who if any of us made it to the roof of the world.

We needed that window but we also feared it. A weather window could just as easily be a weather trap. We had all marvelled at the awesome speed at which conditions can change on Everest. A clear blue day can and frequently does deteriorate into a savage blizzard in less than an hour. That window can slam shut as fast as it opens, and Everest's five-lever deadlock flips into place to secure it.

It was a humbling fact, the mountain's ultimate trump card, and the reason why no one, no matter how brilliant a climber they are, can be totally sure of success. We could try our best to predict what conditions would be like for our summit attempt, but ultimately we would be in the hands of fate.

The possibility of a second attempt for any of us was one that we hardly discussed. We were all aware that the recovery period following an unsuccessful climb to 8,000 metres would almost certainly push us beyond the ten-week period of the expedition. We accepted we would have one chance, and that was it.

Finally Simon announced his decision, making a tour of the camp and telling each one of us individually in our tents (cynically, I interpreted this move was a tactical one to prevent potential protests if we were told *en masse*).

Brian, Barney, Al, Kees and myself would go first, leaving in two days. Simon, Sundeep, Tore and Roger would follow on three days later. Inevitably the teams were dubbed the 'A' team, and the 'B' team.

There were no dissenting voices but Tore, particularly, was frustrated to hear he would be spending more time at base camp. He, more than any of us perhaps, was getting increasingly depressed as each day of inactivity crawled by. Sundeep and Roger took the decision as well as they could, but they too found it hard to contemplate more days at base camp while the 'A' team were on the mountain.

There was only the slightest hint, but it was there nevertheless, that Simon's decision was partly a political one. Himalayan Kingdoms had a lot to gain in publicity terms if Brian reached the summit; his status as an actor would ensure widespread news and print coverage in addition to our film.

Was that why Brian and our film crew had been given the prized first slot? To give us the first, and best, chance with the maximum resources in place? The question was never aired publicly, but most of us, particularly the 'B' team, believed it was a possibility.

Brian was as sanguine and relaxed as ever. Like Al, his temperament was perfectly tuned to the long waiting days at base camp. Unlike the rest of us, Brian did not allow himself to get frustrated, he accepted the inactivity for what it was – part of the whole process.

'We're climbing the mountain,' he told me, 'even when we're sitting here. We're getting strong, getting ready. A good day here is just as valuable as a good day high up – it all helps. There's no point in moving until we're sure the conditions are right.'

So saying, he would retire, the very model of calm, to the 'Himalayan hotel' dome tent for some classical music and a browse through a book. And it wasn't just an act; Brian really was capable of relaxing in this situation. I greatly admired the strength of mind and maturity this revealed. Brian understood perfectly the importance of the 'waiting game'. He could shrug off the pressure when the rest of us were buckling beneath it, perhaps a trick which he has developed from years of acting where the ability to control first-night nerves is paramount.

Halfway through our waiting time at base camp a surprising rumour began to circulate that Richard, the *Financial Times* journalist, was coming back to join the expedition. It originated from the Indian team who were in daily radio contact with Kathmandu. In one of their communications they had received a message from Richard via the Indian embassy there to say he was intending to return.

Simon sent back a strongly worded radio message indicating in blunt terms that in no circumstances should Richard seek to rejoin the expedition. Having one fewer member to account for had altered Simon's logistics on the mountain. Put simply, there was no food or oxygen now in place at the high camps for Richard, and it was too late to alter that. Simon's message elicited no response.

'Hi boys!' Three days later, Richard sauntered into camp, having hitchhiked across the Tibetan plateau from Kathmandu.

'I specifically sent a radio message to Kathmandu instructing you not to come back!' Simon told him, frostily.

'You're not having your fucking tent back!' Brian chipped in.

It was hardly the friendliest of receptions.

I had seen this 'odd man out' syndrome on other expeditions and now Richard was experiencing it in its bitchiest form. The chemistry of teams adjusts itself and changes in subtle ways once one of the number has gone. When that person tries to reintroduce himself unexpectedly, he invariably finds himself alienated and 'frozen out' – no matter how popular he had been in his earlier incarnation.

Richard was barred from going any higher than advance base camp, but he decided to stick with the team to carry out his professional obligations to his newspaper. This impressive display of professionalism meant that he was one of the only journalists on hand to file reports when the storm swept in just days later.

Knowing that we would be leaving imminently, I gave a small parcel of letters to Sundeep for safe keeping. As the weeks had passed, I had realised that we could take nothing for granted on our summit push. Something as simple as an avalanche could kill us just by chance. I had written a number of brief 'goodbye' letters which I now gave to Sundeep.

'Could you post these for me if I don't come back?' I asked him.

He looked down at the slender pile of letters in surprise.

'Of course.'

It may seem a morbid thing to have done, but I was actually happier leaving for our summit attempt knowing that those letters would reach the people I loved in the case that anything untoward happened. Not saying goodbye would be the hardest thing of all, I felt.

'Hey, Matt,' Sundeep called after me as I returned to my packing, 'I sincerely hope I don't have to post these!'

'Me too.'

Looking thoughtful, he returned to his tent to store the letters in a safe spot.

The 'B' team waved us off from base camp on 8 May, after a cheesy photo session in which the 'A' and 'B' teams posed uncomfortably, separately, and together. I dislike team photographs and found myself superstitious about the event – I'm not sure exactly why; I also sensed that the rest of the team was reluctant. Perhaps a team photograph is another of those moments, like the flash of nerves I experienced when I saw our names on the climbing permit for the first time, when the vulnerability of the enterprise is suddenly vividly clear.

Those names typed on the list, those confident rows of smiling faces captured in a photograph at base camp – how effortlessly the mountain can scratch them out. And how frequently it does. Team photographs often become obituary shots in the literature of Himalayan climbing, and not a single one of those smiling faces has the faintest knowledge of the fate that awaits him.

Barney more than any of us hated the photographs. He wouldn't even show his face, but put his sunglasses on the rim of his sun-hat and tipped it down so his eyes couldn't be seen. At the time I thought his behaviour was prattish, but later I realised that he probably felt the same as I did, only more so.

Al, too, was uncomfortable with the team shots. He has a collection of similar expedition photographs which are filled with the faces of the dead. But he stood to attention with the rest of us as two members of the Norwegian team took the group pictures.

*

Our third trek up the East Rongbuk was a very different experience to the first two, fired up by the adrenalin rush that this time it was for 'real'. The sheer pleasure of being unleashed from the constraints of base camp seemed like a catapult shot: I almost felt as if I was walking at sea level, and my mind was clear and untroubled.

After our familiarisation climb to 7,000 metres at the North Col, our bodies were now able to take these lower altitudes in their stride. Compared with the thinness of the air at the Col, the East Rongbuk, between 6,000 and 6,500 metres, now seemed to offer rich lungfuls of satisfying oxygen. One month earlier we had been gasping for breath here as we completed the sixteen-kilometre trek for the first time, taking three days to reach advance base camp. This time we would be a lot faster, reaching ABC in two days.

Although there was no yak traffic on the glacier, there were other distractions. On the lower Rongbuk, we caught glimpses of shy Tibetan deer feeding on the tiny patches of vegetation. When we disturbed them, they ran for the safety of the higher ground, scaling the fragile scree slope so nimbly that not a pebble moved beneath their hoofs. On the East Rongbuk we saw no mammals, just a few hardy birds that had arrived with the warmer weather, pecking through the remains of yak fodder for seeds and chaff.

We also saw the Tibetan snowcock, a duck-sized bird that looks like a customised pheasant. Its call is a bizarre cackling sound. Barney told us a tale about a German climber who had shot and eaten one of these birds a few years earlier. Not long after, he was killed whilst crossing one of the melt water rivers in full flood. We left the birds well alone.

Around us, the glacier was showing the signs of the spring thaw. Silty melt water streams were now flowing strongly through the moraine, carving out sinuous routes from the gravel and revealing the milky-white ice beneath. We had to work much harder to keep our feet dry and in some spots only a series of strategically placed boulders enabled us to cross the fast-flowing water.

In places the streams disappeared from sight into sink-holes and ran underground, deep down into the bowels of the glacier. These subterranean streams could sometimes be heard as a rumbling sound beneath our feet, like the sound of a tube train beneath a London street. I looked into one of the sump holes, where the water rushed down into a perfectly round, polished tube of blue ice, large enough to admit a small car. There was the horrifying temptation to jump into it. I wondered what it would be like to be sucked down for a high speed whitewater ride beneath the ice. A bit like a spider getting flushed down a plughole, I decided – but colder.

The warmer days of spring had caused another change; now the steep valleysides above the glacier were far less stable. Rocks which had been frozen in place through the winter were thawed out and loosened – primed to fall down to the glacier below. The resounding crack and clatter of rockfall echoed back and forth, particularly on the lower sections of the East Rongbuk where the valleysides are steepest and most friable.

On two or three occasions we had quite near misses from tumbling boulders. Brian got the closest call, shuffling out of the firing-line as fast as he could, while two killer rocks bounced past just a short distance off.

'That was a close one,' I told him.

'Like walking through a bloody firing range.'

Two sections of the route had altered dramatically, revealing the instability of the shifting terrain. One tennis-court-sized frozen lake had disappeared entirely and the ground around it had collapsed into itself, leaving a twenty-metre-deep hole which we had not seen before. We concluded that a substantial underground cavity had collapsed beneath the spot, swallowing up the lake, and many thousands of tons of moraine. The well-worn path had run straight across the collapsed area and this had now disappeared; we had to take a new track across steeper terrain to regain the stable ground on the other side.

The other change to the face of the glacier was a huge rockfall which had slipped down the valleyside onto the ice since our last journey up to ABC. This was just as impressive as the collapsed cavern, with thousands of new boulders heaped up in a shambolic pile, many freshly shattered and scarred by the impact as they tumbled down. We crossed the area carefully, hopping from one rocking boulder to another and testing each one for stability before committing our weight. Such a massive rockslide would be too fast to outrun if a team were unlucky enough to get caught beneath it.

After a night at the site of the Indian camp, mid-way on the East Rongbuk, we made it to advance base camp in the midst of a light snowstorm on the afternoon of 9 May. All day the wind had been building in intensity, and now it was blowing at force four or five – enough to cause me to doubt that we would be leaving the next morning.

'What do you think are the chances of the weather clearing tomorrow?' I asked Al.

'Not likely at all. From the look of this stuff we're in for a good few days of unsettled conditions,' he replied.

'We'll just have to wake up tomorrow and see how it is,' Barney chipped in, 'but I have to say it doesn't look good.'

Although that none of us was convinced we would be leaving the next day, we still went through the motions of preparing for the summit push. Kees and I sorted through our equipment barrels, checking every last item off the list as we packed our rucksacks ready for a dawn departure.

As darkness fell, a radio call on the southern side of the mountain announced the first fatality of the season. Chen Yu-Nan, a member of the Taiwanese team, had left his tent at camp three on the Lhotse Face to answer a call of nature that morning, but had neglected to put on his plastic overboots and crampons. Wearing just the slick-soled inner boots, he slipped on the steep ice and fell seventy feet into a crevasse. He was rescued by Sherpas, but later died of his injuries.

The Taiwanese leader, 'Makalu' Gau, was at the South Col when the radio call came through from IMAX team leader David Breashears at camp two to tell him that Chen was dead.

'OK – thankyou for the information' – was the Taiwanese leader's reply – a terse response which Breashears found hard to swallow, having just raced up to the foot of the Lhotse Face in an attempt to save Chen and then had the harrowing task of bringing his body back down. Gau announced to Breashears, and the other climbers from Adventure Consultants and Mountain Madness (who were also at the Col waiting to leave for the summit in just a few hours' time) that the news would not change his intention to continue the climb.

The assembled climbers – more than thirty of them, huddled into their sleeping bags to snatch a few hours of restless sleep before their midnight departure.

*

The sound of Kees unzipping the front of the tent woke me at 6.30 on the morning of the 10th. It was a crystal-clear dawn, with the mountain already so brightly illuminated that I had to put on my glacier goggles to be able to look at it.

'Looks perfect,' Kees said.

I laced up my boots and walked over the glacier to where Al and Barney were in conference.

'What's the verdict?' I asked them.

'We're not happy about it,' Al said.

'What?' I was flabbergasted. 'It's one of the best mornings we've had. Let's go.'

'You see those clouds?' Barney pointed up to the north where a milky haze clouded the upper atmosphere. 'The whole system is unstable.'

'We'll hang on here today and wait and see how it develops,' Al said. 'There's no point going up if the weather's going to break tomorrow or the day after, we'll just knacker ourselves for nothing.'

I looked over to the Col, where a string of climbers were already working their way up the ice.

'What about them? They think it's going to be OK.'

Al and Barney shrugged, and that was the end of the conversation. We trudged over to the mess tent to force down a plate of chappatis and jam, resigned to spending a further day at advance base.

As the day wore on, my frustration increased. The sun was as hot as we had known it, so much so that the interior of the tent became

uncomfortably muggy. For the first time on the expedition, we had
to place the sleeping bags on the roof of the tent to cool the interior
down. I already hated advance base after our first two miserable
forays here, and now I had the dread feeling that we would be here
for far longer than we had planned. Unable to concentrate on
reading, I sat outside the tent restlessly pitching stones into the
smiling mouth of a narrow crevasse.

'Patience, Matt.' Brian could see my growing frustration. 'There's
always a window . . . we'll get four or five perfect days. If it's not
now, then it'll come later. We might have to wait until the end of
May. But if Barney and Al say it's not right, then we stay here.
That's the game.'

In contrast to my own depressed state of mind, the Indian team
in the tents next to ours was in a whirl of high excitement. Their
lead climbers were going for the summit that day, the first attempt
from the northern side since the season had begun six weeks earlier.
All morning, they were gathered outside the green canvas army
tents with radios in hand, trying to spot their climbers through
binoculars. Mohindor Singh, the leader, was the most striking figure:
equipped with mirror sunglasses and a magenta turban, he stood
head and shoulders above the rest of his team.

I wandered over before lunch to see them. 'What's the news?' I
asked one of Singh's deputies.

'We have six climbers just approaching the Ridge. Now we are
waiting with bated breath!' he told me. 'Fingers crossed!'

It was exciting to think that the Indians were so high. We had
made many friends amongst their team – largely through the efforts
of Sundeep who, as a fluent Hindi- and Punjabi-speaker, had
naturally become close to them. I found myself caught up in the
excitement of the event and one of the two girls on the team brought
me a cup of tea to sip while we squinted through the tiny binoculars,
trying and failing to spot the climbers.

The Indians had left camp six at 8 a.m. – a departure time which
even I knew was worryingly late. But there was no outward sign
of concern in the Indian team, only an overwhelming sense of
expectation that the day might bring a great success against the
odds.

By mid-afternoon, the weather, and the prospects of success, had
deteriorated. There was a large quantity of spindrift blowing off the
North Ridge, and the summit plume was just detectable as a wispy
tail curling menacingly behind the top. By 4 p.m., three of the Indian

summit team had decided to return to camp six, leaving three more to continue in the ever-worsening conditions.

Brian poked his head out of the tent. 'I wouldn't want to be up there now,' he said. I had to agree with him. Now I was extremely grateful that we were still at camp three.

Then, with virtually no warning, the wind picked up speed. At the same time the summit disappeared behind a broiling mass of cloud and the North Ridge erupted into a maelstrom of driven snow. Less than thirty seconds later we were running for the shelter of our tents as the first furious blasts of gale-force wind came hurtling down the glacier from the Col, ripping the pujah flags from their cairns and carrying loose boxes and rubbish high into the air.

I made it to the tent just seconds after Kees, and we spent the next fifteen minutes clearing out the frozen spindrift which had followed us in.

The temperature had dropped approximately twenty degrees in as many minutes.

As the wind gathered strength, it became abundantly clear that this was a storm unlike any other we had so far experienced in the previous weeks of our expedition. The full wrath of Everest's fury was unleashed all around us, with a blizzard potent enough to lift a climber off his feet and blow him off the mountain like a scrap of paper.

Most afternoons above camp two had seen a deterioration in the weather conditions, with strong gusting winds and frequent snow-fall, but this was in a different and much more deadly league. Wind speeds over 100 miles an hour are not uncommon on Everest during such storms and by 5 p.m. the snow was driving horizontally through the air with sufficient velocity to draw blood from exposed flesh.

As fast as the driven snow collected against the tents, it was spirited away by the wind as it scrubbed the mountain bare. The cloak of fresh snow which had fallen on Everest over the previous days – millions of tons of it – was now airborne and in the grip of far greater forces than those which had deposited it. The snow became granulated hard ice as it flew, beating a relentless drumming tone against the tight nylon skins of the tents, a mind-numbing white noise like the hiss of static.

We soon realised that we should try to get some film footage to convey the severity of the conditions, but how to achieve it without damaging the cameras? The digital format is as prone to freezing and spindrift as any video system, and we still only had the two camera bodies to rely on for our summit attempt.

Cameraman Kees, who has an answer to every technical problem I have ever thrown at him, went for a simple solution; he ripped up a plastic bin-liner and sealed the camera tight inside it with multiple layers of gaffer tape.

'You think that will work?' I asked him.

'It's that or nothing,' he shrugged.

We dressed in our layers of Gore-tex and went out into the storm to film. Wearing ski goggles to protect our eyes from the gravel-hard snow, the first problem was an immediate one – the condensed warmer air from the tent froze on the interior of the goggles, reducing our vision to an icy haze. To have taken them off would have risked eye damage from the snow impact.

There was not much to see or film. The white-out conditions were so all-encompassing that even our own mess tent was barely visible just ten metres away. I tried to take a couple of still photographs with my Nikon but after a single click the LED shutter speed indicator faded and died, the batteries disabled by the freezing temperature.

Brian emerged from his tent and shouted over.

'Any news of the Indians?'

'Nothing.'

In fact the Indian camp had gone horribly quiet after the storm came in. Now they were sitting in the leader's tent, monitoring the radio, hoping against hope that their climbers would have the sense to pull out and get back down to camp six.

Brian stumbled away towards the Indian camp, the bright blue and red of his weather gear disappearing rapidly into the white-out. I was tempted to follow him but I knew that the Indians would not welcome the presence of our camera at this sensitive time, with three tired climbers locked in a life-and-death struggle high in the Death Zone.

My fingers, locked inside three layers of thermal insulation, were now beginning to freeze, as were my toes. Kees, who had to operate the camera with just one layer of gloves, was also losing the feeling in his hands very rapidly. Half blinded by the iced-up goggles, we snatched a few shots of flapping canvas and driving snow before the lens froze over with spindrift. We retreated back into the tent to thaw out. All we could do now was wait for news, hoping not only that the Indians would make it back to camp six but that the climbers on the southern side would be able to retreat to the South Col.

Our 'gut feeling' on the weather had delayed our departure that morning. If we had left as we had originally planned, we would now be trapped in the storm at camp four . . . a far more dangerous prospect.

There was little doubt in our minds, having witnessed the brutality of the storm here, that any team above camp five would be in mortal danger. Even if they had made it back to their tents, their safety would not be guaranteed. No tent could stand winds like these for very long.

Then, at about 6 p.m., with the storm raging harder than ever, whoops and shouts pierced thinly through the screaming wind, along with a metallic drumming sound. I poked my head out of the flaps to see several members of the Indian team milling around outside their tents. At first I thought they were shouting a warning – perhaps they had received news of an avalanche or some other disaster or they were making a noise to enable someone to find the camp.

Then I realised that their screams were of joy.

'They're on the summit!' one of the team yelled over. 'They made it! Three climbers!'

'Great!' I shouted back before retreating into the tent where Kees and I shared our total amazement at this news.

'Jesus! They kept going! Why the hell didn't they turn back?'

Kees checked his watch. 'I think they've got about another forty-five minutes of light.'

The boldness of the Indians truly astounded us. To have battled on to the summit in that storm revealed an incredible tenacity which was either an indication of supreme confidence or a very foolish mistake. Not knowing the strength of the climbers involved, we were unable to second-guess which was the more likely.

But the bottom line was clear even to a couple of novices like us. The three Indian climbers now had between six and ten hours of descent along a technically difficult ridge in a terrible storm and in the dark.

A couple of hours later, one of the Norwegian team came over to give us the latest news from the Indian camp.

'It's not looking good. They can't get radio contact with the three climbers and they haven't made it back to camp six.'

We knew what that meant. Out of oxygen, exhausted from their ascent, the Indians would have had little chance of finding their way down the precipitous North Face in conditions of near-zero visibility. Even with support at camp six, the chances of a rescue on the North-East Ridge were slim to non-existent.

They would be extremely unlikely to survive a night out without protection, particularly as the northern side has precious few places to dig a snowhole for a bivouac.

All that the climbers waiting at camp six could do was shine their torches out into the teeth of the storm in the faint hope that this would guide in the descending Indians.

Meanwhile there was still no news from the southern side, where their base camp, like ours in the north, waited on tenterhooks for advice of the whereabouts of their teams. Radio communications are sporadic and unreliable at best on Everest; in the severe meteorological static of the storm, they almost ceased to exist. Call after call went out, with little hard information coming back.

That night the storm continued to rage, and it decreased only in the early hours of the morning.

We awoke to the bleakest possible news: the Indian climbers had still not returned to camp six. But worse was to follow: on the southern side of the mountain, more than ten other climbers – members of Rob Hall and Scott Fischer's teams and the lone Taiwanese climber, Makalu Gau – were now missing somewhere between the South Col and the summit. Most incredible of all was the news that Rob Hall and Scott Fischer themselves were both in trouble and had not made it back to their high camps. After a full night out in the storm they would be in a desperate condition, and undoubtedly frostbitten if they were alive at all.

The news that Rob Hall was in peril was greeted with disbelief and shock. Hall was the best – the ultimate practitioner at this deadly game. What set of circumstances had put his life on the line? Many present at camp three simply did not believe that the reports were accurate.

As the day wore on, pieces of radio conversations filled in more of the details as both the north and south base camps tried desperately to find out who was still alive and where they were. There was talk of rescue, but immediate help could only come from the highest camps where the surviving climbers were already exhausted from their own battle against the elements.

How could it all have happened?

Rob Hall's team had left the South Col for their summit attempt at
11.30 p.m. on the 9th. They were bang on schedule and conditions
were clear after an earlier strong wind had blown itself out a few
hours before. By midnight, Scott Fischer's team were also on the
trail, following the crampon tracks of the earlier climbers up
the shoulder of the South-West Face towards the South-East Ridge.

Both teams were operating to the 'turn-around' principle, by
which they would turn back at a pre-designated time if they had
not made the summit. This 'golden rule' was one which both Hall
and Fischer normally regarded as sacred but, in a break from their
usual operating practice, as they set out from the Col neither leader
had announced a firm 'turn-around' time to their clients. The two
most talked-about hours were 1 p.m. and 2 p.m., but in the subsequent accounts of the summiteers it is clear that no one was sure
which would be applied.

One of Hall's American clients, Doug Hansen, a postal worker,
had experienced at first hand the hard reality of a 'turn-around'; in
1995 Rob Hall had turned him back just 100 metres from the
summit. Now Hansen had returned for another try.

By 4 a.m., the two teams, each with climbers ascending at different rates, were intermixed into one straggling line. This
'bunching' had the inevitable effect of slowing everyone's pace, and
left many of the faster climbers, who had orders to stay with their
teams, in the frustrating position of having to wait in the sub-zero
temperatures until their comrades caught them up.

The first serious delay came at about 28,000 feet, at one of the
sections where the ground is steep enough to justify fixing ropes for
security. The original plan, as described by journalist/climber Jon
Krakauer in his book *Into Thin Air*, had been for two Sherpas from
both Mountain Madness and Adventure Consultants to join forces
and fix the ropes in advance of the two teams. This would have

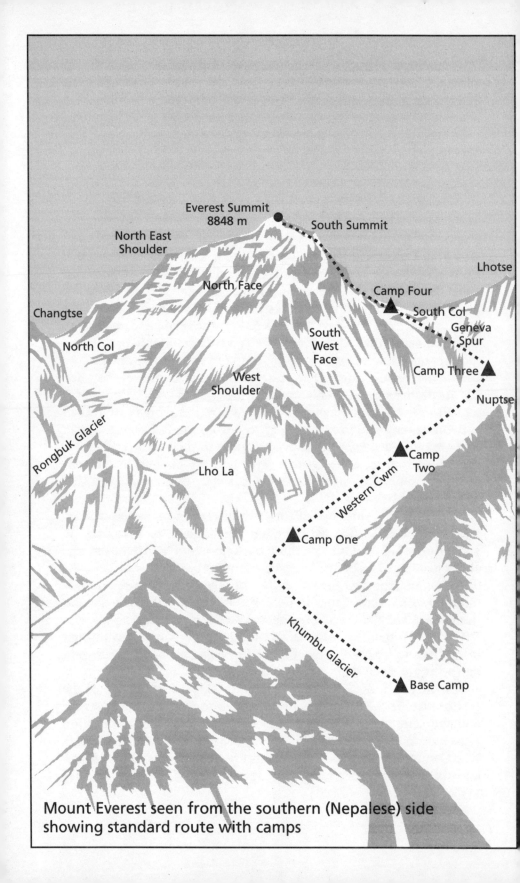

Mount Everest seen from the southern (Nepalese) side
showing standard route with camps

entailed their leaving camp four at least one hour before the main body of the climbers departed. In fact, for whatever reason, the plan had failed and no fixed ropes were in place.

By mid-morning the slow progress was beginning to worry climbers in both teams. Increasingly chilled from standing in the queue, and already exhausted after eleven hours of ascent, three of Rob Hall's clients – Stuart Hutchinson, Lou Kasischke, and John Taske – decided they would abandon their summit attempt. They went down to join Frank Fishbeck, who had already returned to camp four some hours earlier, and Beck Weathers, who had also halted his own ascent after experiencing problems with his eyesight. Unlike Fishbeck, Weathers had been too high to return to camp on his own and was now waiting alone lower down the slope for the team to pick him up on its way back down. Hall sent two Sherpas, Kami and Lhakpa Chhiri, down with his disappointed clients.

There were now seven fewer climbers in the line, but still almost thirty people, including the Taiwanese contingent, were heading up. Inevitably, with such an unwieldy group, there were more delays ahead, particularly as the two cruxes of the South-East Ridge (the south summit and the Hillary step), were still to come.

By noon, the lead guides, Neal Beidleman, Anatoli Boukreev and Andy Harris, were still fixing ropes to the south summit. One hour later Boukreev led the steep ice of the Hillary step and fixed that too. The first of the climbers began to filter up the exhausting pitch on to the final summit ridge.

Boukreev, the Khazak hard man who, unlike all of the other guides, was not using supplementary oxygen, was first to summit at 1.07 p.m. Jon Krakauer, the fittest, fastest and most driven of any of the clients, was ten minutes behind him at 1.17 p.m. In the next thirty minutes, guides Andy Harris and Neal Beidleman also made it, followed by Martin Adams and Klev Schoening – two of Scott Fischer's clients.

They saw no signs from the summit that the weather was about to deteriorate. A few clouds were playing around the lower valleys but no more than would be considered usual during a Himalayan afternoon.

Congestion at the Hillary step further slowed progress for the remaining climbers but by 2.15 p.m., Lopsang Jangbu, Sandy Pittman, Charlotte Fox, Tim Madsen and Lene Gammelgaard were at the summit. Rob Hall, Mike Groom and Yasuko Namba were not far behind them.

Hall called down by radio to base camp manager Helen Wilton and doctor Caroline Mackenzie, who were waiting anxiously for news ten thousand feet lower down the mountain. 'Rob told us he was on the summit and that it was quite cold,' Mackenzie recalls. 'Then he said he could see Doug [Hansen] coming up.'

His words gave the base camp team the impression that Doug Hansen was just a few steps away from the summit, but that was not the case. In fact Doug Hansen was still struggling near the Hillary step, close to the end of his energies but still pushing himself at a snail's pace for the top.

By 3.15 p.m., Neal Beidleman – the Mountain Madness guide who had been waiting on the summit with three clients for Scott Fischer to arrive – decided he could wait no longer. Beidleman had no radio and could not determine where Fischer was. With his clients showing the signs of hypoxia, he began the descent. In fact Fischer did not make it to the top until 3.40 p.m., in a dangerously weak condition and with the storm about to break. He didn't linger.

Rob Hall stuck it out on the summit until 4 p.m. when Doug Hansen finally arrived. He had been on the top of Everest for nearly one-and-a-half hours by the time Hansen painfully made his way to the summit that he had so narrowly missed achieving the year before. Whether Hansen had the mental acuity left to realise where he was, or to feel any sense of jubilation, will never be known, because almost as soon as he got there, Hall turned him right round again and they began the descent.

It didn't take Hall long to realise that he had an extremely serious problem on his hands.

In two radio calls, at 4.30 p.m. and 4.41 p.m., Hall informed his team that Hansen had run out of oxygen and was dangerously exhausted. Down in base camp, members of his team heard him calling for 'Harold' (his guide Andy Harris) to come back up with oxygen.

Hearing this news, and unsure whether Harris had heard Rob Hall's plea, Adventure Consultants doctor Caroline Mackenzie ran across to Scott Fischer's base camp and asked them to radio up and determine whether any of the Mountain Madness team could help. In the ensuing radio conversations it became clear that Scott and his team were also in serious trouble and in no position to offer assistance to Hall.

'That was when we realised the scale of what was going on,' Mackenzie said.

History was now repeating itself. Hansen had run out of energy after turning back the previous year but on that occasion he was lower on the peak. Now, one lethal barrier still lay in front of Hall and Hansen, the Hillary step, the steep ice climb which no semi-comatose climber could possibly descend.

With Doug Hansen now in an advanced state of exhaustion and the storm rising, as he descended into the white-out, Rob Hall was faced with two choices: he could abandon Hansen and attempt to save his own life by a fast descent. Or he could attempt to bivouac with Hansen overnight in the hope that the storm would pass and enable them to escape the following day. Hall must have known he was in a life-threatening situation – his many years of experience would have told him that – and he certainly knew that his client Doug Hansen was in mortal danger, being in a state of near-collapse, and also much less experienced in the skills of survival in extreme conditions. They were both exhausted, probably dehydrated, and with their oxygen supplies running low if not already empty.

During two calls between 5.30 and 6 p.m., members of Hall's base camp team implored him to save himself. They were in no doubt at all that, without oxygen, Hansen would die and it was now abundantly clear that Hall, too, was in danger. Caroline Mackenzie was one of Hall's team who spoke to him during those calls.

'I asked Rob if Doug was still conscious and he said yes, he was. I think that was why Rob felt he couldn't leave him. Doug was hypoxic but he was still conscious. There was no way Rob could leave him like that.'

Andy Harris, the Adventure Consultants guide, moved up from the south summit with two full oxygen cylinders, but with darkness falling and the storm at full tilt, no further radio conversations were heard from Hall until the following morning.

In the dark, Hall and Hansen could not continue. With fatigue compounding the chances of a slip, with visibility reduced to just a few metres, and with life threatening drops on either side of the route, the best Hall could hope for was to find shelter . . . perhaps to scrape a hollow in the snow and wait for the blizzard to end.

That night can only be imagined in the darkest corners of the mind. Others have described their experiences in similar circumstances and perhaps, in their words, we can get a glimpse of the horror of a night out in an Everest storm.

This is how Peter Habeler, Reinhard Messner's partner for the

1978 first ascent of Everest without supplementary oxygen, described his own survival in a similar storm:

> What it means to survive a stormy night at such an altitude can only be imagined by somebody who has personally experienced it. Even under the most favourable circumstances every step at that altitude demands a colossal effort of will. You must force yourself to make every movement, reach for every handhold. You are perpetually threatened by a leaden, deadly fatigue. If you are exposed in such a situation to a storm, with squalls which reach a maximum speed of 130 kilometres an hour; if a heavy snowdrift sets in, so dense that you can no longer see your hand in front of your face, your position becomes practically hopeless. You must cling on firmly to the ice in order not to be hurled off the mountain. Everybody is left to his own resources. If something happens to you, help is out of the question. Everybody has enough to do in trying to save themselves.

But Rob Hall was not in a position to think only of his own survival. He had a professional and moral duty of care to Hansen which meant that leaving him was not an option. Setting aside the personal relationship which had built between the two men, this 'code of conduct' alone was enough to keep Hall there – if the weather was giving him a choice at all.

Elsewhere, amidst confusion and a general breakdown of communications as radio batteries died and headtorches gave their last glimmer of light, others were also finding it nigh on impossible in the white-out to find their way back to the camp on the South Col.

The main group of climbers – eleven of them in total – was wandering the Col from side to side, blinded by driven snow and unable to find their tents. The problem was compounded by the fact that in the darkness it was impossible to wear ski goggles or glacier glasses (which are both heavily tinted), thereby exposing the eyes directly to the stinging fragments of airborne ice.

Two of the group – Neal Beidleman from the Mountain Madness team, and Mike Groom from Adventure Consultants – were guides. They had two Sherpas to assist them with the seven clients. Having lost their bearings they wandered the Col for two hours, becoming increasingly disoriented and exhausted. Finally the two guides realised that to continue was futile until visibility improved. They found the shelter of a small rock and grouped together in a huddle to preserve as much body warmth as they could.

In the tents of camp four, just a few hundred metres away, the luckier members of the ill-fated summit day lay, for the most part, comatose in their tents. The only climber with the strength to push himself out into the white-out blizzard to try and guide in the lost climbers was Scott Fischer's guide – Anatoli Boukreev.

Boukreev had been hired for $25,000 US dollars to assist Scott Fischer and the Mountain Madness team but his guiding tactics on this ill-fated summit day had been unconventional to say the least. In agreement with Fischer, he had climbed without using supplementary oxygen and had therefore been less able to wait around to assist the slower members of the group on their descent. Without the benefit of the extra oxygen, Boukreev was more vulnerable to the cold and to the ravages of altitude and this made a fast descent desirable. By 5 p.m. he was back in camp four at the South Col, preparing extra oxygen and liquids for the descending climbers who were now fighting their way through the blizzard.

Although members of Fischer's own team would later question Anatoli Boukreev's actions in descending so quickly from the summit to camp four without waiting to assist any clients, Boukreev became belatedly one of the heroes of the hour once he realised the real scale of the mounting disaster.

Even though the blizzard had now reduced visibility to just a few metres, and despite the exhaustion of having climbed to the summit just hours before, Boukreev found the strength to go out on two attempts to find the lost climbers. He went alone, for there was no one else at the Col with the strength to join him. At that point, Boukreev later recalled:

Visibility was maybe a metre. It disappeared altogether. I had a lamp, and I began to use oxygen to speed up my ascent. I was carrying three bottles. I tried to go faster, but visibility was gone . . . it is like being without eyes, without being able to see, it was impossible to see.

Not surprisingly, Boukreev was unable to locate any of the lost climbers in the raging storm and he had no radio to guide him to anyone out in the void. He returned to camp four to await events.

Just before 1 a.m., Scott Fischer's guide Neal Beidleman staggered in with three of his clients, having taken advantage of a brief lull in the storm which enabled him to see the tents of camp four. He told Boukreev where he would find the others, huddled exhausted and hypothermic at the far end of the Col. Then Beidleman himself collapsed into his sleeping bag unable to move.

The Khazak went out once more into the teeth of the storm and, having noticed the dim glow of a headtorch, did finally manage to locate the group. Boukreev managed to get three more climbers, including Sandy Hill Pittman, back to the camp, and in so doing he undoubtedly saved their lives.

That left a total of seven climbers unaccounted for on the southern side of Everest as the night wore on. Rob Hall and Doug Hansen were somewhere near the south summit with Andy Harris either with them or not far away. Scott Fischer was on a ledge about 1,000 feet above the col with the Taiwanese climber 'Makalu' Gau. Beck Weathers and the Japanese climber Yasuko Namba had been given up for dead, last seen on the South Col.

On the northern side, the three Indian climbers from the Indo-Tibetan border police team were also out in the full force of the storm with no shelter, no oxygen and no prospect of rescue.

The Indian climbers were Tsewang Smanla, Tsewang Paljor and Dorje Morup, three out of the massive forty-strong team alongside which we had climbed on numerous occasions over the past weeks.

In a desperate predicament, and faced with the impossibility of continuing, most climbers will opt for an emergency bivouac to try and survive a night out. Any source of shelter from the wind and cold is better than nothing, but the potential *degree* of shelter depends on the specific terrain. At its best, a sizeable hole can be cut with an ice-axe into a hard bank of snow or ice, at its worst a climber might resort to lying beneath an overhanging rock or scraping a shallow 'grave' to lie in.

But Everest is not a good mountain on which to be seeking a bivouac site and the higher you happen to be, the fewer the options are. Even during 'good' weather, so much wind rips across its slopes that deep drifts of snow are rare. Where banks of solid ice can be found, it is likely to be as hard as iron, requiring a high expenditure of energy to excavate a space to crawl into. An ice-axe is a useful tool in such circumstances but its cutting blade is just a few inches across. Again this increases the task of cutting a decent shelter.

Given the very daunting problems of finding a bivouac site, it is surprising how many climbers *have* survived bivouacs above 8,000 metres . . . something which early expeditions to Everest would have considered a preposterous idea.

During the American expedition of 1963 Willi Unsoeld and Tom Hornbein had made the first ascent of the West Ridge, reaching the summit at 6.15 p.m. They survived an emergency bivouac at 8,500 metres and Unsoeld lost nine toes to frostbite as a result.

In September 1975, during their successful first ascent of Everest's South-West Face, the renowned British climbers Dougal Haston and Doug Scott sheltered in a snow hole near the south summit of Everest having run out of daylight for their descent. Although they had no food and no sleeping bags they did have a small stove and a bivouac sheet. They spent the night fighting to keep warm blood circulating through their extremities in the desperate attempt to prevent frostbite. Dougal Haston described what must have been the worst night of their lives in Chris Bonington's book *Everest the Hard Way*:

> There was no escaping the cold. Every position was tried. Holding together, feet in each other's armpits, rubbing, moving around the hole constantly, exercising arms. Just no way to catch a vestige of warmth. But during all of this the hours were passing. I don't think anything we did or said that night was very rational or planned. Suffering from lack of oxygen, cold, tiredness but with a terrible will to get through the night all our survival instincts came up front. These and our wills saw the night to a successful end.

Their survival was all the more remarkable for the fact that neither Scott nor Haston suffered frostbite as a result of their bivouac . . . a testimony to their incredible resilience and survival skills.

The two ex-SAS soldiers Brummie Stokes and Bronco Lane were less fortunate when they found themselves in a similar situation one year later. They too cut themselves a shelter into a stretch of ice beneath the south summit. Stokes later had to have all his toes amputated, and Lane also lost fingers.

Surviving as a climbing pair is one thing – at least there is the comfort and body warmth of another human being to help you through the night, but surviving as a solo climber in a bivouac above 8,000 metres on Everest has to require a superhuman determination.

One of the few people to be able to claim such a distinction is Stephen Venables. In 1988, as a member of an American expedition,

Venables reached the summit alone after an epic ascent of the Kanshung (East) Face. He was the first British climber to reach the top without the use of supplementary oxygen. He, like Scott and Haston, ran out of daylight hours and was forced to spend the night out; he wrote of the ordeal in the compelling account *Everest: Kanshung Face*:

> I had no intention of dying that night. I was alone just above 8,500 metres but the wind which had frightened me so much by the Hillary step had now died away and the air temperature was probably not much lower than −20c. I was lucky with the conditions and I knew that I could survive in the excellent clothes I wore, but I had to resign myself to the probable loss of toes.

Against all the odds Venables did survive. Back in the UK he later had three-and-a-half toes amputated after frostbite and gangrene set in.

All the above climbers survived bivouacs above 8,000 metres and got away with their lives. With his extensive knowledge of mountaincraft and, knowing full well how many other people had survived bivouacs at these extreme altitudes, Rob Hall must have thought that he had a fighting chance of surviving if he could make it through to daybreak. Whether he believed that Hansen would make it through the night is another question and one to which we will never know the answer. In any case, Hall, acting faithfully according to the unwritten code of mountain guides everywhere, was not going to leave his client while he was still alive.

But whilst in some ways, Hall and Hansen's bivouac was similar to those of Scott, Unsoeld, Lane and Venables, it differed in one crucial respect: none of them had fought through the night against a storm of the severity of the one which raged about the slopes of Everest on that 10th of May.

Venables talks of temperatures around −20°C. Rob Hall and all the other climbers who now found themselves trapped out on the mountain, were fighting −40 degrees and below . . . with a wind of 100 knots blowing every last vestige of warmth from their flesh.

The next radio communication from Hall came at 4.43 a.m. on the 11th. Not surprisingly, his speech was slurred and he sounded disorientated and dazed after what must have been the most horrific night of his life.

He told base camp that he was 'too clumsy to move' and reported that Andy Harris had been with him through part of the storm. He was unsure what had happened to Harris and, when asked about Doug Hansen he replied, 'Doug is gone.'

Thirty minutes later, by patching their base-camp radio set to a satellite telephone line, the Adventure Consultants' support team enabled Jan Arnold, Hall's wife, to talk to her husband from New Zealand. Arnold, who was seven months' pregnant with their first child, had been to the summit with Hall in 1993, and knew, as any Everest summiteer would, precisely how desperate his situation was. 'My heart really sank when I heard his voice,' she later recalled. 'He was slurring his words markedly. He sounded like Major Tom or something, like he was just floating away. I'd been up there; I knew what it could be like in bad weather. Rob and I had talked about the impossibility of being rescued from the summit ridge. As he himself had put it, "You might as well be on the moon."'

With daylight to assist him, and with the worst of the storm now blown away, Hall now began to try and clear his oxygen mask of ice. He had two full oxygen cylinders with him but they were useless unless he could free his regulator and mask. Shivering violently, and with his hands almost certainly already frosbitten, his task must have been unbearably frustrating and painful.

But by 9 a.m., Hall did manage to free the obstruction in his breathing equipment. He plugged into the oxygen for the first time since the previous afternoon and this news brought a burst of optimism to those who waited on tenterhooks below.

The radio calls continued, as members of Hall's team and fellow climbers tried to bully him into moving down the mountain towards camp four. Helen Wilton, Adventure Consultants' base camp manager told him, 'You think about that little baby of yours. You're going to see its face in a couple of months, so keep on going.'

Ed Viesturs, a member of the IMAX team and a close friend of Hall, spoke to him several times as the day wore on. 'Rob, you gotta get moving. Put that pack on, get the oxygen going, get down the hill.'

Viesturs used humour to try and get a response out of Hall: 'We're going to get down, and we'll go to Thailand, and I'll get to see you in your swimsuit with your skinny legs.' And, 'You're lucky, Rob, your kid's going to be better looking than you.'

Hall responded to the chiding, as Viesturs recalls. 'He laughed. He said, "Geez, thanks for that."'

By ten o'clock that morning, five Sherpas carrying extra oxygen and flasks of hot tea had set out from camp four in a last-ditch attempt to rescue Hall, Fischer and 'Makalu' Gau. Their actions were heroic to say the least, particularly as they were still physically exhausted from the rigours of the previous day.

They found Scott Fischer and 'Makalu' Gau on a ledge about 400 vertical metres above the Col. Fischer was alive, just, but he did not respond to the Sherpas and they decided he was too close to death to be rescued. The Taiwanese climber was in slightly better shape and the Sherpas were able to rouse him to a semi-conscious state after giving him tea and oxygen. Cradled between three of the Sherpas, Gau was able to stagger down to camp four.

Meanwhile Ang Dorje and Lhakpa Chhiri bravely continued up towards Hall, determined to reach him if they possibly could. Risking their own lives, they fought on until high winds defeated them approximately 300 metres below Rob Hall's position. The Sherpas could do no more . . . no human being could. It was 3 p.m., and the New Zealander now had just hours to live.

Just before nightfall, at 6.20 p.m. Hall made his last radio contact with the world. Fittingly, the final words he spoke were to his wife.

'Hi, my sweetheart. I hope you're tucked up in a nice warm bed. How are you doing?'

'I can't tell you how much I'm thinking about you,' Jan Arnold replied. 'You sound so much better than I expected. Are you warm, my darling?'

'In the context of the altitude, the setting, I'm reasonably comfortable,' Hall told her.

'How are your feet?'

'I haven't taken me boots off to check, but I think I may have a bit of frostbite. . . .'

'I'm looking forward to making you completely better when you come home. I just know you're going to be rescued. Don't feel that you're alone. I'm sending all my positive energy your way!'

Hall's last words to his wife were unbearably poignant, 'I love you. Sleep well, my sweetheart. Please don't worry too much.'

Hall did not speak on the radio again and within a few hours he was dead.

*

At camp four on the afternoon of the 11th, the scene was not unlike the aftermath of a battle. The surviving climbers were in a state of shock, their tents ripped and half destroyed, everyone trying to come to terms with the catastrophe that had come out of the blue. In the normal run of events, the climbers would have descended that day following their summit attempt. As it was, they did not have the strength. Breathing oxygen from the IMAX tents (given without hesitation by IMAX leader David Breashears even though it threatened the success of his own multi-million-dollar expedition), they lay in the ever-strengthening wind in a state of mental and physical paralysis.

Then, at about 4.30 p.m., as one piece of bad news seemed to follow another, a single, astonishing ray of hope came out of the blue.

Beck Weathers rose from the dead.

The Texan pathologist had been unconscious and without shelter for more than fifteen hours after passing out during the storm of the previous night. Like Yasuko Namba, who lay nearby, he had been considered beyond help and left to die. Weathers later recalled, 'I'd lost my right glove. My face was freezing. My hands were freezing. I felt myself growing really numb and then it got really hard to stay focused, and finally I just sort of slid off into oblivion.'

Having entered that 'oblivion', and with his body core frozen to within the tiniest possible margin of the point at which death would be inevitable, Weathers recalls nothing whatsoever of the long hours that followed as his body was battered by the freezing hurricane-force winds.

Then, incredibly, some primeval survival instinct fired up a spark of life in the deep-frozen core of Beck Weathers' brain. Breaking the crust of ice crystals that coated his face, he was able to open his eyes for the first time. What he saw shocked him into consciousness.

'Initially I thought I was in a dream,' Weathers told his fellow team member Jon Krakauer, 'When I came to, I thought I was lying in bed. I didn't feel cold or uncomfortable. I sort of rolled on to my side, got my eyes open, and there was my right hand staring me in the face. Then I saw how badly frozen it was, and that helped bring me round to reality. Finally I woke up enough to recognise I was in deep shit and the cavalry wasn't coming so I better do something about it myself.'

In fact the 'cavalry' had already been, and pronounced him as good as dead. Two rescue attempts had reached Weathers where he lay and both had decided that to try and drag him into camp would merely prolong the inevitable.

Now, squinting half-blind into the wind, Weathers made a guess where the tents of camp four would be and stumbled towards them. With his right arm frozen out in front of him, and his face still largely covered with ice, he made a gruesome sight as he reached the tents, reminding the awestruck climbers at the camp of a 'Mummy in a low-budget horror film'.

But this was no cheap piece of fiction. Weathers was suffering from the extreme ravages of frostbite and exposure, and in the opinion of Stuart Hutchinson, the doctor that examined him, 'None of us thought Beck was going to survive the night. I could barely detect his carotid pulse, which is the last pulse you lose before you die. He was critically ill. And even if he did live until morning, I couldn't imagine how we were going to get him down.'

To the utter astonishment of his fellow climbers Beck Weathers did survive the night. And not only that. Like 'Makalu' Gau he recovered sufficiently to stand on his own two feet the next morning. He had to, it was his only hope of survival.

On Sunday the 12th, the descent began. Metre by metre, 'Makalu' Gau and Beck Weathers were supported off the South Col, down the Geneva Spur and right down the Lhotse Face to camp two. It was a rescue of epic proportions, given the immensity of the terrain and the appalling physical condition of the injured climbers. In this as in many other aspects of the story, Weathers and Gau were lucky. Two waiting teams of extremely strong climbers, the IMAX team of David Breashears and the Alpine Ascents team of Todd Burleson, climbed up to assist the exhausted Sherpas with their task.

Meanwhile, at base camp, the final piece of the rescue was being put into place. Guy Cotter, an Adventure Consultants guide who had come across from nearby Ama Dablam to help co-ordinate moves to fight the crisis, had managed to persuade the Nepalese Army to fly a helicopter up from Kathmandu to airlift Weathers and Gau to hospital.

Helicopter evacuations from base camp are not unusual, but Weathers and Gau were in too ravaged a state to be brought back through the maze of crevasses of the Khumbu icefall. If it happened at all, the rescue would have to happen in the Western Cwm, at an altitude which would endanger the pilot and his machine.

The pilot, Lieutenant-Colonel Madan Khatri Chhetri, flew his French-made B2 Squirrel up the icefall and circled above the waiting climbers at just a shade under 20,000 feet. To say that he was pushing the operational envelope of his aircraft would be putting it mildly. The last helicopter to fly into the Cwm had crashed on the glacier below.

The rescuers had created a giant red cross in the snow, etched into the white surface by dribbling Kool-Aid drink out of a bottle. The Nepali pilot hovered above it and 'Makalu' Gau was loaded on board. Half an hour later the courageous pilot returned for Beck Weathers.

Lieutenant-Colonel Madan's action was the last in a long line of heroic actions which in combination saved the lives of the American and Taiwanese climbers. A couple of hours later the two men were being treated in a Kathmandu hospital, and they were then evacuated to their home countries.

*

On the northern side of the mountain the storm had also taken its toll, but the central story which had emerged was not at all like those from the southern side where heroism and selfless action had saved lives which would otherwise have been lost.

In the north, a climbing team in desperate need of help after failing to return to their top camp were passed by a team whose priorities lay with their own summit bid and not with an attempt at rescue.

The climbers in peril were the three Indians of the Indo-Tibetan border police team who had failed to return to camp six at 8,300 metres after their announced summit success of the afternoon of the 10th.

Like most of the summiteers on the southern side, the three Indians on the North-East Ridge were still alive as day broke on the 11th. Frostbitten, their oxygen finished, they were in desperate need of fluids and oxygen if they were to stand any chance of survival. Down at camp three, their distraught leader, Mohindor Singh, kept a vigil at the radio in the tent next to ours, hoping against hope for a miracle. The Indian leader knew, as we all did, that the chances of surviving a second night out would be negligible for the three climbers, but *if* they could somehow make it back to camp six then at least there would be a fighting chance of saving one life and perhaps more.

The conditions were too severe to allow a rescue party from the Indian team to go up and in any case their arrival would have been too late; the distances involved on the northern side are greater than those on the southern. To get a rescue team from where we were at camp three to camp six would take a minimum of two days, or even three if the winds remained strong.

As luck would have it, a team of five strong climbers – two Japanese and three Sherpas – was about to stumble upon the Indians. They were equipped with oxygen, fluid and food – all the ingredients for a rescue. The Japanese climbers were twenty-one-year-old Eisuke Shigekawa and thirty-six-year-old Hiroshi Hanada from the Japanese-Fukuoka Everest expedition.

The Japanese team had made no secret of their intention to summit on 11 May. The complicated pyramid of logistics involved in any summit attempt means that it actually makes good sense to work *backwards* from a given summit day when calculating the supplies of oxygen, gas and food which have to be portaged on a tight schedule to the higher camps. Most Everest expeditions work this way – but most have the flexible attitude that although everything should be ready for a given summit day, other factors will probably cause delays.

Ironically our own original proposed summit day had been 10 May, but the bad weather in the days prior to that date had delayed our departure. The Japanese, more committed than most to their pencilled in 'ideal' date of the 11th, seemed hell-bent on summitting that day almost regardless of what the weather was going to do.

Having sat out the storm at camp six (which in itself must have been a terrifying experience) on the exposed North Face, the Japanese team, apparently ignoring the fact that the weather was still obviously very dangerously unstable, left the 8,300-metre-high base on schedule not long after midnight on the 11th.

By 8 a.m. the five climbers had climbed up the steep cliffs of the yellow band and reached the first step – a twenty-metre-high cliff which is the first of the major obstacles on the North-East Ridge. Here, to their surprise, the Japanese team came across one of the Indian climbers, who was badly frostbitten and clearly suffering from the ravages of acute mountain sickness after a night out without oxygen. No communication passed between the Japanese team and the stricken Indian. According to the lead climbing Sherpa, who later spoke to journalist Richard Cowper about the incident, the Indian just 'made a big noise'.

The Japanese team hardly paused. Leaving the Indian lying in the snow, they continued their climb towards the summit. Later, at the top of the second step, the Fukuoka team found the other two Indians, also horrifically frostbitten and close to death.

Again they continued. Again as the lead Sherpa Kami later confirmed to Richard Cooper in an interview, they made no attempt to assist the Indians but carried on into the worsening wind towards the summit. The fact that they made it at all speaks for just how determined the Japanese team were to reach the top on such a marginal day, as the rescuers on the southern side had found as they attempted (and failed) to reach Rob Hall on the south summit. In a howling gale, the Japanese summitted just before midday and began their descent, which would once more take them past the Indian climbers.

Down at advance base camp, all was confusion. The Indian team were frantic for news of their missing team members and whether or not any rescue attempt was to take place. At 4 p.m. on the 11th, just after Sundeep, Roger, Tore and Simon arrived at the camp, Indian leader Mohindor Singh asked Sundeep to accompany him as translator to the Japanese leaders' tent where vital radio communications were being made.

'Singh was desperate to get news of his climbers,' Sundeep recalls, 'and he knew there was a chance that at least one might be rescued by the Japanese climbers as they descended.'

The Japanese leader radioed up to camp six where the first of the returning summiteers arrived sometime between 5 and 5.30 p.m. Due to some confusion, perhaps a result of the fact that information was being exchanged via radio link with poor reception and that the conversation was a three-way one in Japanese, English and Hindi, the hope of rescue was not at this stage dashed.

'The radio call definitely gave myself and Singh the impression that one of the Indian climbers was being helped down – that he would arrive at camp six within the next couple of hours,' Sundeep remembers. 'In a way, that was the big mistake. If they had told Singh from the start that no rescue was possible then the situation would have been different. As it was, the first Japanese climber back to six – and then the second too – both gave the impression a rescue was under way.'

But as the remainder of the five-strong Japanese team reached camp six, and still with no sign of any of the Indian team arriving, the penny finally dropped.

'By about 8.30 p.m., when it was dark,' Sundeep continued, 'Singh and myself finally realised the truth. There had been no rescue. In fact there had been no rescue attempt at all. That was when we realised that all three climbers would certainly be lost.'

Singh returned to his camp to give the dreadful news to his heartbroken team. Sundeep reported back to us in the mess tent.

'That's it,' he told us, 'there's no chance of any rescue now. We have to assume the Indians are dead.'

The meal that night in the frozen tent was one of unparalleled misery. Most of us sat, wrapped in our own morose thoughts, pushing forkfuls of oily noodles round a dirty plate and mulling over the fate of the Indian climbers.

The next day, incensed by the way in which the Japanese had apparently ignored his stricken climbers, Singh called a meeting of all the other expedition leaders (but not the Japanese leader Koji Yada) in his tent on the morning of the 12th. The session was tape-recorded by the Indian team. He ran through the events of the previous two days and informed the gathering that he wanted to issue a joint statement, to be agreed by all present, condemning the Japanese for their failure to try a rescue.

Having listened to the account, the other leaders (who included some extremely experienced Himalayan climbers) did not agree with Singh's proposal. Some had doubts that the Indian climbers could have been rescued at all, others recalled similar incidents from their own climbing careers where they had had to leave living climbers behind who were beyond saving.

Our own expedition leader, Simon Lowe, was one of those present:

> Basically Singh wanted us to slam the Japanese for what they'd done, but although we had huge sympathy with his point of view, we had no first hand knowledge of what had happened. Also, we couldn't ignore the fact that the root cause of the tragedy was in their own actions. The Indian climbers put themselves in jeopardy.

Notwithstanding this disappointment, Singh did issue a press statement of his own, complaining of the Japanese actions.

By the time the Japanese team returned to advance base camp, the news that they had ignored the dying Indians had whipped up a storm of protest which spread right across the world.

Richard Cowper, the *Financial Times* journalist with our expedition, interviewed the two Japanese climbers and their Sherpas for a condemnatory article which appeared the following Saturday in the UK, and which considerably fuelled the debate. Asked why they had offered no assistance to the dying Indians, Shigekawa told Cowper, 'We climb by ourselves, by our own efforts, on the big mountains. We were too tired to help. Above 8,000 metres is not a place where people can afford morality.'

Hiroshi Hanada added, 'They were Indian climbing members – we didn't know them. No, we didn't give them any water. We didn't talk to them. They had severe high-altitude sickness. They looked as if they were dangerous.'

Later the Japanese team released a statement claiming that Kami Sherpa had helped free one of the Indians – probably Tsewang Smanla – from a tangle of fixed ropes near the second step. They also announced that there had been no indication at the summit that the three Indians had been there at all – a startling accusation which only compounded antagonism towards themselves at a time when feelings were already running high.

(In fact the Japanese were right in this assertion, the Indians had not been on the summit when they had radioed back to their leader to report success. If they had been, they would have been standing right next to Hall, Lopsang and Doug Hansen . . . who reported no sign of them at all. It is now believed that in the conditions of limited visibility they mistook a lower pinnacle for the summit and in fact reached a high point about 150 metres from the top.)

The Japanese attitude created an ugly mood amongst the teams at camp three – not least our own. Brian was outraged at their behaviour and threatened, 'I'll rip the flag off their pole and piss on it.'

Al took a different view. 'All this talk about rescue is crap. There's no way the Indians could have been rescued from where they were, no matter how many people tried. There wasn't much the Japanese could have done.'

Cowper wrote in his article:

No one believes for one moment that the Japanese could have saved all three Indians. But most mountaineers I spoke to say that if all five members of the Japanese team had concentrated on the one frost-bitten Indian at the first step then one life would surely have been saved.

At the time I agreed with him.

On the 13th, I hung around the Indian mess tent like a vulture waiting for the surviving Indian climbers to drag themselves back into camp. They moved like men returning from a war – shattered figures devastated by the loss of their friends. The leader Mohindor Singh came out of the tent and put his arm around one of the returning climbers as he stood in front of the cairn of prayer flags, his shoulders heaving as he sobbed with tears. Kees was asleep in the tent at that point so I shot the sequence, zooming in for a close up on the faces of the weeping men and trying to switch off the little voice inside me that was telling me I really shouldn't be doing this.

Later I asked Singh if I could interview him for the film but he was too stricken with grief at that point and told me he would talk in a couple of days. After I thought about it, however, I realised that to interview Singh would be a pretty gross intrusion while he was still mourning the deaths of his team members, and I didn't raise it with him again. I did, however, interview members of our own team to try and get an insight into how the catastrophe had affected them. Kees and I squashed into Sundeep and Roger's tent; ghoulish though it may seem, I wanted to record their reactions to the increasingly bad news from above.

Roger spoke first:

We accepted that people might die this year on Everest. But it's one thing to accept that intellectually, and another to be sitting here in our tents knowing that people are dying up there on the mountain.

Sundeep was also beginning to question his motives for the climb:

It makes you think about how much you want the summit. What you're prepared to risk – what you're prepared to lose.

There was a growing awareness that the events of this twenty-four-hour period were likely to affect us for a long time to come. Our strategy had already been knocked massively out of shape by the unsettled weather of the last few days, and now the deaths caused by the storm would take a deeper toll on the already vulnerable nerves of the team.

8

For the next four days, the bad weather continued to pin us down at camp three, with no sign of any change. Our entire team had now been stuck at 6,450 metres for seven days, far longer than had originally been planned. Physically we were deteriorating every day, and yet we still had no firm idea of when we would be going for the summit. Each day, we went to sleep clinging to the hope that the next morning would give us our 'weather window'. Each day dawned with high winds and snowfalls, condemning us to more time on our backs in the freezing camp.

The original plan had been so effectively destroyed by the storm that most of us could barely remember what dates we had originally set aside for our summit attempt. The very fabric of the expedition was in danger of being ripped apart. Team 'A' was now tired and debilitated; Brian particularly had been very deeply affected by the deaths on the mountain and felt that the bad weather was likely to continue for a while as he told me in an interview we filmed in his tent:

We're all very frightened. This has knocked us all for six. We've got to treat this mountain with a great deal of respect.

Kees and I were also nervous and on edge; our film was heavily dependent on getting footage from high on the mountain and as each day passed that possibility was looking more remote.

The camp, like us, seemed to be falling apart. The mess tent was now damaged and offering even less protection than before. The crevasse in front of our tent was widening as the weather warmed, swallowing up rocks and threatening to engulf Nga Temba's tent. The toilet was now a veritable mountain of shit, and foul smells were drifting out of the crevasses where generations of waste had been dumped by previous expeditions.

All the minor ailments that we had lived with since arriving in Tibet now flared into irritating infections. Sore throats, split fingers, mouth ulcers, blisters, diarrhoea, piles ... we all had our problems and sitting on our backsides was only making them worse ...

Team 'B', having arrived later to advance base, was generally in better condition, both mentally and physically. Their bodies had endured fewer days above 6,000 metres, and they could see how feeble team 'A' was beginning to look. The weather continued to be unstable, with high winds and snowstorms most afternoons.

Even so, it still took me by surprise when Simon called a meeting in the mess tent and announced that he was proposing to let the 'B' team go first.

'You can't do that!' I protested, seeing our whole enterprise suddenly threatened.

'Why not?' Simon replied, icily calm.

'Why change the plan?'

'You guys aren't showing any signs of leaving for your summit push,' Roger pointed out, 'and while we're waiting here we're running our bodies into the ground. If you won't take the risk on the conditions, we will. It doesn't make sense for us to wait here any more.'

I could see his point. Our own team, or more particularly Al, Brian and Barney, had shown extreme reluctance to leave until they were totally convinced the weather window was right. There had even been talk of retreating again to base camp and waiting for another push, but I wanted to avoid that at all costs. I had a suspicion that Brian would not be up to another long haul up the glacier no matter how much rest he got down low.

Now, the 'B' team were upping the ante, and putting us under pressure to get off our asses and move – or step aside and let them through.

'It's like Simon says,' Sundeep pointed out, 'we can sit here for ever waiting for the perfect day. We won't climb the mountain sitting at advance base camp.'

'I don't see what the panic is,' Al put in, 'we've still got nearly two weeks before we have to be out of here. There's more time left than you think, and the best conditions are often towards the end of the month. We can blow it by being too impatient.'

'I agree,' said Brian, 'it's way too windy at the moment and it's way too cold. With the filming, we're going to be in for long periods of standing around. Kees is more than likely to get frostbitten fingers if we go now and he tries to shoot.'

Brian was right, but his words gave the 'B' team more ammunition.

'That's true,' said Simon. 'The filming does take more time. If the conditions are a bit marginal, then it doesn't make so much sense for the filming group to be in that slot. You need super perfect conditions.'

'Hang on a minute!' I had to fight our corner on this one. 'That isn't the case. You've all seen how fast we've been working. I agree that on the glacier we held things up quite a bit when we were shooting but on the summit push it'll be mostly Al going on ahead and filming Brian coming up. Like he did on the Col. The reason Kees and I are there is to do the interviews and stuff in the evenings at the camps, when it doesn't affect our speed at all.'

'Keep your hair on, Matt, no one's saying the film team are slower,' Simon told me. 'But you have got more gear to carry and you will risk frostbite if you have to take gloves off to film in the coldest conditions.'

'OK. But I resent the implication that we are slower, because we're not.'

Simon concluded the meeting in his usual diplomatic style:

'All right. Well, in any case, there's no decision we *can* make until the weather clears up a bit.'

'So which team's going first?' Tore, the Norwegian, was, like Roger and Sundeep, itching to get into the summit push.

There was a pause while Simon looked over to Barney.

'I'll have to have a chat with Barney and Nga Temba about it,' he said, 'and we'll let you know.'

This inconclusive end left us all unsettled. In the tent that night I found it extremely difficult to sleep, worrying that our slot was about to vanish, leaving us to deteriorate gradually here until we had no strength left. I came up with a rearguard action if it turned out that the 'B' team were given the go-ahead to leave first; this was the decision to send Kees up with them, so that at least some of the high-altitude filming could take place.

I also resolved to give Sundeep, the 'B' team member I judged most likely to make the summit, a lightning course in handling the video camera. It was a very long shot but if I gave him the spare Sony, he might just be able to shoot something if they got lucky with the conditions and topped out.

But by the evening of May 14 no decision had been announced. The conversation had not been raised again, and in fact, I needn't have worried, for conditions were about to clear.

*

On the morning of the 15th, I awoke to the unmistakable sound of equipment being sorted and packed in Brian and Barney's tent next door. Kees had woken earlier and was probably having his first cup of tea in the mess tent. Although it was still too early for the sun to hit the fabric of our tent, I could sense by the brilliance of the reflected light off the glacier that the sky was clear.

I poked my head out of the front of the tent. Barney was there, with his blue equipment barrel by his side.

'What's the news?' I asked him.

'We're on.'

A massive shot of mixed adrenalin and dread ran through my body. The thought that we would finally be leaving filled me with contradictory emotions: I was pleased that something was happening at last, when just a couple of days before I had been fighting to keep our 'number one' slot. But we had spent so many days now at advance base camp that we were used to the inactivity. My body felt stiff, unfit and unready for the challenge. My mind was also unprepared. The sense of purpose, of focusing on a single recognised objective, had been thrown by the events of the storm. All the confidence, impatience and optimism I had experienced on leaving base camp was now replaced by the leaden sense that we were out of condition and out of time.

I was acutely aware of the amount of body weight I had lost. It seemed to have fallen off me in this last week living at 21,500 feet on a deficient diet and with an appetite which was feeble at best. My legs, never abundantly endowed with meaty tissue, were now as skinny as two sticks of celery. My midriff was likewise reduced; pinching the skin of my stomach between two fingers raised not an ounce of fat.

I estimated I had lost at least 10 kilogrammes, which worked out at more than a kilogramme a week; but I didn't really know how this would affect my performance. Perhaps if the muscle were still intact, I would not notice any difference? Or, more worryingly, would I suddenly run out of steam high on the mountain? The only solace was that all my fellow climbers were in the same state.

Everyone had lost a comparable amount of weight, in Brian's case perhaps as much as fifteen kilogrammes.

Advance base camp had been a haven from the storm, and like a creature who has hibernated for too long through a cold winter, the prospect of leaving this place of security was deeply unattractive. Here was safety; up there was danger, as the storm had so tragically reminded us.

I retreated back into the tent and lay down for a few precious moments, trying to banish the apathy which threatened to overwhelm me. The very last thing I wanted was to push myself back up the Col, particularly as the recent heavy snows were still sitting ready to avalanche at the first warming of the weather . . . like today for example.

Simon shook the tent. 'Wake up, Matt, you're leaving in half an hour.'

I realised that the longer we were delayed, the better the chance of the Col avalanching on us. I got dressed in double time and was soon outside with the others preparing my rucksack of gear.

There was none of the banter and camaraderie with which the 'B' team had seen us off from base camp. Now, they were in sombre mood, no doubt contemplating the stressful extra days they were about to have waiting here. Their bid to take over our slot as team 'A' had so nearly succeeded and now all four were looking as if they regretted not pushing a bit harder.

There was no sense of excitement or anticipation. The storm, and the knowledge of the fatalities it had caused, weighed heavily on us all as we shouldered the packs and checked over our equipment lists for the final time.

We shook hands and there were a few muttered words of encouragement. Even Brian, normally the loudest of us, was strangely quiet as we plodded very slowly up through the other camps on the strip. As we passed through the Indian tents, they were already packing to begin their evacuation.

All five of us were moving slowly and it was a relief to have a rest when we reached the permanent ice before putting on the crampons and starting up the plateau before the Col. On our first trip here, the plateau hadn't bothered me at all; now, with the sun radiating strongly off the ice, I felt trickles of sweat soak my back as the temperature rose. We all stopped frequently to apply glacier cream, stuffing it into our ears and noses which experience had taught us were particularly vulnerable to the ferocious radiation.

I had always considered the plateau to be flat, but now I realised it is not. It runs in a steady rise, which now took its toll on my weakened legs. I drank regular sips of juice from my bottle, and stuffed down a couple of toffee crisps, but could not detect the burst of energy which these normally give.

After three hours we reached the base of the Col where the weather took a sudden turn for the worse. A black cloud swept without warning into the sky above the snow ridge and a wind whipped straight down the face at high speed. It began to snow, then hail, and against my skin I could feel my sweat-soaked inner thermal shirt beginning to cool down uncomfortably.

I was missing a couple of important images from our first trip up the ice wall, specifically a shot of Brian approaching the Col, and something from the bottom of the wall to show how intimidating the hanging glacier is to anyone looking up at it. We brought out the camera and filmed these quickly as the weather conditions changed again to reveal bursts of sunshine through the sporadic cloud.

Then we threaded on our harnesses and began the climb. With three hours of exertion behind me since advance base, my legs now felt better in tune and I found I was moving fairly fluidly. The muscle fatigue which had set in after our prolonged period of lying on our backs was easing off. To my relief I found I was still reasonably fit.

The condition of the snow was my main concern. The storm, and the unstable weather of the last few days, had dumped millions of tons on to the Face. It was sitting on top of wind-polished ice, and therefore liable to avalanche without warning. We moved as fast as we could to reduce our exposure time, but it still took us a further three hours to reach camp four.

Kees was the first to reach our tent. 'Take a look at this!' he exclaimed.

I stooped down to look into the tent, which we had carefully cleaned before we left after our first acclimatisation climb to the Col.

The interior was in a disgusting state, with discarded tea bags, foil soup packets and other rubbish stuck fast into frozen puddles where liquids had been spilled and left. In the foyer, yellow stains marked where urine bottles had been tipped out carelessly on to the ice, and the floor of the tent itself was now sagging into a deep hollow where body warmth had frozen down into the carefully flattened platform. The fabric of one side wall had been scorched by a gas stove, and several jagged rips marked where crampons had been worn inside. Our sealed packs of food had been ripped open and plundered.

Al came over and took a look. 'Fucking toerags,' he said. 'I told you this would happen. We've had squatters.' His own tent was in a similar mess.

'Who the hell has left them in this state?' Brian was outraged.

'People must have used them for refuge in the storm.'

Al was right again. Our camp was one of the best set up and the best stocked at the North Col. During the chaos of the storm, with teams in disarray retreating off the mountain, it was hardly surprising that some had sought shelter in what amounted to a free hotel.

'Or it could be the International team.'

That was another possibility. Late in the season a mixed international team had arrived at advance base camp. Their tactics seemed a world away from the the structured logistics of Himalayan Kingdoms, and as far as we could see, they were essentially a group of individuals who had bought their way into a shared permit. Rumours flew around the camp that they might try 'squatter' tactics – utilising the vacant tents of other teams rather than carrying their own.

I preferred to believe that our tents had been used during the storm. At least that might explain why someone *in extremis* could leave them as such an unbelievable tip.

Now we had to expend valuable energy clearing them out and making our base habitable as far as we could. An hour later we were ready to start rehydrating our bodies after the climb. It struck me that we would be in serious trouble if camps five and six had also been plundered. If our oxygen supplies were gone then our summit attempt was as good as over.

That night at the North Col was a restless one, accompanied by a buffeting wind which beat sporadically against the tent.

Now that the previously flat floor of our Quasar had been melted out into a deep scoop by other occupants, it was no longer possible to get a comfortable sleeping platform. No matter how many positions we tried, the slope always won, pitching Kees and myself into an undignified and sleep-defying tangle in the central dip. In the early hours of the morning we rearranged the entire tent, placing the rucksacks in the centre to reduce the slope. It worked well enough to allow a few hours of fitful sleep.

At dawn we began the morning ritual of firing up the gas cookers and preparing tea. By 8 a.m. we were out in the full glare of the early morning sunshine, interviewing Brian as he prepared for the long day's climb up the North Ridge. He was looking fit and rested, even though, as usual, he had eaten very little for breakfast.

'It's going to be a hard day, but if we can do it, we'll be on oxygen from camp five onwards. Then it's follow the yellow brick road to the top!'

We all looked over the dip in the Col to the vast flank of the Ridge which awaited us. A fixed rope was visible on the lower reaches, but it was too far away to be seen on the higher slopes. One of the other teams had left at dawn, two hours before. Now they were just a line of tiny dots, about a quarter of the way up the snow-laden part of the Ridge. It was Brian who pointed them out.

'Look at that team! They've stopped. They're hardly moving.'

Kees framed up a shot on the end of the zoom lens and filmed them, ominously motionless, against the enormous reflected light of the ice. Whatever kind of personal hell they were going through we would find out soon enough.

To their left, we could clearly see the fast-blowing spume of ice crystals shooting off horizontally over the edge of the Ridge.

'There could be a lot of wind today,' said Al. 'Best be off.'

That was the nearest we got to a tactical discussion about the day ahead. Barney had not been on the North Ridge before, and Al was preoccupied with sorting out the camera. On the first time up the Col, and even the first time up the Rongbuk glacier, we had always talked the problems through in advance. This time, we didn't even think about a discussion, perhaps because the Ridge looked so simple that we didn't anticipate any problems.

We packed our climbing gear and sleeping bags into the rucksacks, put the filming gear into safe, padded parts of the packs, and filed out of the camp. Al took over from Kees for the day's filming.

The route dropped down into a dip in the Col and then crossed the crevasse marking the divide between the solid rock of the Ridge and the compacted ice of the hanging glacier. The dip looks insignificant from the North Col camp, but the rise on the other side was steep enough to make me draw hard for breath. Despite the freezing wind, I found myself sweating inside my many levels of clothing, and after half an hour I was already stripping off an outer layer to let my skin breathe.

'There's the Catalan rope coming up from the western side!' Al pointed out the fixed line dropping down on the opposite side of the Col. Alone amongst the teams, the Catalans had chosen to attempt the Col from the western, more avalanche-prone side. It was a bold gesture but they had found it hard going and had only just made it to the Col as we were coming up for the second time.

Well over 7,000 metres now, we were climbing at the upper limits of what most acclimatised climbers can handle without supplementary oxygen. The Ridge is not particularly steep compared to the ice wall leading to the North Col, but at this rarefied altitude it is relentless and continuously demanding.

Every abrupt movement was punished with a wave of dizziness, and the only way to continue moving forward and up was to move smoothly and slowly, raising each boot just a few inches at a time into the sharp-edged steps which had been cut into the ice by the cramponed boots of our fellow climbers.

The fixed ropes and their anchors became waymarkers: targets to make within a certain number of steps. I began on a system of fifteen continuous steps, followed by about a minute of deep breathing to recover. After an hour it fell to ten steps and about three minutes of recovery. Brian was also moving slowly, planting each cramponed foot in slow motion into the ice step above and pausing to look out over the views to Nepal, which were now opening up and becoming more spectacular with every rope length we passed.

Back to the North, the elegant South Ridge of Changtse was also gradually revealing more of itself, leading the eye up to the pyramidal summit, with its complicated cornices of ice.

Al and Barney seemed less affected by the altitude, Barney patiently shepherding Brian up, and Al moving out away from the fixed ropes to film when the wind allowed him to do so. Once again, I was thankful that we had Al with us to cope with the camera; I was not at all sure that Kees and I could have found the extra reserves of energy to devote to the filming.

After a while, I lost all track of time, locked into the simple physical battle to gain height and tick off the fixed ropes one after the other. I began to play another mental game, rationing sips of drink and bites of food against the passing waymarkers of the fixed ropes. One rope's length earns a rest for five minutes, two rope lengths a sip of juice, three a chunk of chocolate and so on. I even rationed my right to enjoy the view; that was a luxury which could only be earned every four ropes.

Al broke the spell, snapping me back to the moment.

'There's the body of a Spanish climber just up ahead to the right of the Ridge. Do you want to film it?'

His words took me by surprise, I hadn't known about the body.

'How long has it been there?'

'Years.'

'How did he die?'

'No idea. Could have been anything. Storm, a fall.' Al's voice did not betray the slightest flicker of emotion. And for that matter, nor did mine, despite the fact that I had never seen a dead body up close before. I caught my breath and decided that we should at least have a look.

We found the remains of the climber amongst the rocks about fifty metres away from the main route up the Ridge. All that remained was a sad, tattered bundle of ripped clothes, and the bare bones which had once been a living human being. The wind was blowing at the shreds of fabric, still trying to tear them away from the body. A few rocks had been placed on the remains as a makeshift grave.

Looking back down to the camp on the Col, which was less than an hour away to a descending climber, I wondered how it was that he could have died so close to safety. Did he descend in a storm and lose his way? Or did he pause to rest in this spot and then lose the strength to continue?

'Do you want to film it?' Al was unpacking the camera.

Ethically I was resistant to the idea, but I knew the shot could be a powerful addition to the film; the corpses which lie on Everest's higher slopes are a part of the reality of the mountain regardless of whether I thought it was acceptable to film them. To ignore them in the film would be missing one of Everest's most potent messages: if you die here, this will be your resting place for eternity.

'Yes. Try and get it in a wide shot.'

Al filmed a variety of different shots, panning down the North Face, and trying hard to keep the camera stable in the fiercely gusting wind. Then we picked our way back through the rocks and rejoined the others back on the Ridge where they had been resting.

By late morning we were ready for a longer break. We stopped at a small rocky ledge where the five of us could sit together. I wasn't at all hungry but I forced down a tin of tuna salad, some crackers and a mouthful of cheese. Apart from the occasional comment on the view there was little conversation between us, for every part of our faces were covered by balaclavas and the hoods of our down suits. Where the wind found a scrap of skin to torment, it lost no time in freezing it.

There was no doubt the westerly wind was rising as the day, and the climb, went on. As we started out once more up the fixed ropes, I noticed that pea-sized stones were skittering across the ice and blowing off towards the east. Ice debris kicked out by climbers above no longer fell towards the climber below, but flew off the same way as the stones, horizontally over the drop to the East Rongbuk. The loose straps on Brian's pack were flapping wildly, and the top strap on my own pack was doing the same, flicking into my face with some force at every gust. I stopped and took off the pack to tie it up.

Back into the routine: clip on to the rope, ten steps, then rest. The hours passed, and we became spread out over two rope lengths or more. Brian seemed to be getting slower but I was happy with the progress we were making. The camp at the North Col was now far beneath us, and the top of the snow ridge seemed to be just a couple of hours away. Just above there, hidden somewhere in the rocks, I knew, was the safety of camp five, where we would rest before the further challenge of the climb to camp six and beyond.

Getting Brian on to the oxygen at camp five was one of the last major hurdles, I thought. If he kept his promise to use it, and we got the weather window, then there seemed little reason why a summit attempt should not go ahead. He seemed to me to be still going strongly, and showing no signs of altitude sickness even on this, the highest of day climbs so far. For the first time since the storm struck, I was allowing a chink of optimism to creep in.

At 2.30 p.m. we began one of the steeper stages of the Ridge, a rope's length of glass-hard ice into which shallow steps had been chipped. The change of gradient slowed us down even more, until we were gasping for air after virtually every step. Kees was falling further behind the group, and I waited at the top of the steep section for him to catch up.

We continued together towards the other three, who had stopped above where the gradient eased off. I assumed this was a stop like the numerous others we had taken during the day, and took off my pack for a drink.

Brian was the first to speak, his voice raised against the wind.

'We're just having a bit of a discussion here, Matt, which you ought to be a part of.'

'What's up?'

'I think we've got a problem.' It was Barney who took over. 'We should be almost at camp five by now, but we're still only two-thirds of the way up the Ridge.'

'If that.' Al came into the conversation. 'You could argue that we're only halfway up, and we've been on the go for five or six hours.'

'Then we'd better pick up some speed. We'll be there in a couple of hours.' I took a swig of juice, still unaware of the true implications of what they were saying.

'It's not as simple as that,' Al continued. 'If you look up the Ridge you can see a couple of the tents of camp five.'

He was right. The red and yellow dots were just visible amongst the jumble of rocks.

'And now take a look down to the Col.'

I did as he asked but couldn't see what he was getting at.

'So?'

'So the tents are roughly the same size. I don't think we are nearly there at all. I think we're only just halfway.'

Barney came in again. His voice as casual as ever, conveyed none of the seriousness of his words:

'If we keep going at this rate, and we're bound to get slower, we'll be in after dark. The wind could get up and then we'll have fingers and toes going. Could turn into a bit of an epic.'

He turned his face away, unable to meet my eyes.

I looked up at the remaining stretch of Ridge above us, scarcely able to believe what I was hearing. In my judgement, we had cracked the majority of the climb. The rock section was just an hour away, wasn't it? Brian was tired, agreed, but no more so than he had been on the Col. There had not been the slightest hint from Barney or Al that we were heading for a problem.

'So what are you proposing?'

There was a long, awkward pause before Barney spoke.

'We're thinking about heading back down.'

'Heading back? But we're almost there! What's the point of that?' The wave of anger swept over me in an uncontrollable wave. 'We're here to climb, aren't we?'

The rushing of the wind was the only reply.

'And if we do go back, what's going to happen then?'

'Well.' An even longer pause. 'That'll be it.' Barney delivered the killer line, the death sentence on the film and all I had hoped it would be.

'That's it? After all this work? That's it? You can't be serious, Barney! We have to make a summit attempt. This is pathetic!' I was ranting. 'Brian. What about you? You can't let it end like this, can you?'

Brian was putting a brave face on it. 'We'll go back down, have a good night's sleep and some food and try again tomorrow.'

Barney looked away and I knew why. Even I, as a novice at altitude, knew that there was no way Brian would be up for another attempt at the Ridge, no matter how much food and sleep he got.

'We've just been too slow. And if we're too slow here then we'll be in trouble up high.' Al was backing Barney.

I gestured up towards camp five and the tents which could so clearly be seen. 'But this is fucking bullshit! There's the camp. All we have to do is keep going and we'll be there. We're nearer to camp five than we are to the Col, for Christ's sake!'

I was almost in tears with the frustration.

'I know that's how it looks, but the distance is foreshortened.' Al was as calm as ever. 'If we take Brian up there we might not get him back down. He's too slow. And Kees is looking knackered as well.'

'So why didn't either of you say anything this morning? If we had to move fast, then why not tell us? Why didn't you point it out when we stopped for lunch? You must both have known it then, didn't you?'

No one replied.

'And what about the film? How is the viewer supposed to understand a copout like this after all the gung-ho talk? Every piece of material we've shot is leading towards a summit attempt. Everyone knows that attempt can fail but the least everyone is expecting is for Brian to have a try. At the moment we haven't even made as much ground as Brian made in 1990. If we shoot you turning back now, all the viewer is going to see is you jacking it in on a beautiful blue sky day three days beneath the summit! And at that point they're going to think "what the fuck was the point of all that?" just like I'm thinking now.'

I have never been angrier. The only reason I had taken on the film was that I had believed it would go further – much further – and harder than 'Galahad of Everest'. Brian had convinced me, Himalayan Kingdoms had convinced me, and, in turn, I had convinced the commissioning editors of Channel 4 and ITN that we would be filming where no one had ever filmed before. What was I going to tell them now?

The one thing I didn't want to do was make a remake of someone else's film. That was why the summit attempt was so important; to film Brian in the Death Zone and making an all-out attempt on the summit was the very essence of the production and all my hopes.

Now I was left with a flop. In those moments I truly doubted that I had a film at all. Who in their right mind would want to watch an Everest film which ended in a casual conversation before the real climbing began? The way the three of them were talking, it was sounding like a decision to pack up a summer's picnic after a few spots of rain.

'There's no point in getting nasty about it.' Barney was on the defensive. 'We're not going to get Brian into a situation where his life is in danger.'

'I know. And I agree about that. The last thing I want is Brian, or anyone, to be out of their depth. But Brian's been much higher than this before and he's in good condition. There's no technical ground here, and things could look better once we reach five and the oxygen. Let's *try*. That's the least the viewer has to expect. We still have time.'

But Barney was not to be moved, and neither was Al. My protests went against their combined years of experience which told them we were heading for a problem.

As our argument continued, an extraordinary thing happened. Al spoke some words which would come to haunt us over the following days. From the late morning onwards we had been followed, and occasionally overtaken, by two climbers who were also beating a path up the Ridge to camp five. Now they trudged past us, looking very tired. One was a young guy with Slavic features, a Hungarian who looked in his late twenties. The other was an older, bearded man who we recognised as an Austrian, Reinhard Wlasich, a climber several of our team had spoken to at advance base camp.

'Those two are moving too slowly as well,' Al commented after they had passed. 'Chances are they're going to die.'

Seen in the context of the prevailing conditions there was not the slightest reason to think he might be right. I dismissed his chilling comment as a throw-away line. For the moment my attention was focused on our own situation and the devastating news that Brian's third Everest attempt was effectively over before it had begun.

'So that decision is final, then? This is it?'

Barney looked to Al for confirmation. 'Yeah. We'd best go back.'

'In that case we'll have to film a conversation between you where you give us the reasons for the decision.'

Kees brought out the camera and filmed as I interviewed Brian, Barney and Al. Brian was still talking about trying again the next day but I don't think even he really believed it, because in the same breath he proposed another plan:

'Let Al take over. I'll give him my prayer scarf to put on the summit, keep my promise to the Dalai Lama.'

We packed the camera away and prepared in silence for the climb down. The atmosphere was extremely tense, it was only by a narrow margin that the confrontation hadn't become an all-out row.

Before we started the descent, I took one last look up the slope towards the two ascending climbers who would be the only people left on the Ridge once we were gone. They were stationary, bent over their ice-axes against the force of the wind, about two hundred metres above us. Far beyond them, the tents of camp five were beckoning; they would be there within a couple of hours I thought, envying their luck.

Then we turned away from the North Face above us and began the retreat to the Col. Al and I moved in front with Kees moving a little slower and Barney assisting Brian at the back.

My mind was in shock, numbed with a combination of anger and frustration. In thirty minutes flat, five months of training, planning and climbing had been brought to an ignominious end which had come out of nowhere. All the momentum had resulted in nothing; phenomenal levels of motivation and belief in the project were what had fuelled us this far . . . and now they were revealed as a complete waste of time.

What now? How to salvage a film from the wreckage? My mind was busy running through the options as we continued down to the Col. By rights we should now all descend, leaving the way clear for the second team to come up behind us for their attempt. If any of us chose to continue the climb we would be overlapping with Simon and Co., and thereby reducing their chances. At least that was what my oxygen-depleted brain was telling me.

In fact, as I realised after reaching the Col, that logic was adrift. The 'B' team weren't coming up to the Col tonight; they were due up the next day, leaving the possibility that some members of our team *could* still make a dash for the summit and – as long as we could clear out of camp six quickly on the way back – have no adverse affect on the others.

The possibility of turning my anger into something more useful was beginning to evolve. If I could channel this frustration, convert it into a positive rather than a negative force, then perhaps the situation would improve.

Twenty minutes of 'anger control' later I had a question for Al.

'How do you feel about the two of us going for the summit?'

Al took his time taking off his snow gaiters while he considered it. If a flicker of doubt crossed his mind, he was kind enough not to reveal it.

'All right. But what about the film?'

'We can shift the focus of the film on to you. We've already got quite a lot of good interview and diary stuff with you and Brian can give you his Dalai Lama scarf to put on the summit pole like he said.'

'We'll have to check it out with Simon. How do you feel about going back up the Ridge after today?'

I knew what Al was questioning. Effectively we had blown an entire day's energy on our abortive journey up the Ridge, energy that might be needed further down the line.

'I reckon we'll be all right if we get an early start.'

By the time Barney and Brian got back down to the Col, Brian was completely drained. His energy reserves were depleted to the point where he could barely make it back up the small rise into the camp. I realised with a sense of shame that Barney and Al had been right about Brian's condition; he had looked strong on the Ridge but was actually weakening faster than he seemed. Looking at him now, as we filmed him collapsing on to the ground beside the tents, I was filled with remorse; nothing – not even my precious film – was worth pushing Brian into danger for. Barney and Al were perfectly right to pull Brian out of the climb when they did.

When Barney handed Brian a drink bottle, he barely had the strength to lift it to his lips. But he did have the ability to utter a few words once the camera was running.

'I haven't got the strength to go back up. Al, you take over for me.' Then he collapsed in a coughing fit by the tent, looking dazed and shattered.

Later, we radioed down to base camp and reported the day's events to Simon. He was as laid-back as ever and didn't sound at all surprised to hear that Brian's attempt was off. Barney gave me the radio to put my proposal.

'Al and I want to carry on and try and film as high as we can. Is that OK?'

I could feel my pulse thudding in my temple during the slight pause.

'Yeah. I've got no problem with that. What about Kees?'

'He's going down to shoot at base camp with Brian.'

'All right. Good luck. Give us a radio call from five tomorrow night.'

Still stunned by the speed at which events had developed, I went back to the tent where Kees was brewing tea. The entire shape of the expedition had changed in just a few hours. Al – not Brian – was now the motivating personality we would follow in the film to the highest slopes of Everest. I was extremely thankful that we had taken the opportunity of filming with Al at earlier points in the previous weeks. If we had no material featuring him, then his late entrance into the film would be extremely confusing for the viewer. Luckily too, Al's blunt, practical personality came over strongly on camera.

But there were still important questions about the extra shots and sequences we would need to cover Al's ascent properly. Not least of these was how Al would be filmed on the summit. I filed that question away under 'to be resolved' in my mind, and took the earliest opportunity to sleep.

9

We crammed into Brian's tent the next morning and filmed him handing his scarf to Al. The symbolism of the handover was more than just a token gesture. Brian had made a promise to the Dalai Lama at an audience he had had with the great man in his Daramsala headquarters that he would endeavour to place the scarf on the summit pole. He had failed twice to carry out the pledge. Perhaps the scarf would reach the top on this third try.

'Say a prayer for world peace,' Brian told Al, grandly '*Om mane padme hum*, hail the jewel in the lotus!'

One hour later we said our goodbyes. Kees took one of the cameras down with him to film Brian's descent, and to shoot any radio conversations at base camp. Al and I packed our rucksacks and clipped on to the fixed ropes to set out again up the North Ridge.

The wind was stronger than the previous day, gusting more powerfully across the Face. Nevertheless, we moved consistently, plodding up the incline without the long, dangerously slow pauses which had characterised the previous day's climb. Mentally I was far better prepared for the Ridge; the need for speed was now firmly planted in my mind, and I concentrated on finding a rhythm which could be sustained without exhausting my legs.

Al forged ahead in silence, moving as strongly as ever, and pausing only to make tiny adjustments to his headgear and wind suit to keep the worst of the wind off his face.

This time I abandoned the technique of counting out the steps between each breath, it was too demoralising when the numbers began to fall. Instead, I fixed my eyes on landmarks on the Ridge – prominent rocks, or the bright orange splash of oxygen cylinders, and set myself time limits to reach them.

All the complacency of the previous day was gone, I was hypersensitive to the fact that my performance today and tomorrow would

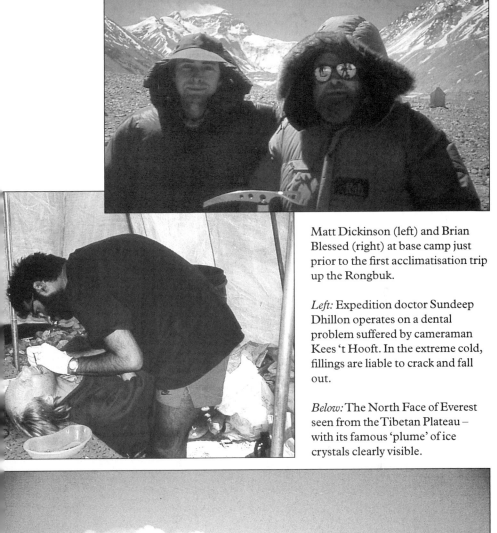

Matt Dickinson (left) and Brian Blessed (right) at base camp just prior to the first acclimatisation trip up the Rongbuk.

Left: Expedition doctor Sundeep Dhillon operates on a dental problem suffered by cameraman Kees 't Hooft. In the extreme cold, fillings are liable to crack and fall out.

Below: The North Face of Everest seen from the Tibetan Plateau – with its famous 'plume' of ice crystals clearly visible.

The North Face of Everest seen from the Rongbuk Monastery. The mountain dominates the valley even though it is still twenty miles distant.

Below: Film cameraman Ned Johnston shooting with his 16mm camera on the Rongbuk Glacier.

Bottom: Members of the Sherpa team pictured at the Pujah ceremony held prior to leaving for the mountain.

Advance base camp at the head of the East Rongbuk Glacier at an altitude of 6,450 metres. In the background can be seen the intimidating ice cliffs of the North Col.

Members of the Himalayan Kingdoms team climbing on the North Col.

Above: The 'B' team pictured at base camp. From right to left; Sundeep Dhillon, Simon Lowe (expedition leader), Richard Cowper, Tore Rasmussen, Roger Portch.

Above left: The North Face of Everest as the storm clouds rolled in on 10 May.

Left: The North Ridge of Everest (seen left) leading to the North-East Ridge (seen on skyline). The summit is top right. The First and Second Steps can be seen as bumps on the Ridge.

Sherpa Lama, Ang Tsering and Rob Hall at Pujah ceremony on the southern side of Everest.

Right: Beck Weathers, member of the Adventure Consultants Everest expedition on the southern side of the mountain. Weathers' miraculous recovery – and rescue from the mountains – is one of the most extraordinary stories ever to emerge from Everest.

Below: The helicopter evacuation of 'Makalu' Gau from base camp on the southern side of the mountain – one of the highest helicopter rescues ever performed.

Rob Hall's team at Everest base camp on the southern side of the mountain (April 1996).

Brian Blessed (seen at rear) and team proceeding up the North Ridge. High winds are blowing ice crystals off the skyline above. The attempt failed several hours later when it was realised the group was travelling too slowly.

The final summit ridge with the summit seen mid-frame. Lhakpa leads the last one hundred metres of the climb. (Photo taken with throwaway 'fun camera'.)

Mingma, Gyaltsen and Matt Dickinson on the summit of Mount Everest. (Photo taken with 'fun camera'.)

be watched like a hawk by Al. Just as Brian had been, effectively, turned back, so could I be, if Al saw any weakness on my part. He knew how little high-altitude experience I had, and it was not in his interest or mine to pretend I was up for a summit attempt if it was going to lead me into trouble. His instincts as a guide would never let that happen.

Surprisingly, my mind felt a lot sharper that the day before. Perhaps the height gain we had made was not a waste after all. Although we had expended a significant sum of energy on what was apparently a wasted day, the extra acclimatisation we had forced on our bodies now felt like a bonus as we rose towards 7,500 metres without oxygen for the second time.

'Climb high, sleep low' is the often quoted maxim, and that was what we had done.

It took us just three hours of almost continuous climbing to reach the high point where Brian turned back; less than half the time it had taken us the day before.

Then the wind really began to pick up force, pelting us with pebbles of dark rock and chunks of ice. It was fortunate it came at us from the western side, for if it had been a headwind it could have stopped us in our tracks. During the stronger blasts it was completely impossible to continue moving; the force was strong enough to blow us off our feet. We bent down low against the Ridge, all crampon points firmly entrenched into the ice for stability.

I noticed that Al had clipped himself on to the fixed rope, something he had done only rarely during the past weeks of the expedition. He realised, like I did, that the wind was vicious enough to blow us off the Ridge without the security of the lifeline.

Our speed diminished dramatically and it took us another one-and-a-half hours to make it to the top of the snow section. We could have done with some shelter for a rest but there was none. The North Face does not offer natural sanctuaries from the wind. Instead, we sat in the full thrust of the jet stream as we rested, barely able to shout at each other above the noise.

Five minutes was all we could stand, and at that point our feet and hands were already turning numb. We started up through the rocks, following the wind-worn ropes which from the look of them had been there for years.

Mentally, I was expecting camp five to loom up pretty quickly but the foreshortening effect of looking directly up the line of the Ridge had made the tents seem significantly nearer than they actually were. Barney and Al had been right again, camp five was definitely not an easy walk from the top of the snow.

In fact the terrain was tiring; with frequent big steps up, and loose rocks underfoot. Finding any regular rhythm was out of the question. The fixed ropes were a liability, snagging our crampon spikes and often complicating the route-finding. Many of them had been laid when the Ridge was still under snow, and now it was gone, the ropes were flapping loosely in the wind, with their snow anchors banging uselessly on the rocks.

During one of our frequent stops, I watched a jet-black bird, a chuff, using the updraft of the wind current to gain height. These carrion eaters are attracted to the higher slopes for just one reason: the rich pickings left behind by climbers at abandoned campsites. As winter comes to an end, left over food supplies, and human bodies, are exposed as their snow cover melts.

Spring is a good time in the Himalayas if you are a scavenger with wings.

I found it amazing that such a tiny creature could fight an upward track through winds which had threatened to blow us off our feet; and even more amazing that its lungs could draw enough oxygen to survive at an altitude above 7,500 metres. I wondered what their altitude limit was, and if one had ever flown at the summit.

With its wings shifting and realigning to adjust to every new gust of wind, the acrobatic bird was gaining height incredibly rapidly. It had probably matched our seven-hour climb in as many minutes. Full of admiration, I watched it continue for some moments until it passed out of view amongst the rocks above.

Intent on keeping upright amid the jumble of rocks, I had failed to notice the bank of cloud which had swept up behind us. Now it enveloped us completely, reducing visibility to less than ten metres. The figure of Al periodically disappeared in and out of the gloom, but I preferred the cloud to the wind which had now thankfully died down a little.

Inside the cloud, sound took on a completely different quality. The harsh, metallic clinks of metal against rock became muffled and deadened and, for the first time since leaving the North Col, I realised I could hear myself breathing. The sense of location, of elevation high in the Himalayas, was also completely lost now we were deprived of any visual reference beyond our immediate surroundings. Apart from the incredible thinness of the air and the discarded oxygen cylinders which were scattered along the route, we could have been on a high ridge in the Alps.

'First tents!' Al's voice yelled at me out of the gloom.

Camp five was not what I had expected. In my mind I had imagined it as a flat area on the Ridge with space for ten or fifteen tents. In fact it is not a 'camp' at all in the way that ABC and the North Col are, but is best described as a string of cleared platforms stretching for a quarter of a mile or more up the North Ridge. The more palatial platforms can take four or five tents at most; the majority offer very marginal space for one or two. There is virtually no shelter against the wind.

Since we had no idea exactly where the three Himalayan Kingdoms tents were positioned, the only way to find them was to continue climbing up the Ridge until we stumbled upon them.

I was unprepared for how long this took, and soon found my body was simply not responding. Mentally I had assumed that 'reaching' camp five would mean we would be able to rest. Now, like the squaddie who finds his 'checkpoint' cruelly moving away from him at the end of a forced training march, my mind was bubbling with irrational anger at all this extra work we were having to do. I told myself it could only be another five minutes. Then another half an hour. But an hour later we were still beating a painfully slow path up the Ridge.

Each time we saw tents above, my legs found new strength: surely this is our camp? Isn't it? And each time we realised it wasn't, my morale took a further dive. I began taking frequent stops, slumped on my side and staring out into the gloom. All motivation soaked away as I began to doubt we would ever find our tents. Forcing myself to stand up and keep climbing was getting to be a problem.

Al – who was in better condition – waited for me, passing the time with his favourite hobby, sifting through the debris of old tent sites.

'Looks like the Japs were here,' he muttered, showing me some noodle sauce packaged in a foil sachet.

I grunted a monosyllabic reply but my attention was wandering. An altitude weevil in my head was whispering again, what's the point in finding camp five? Who cares about it? Why are you putting yourself through all this pain? There's plenty of tents around – sleep in one of them instead.

The cloud was clearing, giving us dramatic glimpses of the glacier below. Then Changtse was revealed, and beneath it, the North Col.

I could just make out the miniscule specks of our camp, where team 'B' would now be resting, just one day behind us.

When we climbed up the next small rise, we found the three tents. Unknowingly, we had rested for ten or fifteen minutes just a few metres away. Hearing the noise, Mingma's head popped out.

'Here!'

We sat in front of the Sherpas' tent and drank some hot tea from Lhakpa's thermos. They had spent the last two days waiting for us here, and were as relieved as we were that we had arrived. They had been sleeping on oxygen, which had helped, but they were nevertheless bored, and obviously keen to escape from five.

'Bhaje go back?' Lhakpa used the Sherpa nickname for Brian.

'Yeah. Bhaje knackered,' Al replied.

'And the rest?'

'Simon's coming up tomorrow with Roger, Tore and Sundeep.'

'OK. We go to six tomorrow?'

'Yeah. What do you think of the weather?'

With the professional eye of someone who has spent his life amongst fickle Himalayan weather, Lhakpa looked out of the tent towards the summit. 'Maybe too much wind.'

I was gradually recovering as the tea worked its magic. While Al and the Sherpas talked through details for the following day's climb, I began to notice the squalor our tents were pitched amongst.

The platform was littered with the shredded remains of abandoned tents, with strips of fabric blowing in the wind. Pieces of rope, half buried foil sachets of food and remnants of clothing were embedded in almost every inch of ice. Sharp metal snow stakes were sticking out at crazy angles, attached to lines which went nowhere. Large areas of ice were stained yellow from urine, and frozen faeces were abundantly scattered around.

This mess had obviously been accumulating year after year, as expeditions abandoned their gear, or had it destroyed in storms. It was a depressing location, soiled and spiritless; I was already looking forward to getting out of camp five and we had only just arrived.

A more welcome sight was the pile of oxygen cylinders next to the Sherpa tent, stacked up on a platform which had been cut into the ice. Their presence here represented a huge amount of load-carrying, and was another sign of the utter professionalism of our Sherpa team.

In the tent, we arranged the Karrimats and sleeping bags, and then dragged in a couple of oxygen cylinders. I screwed on my regulator, set the valve to one-and-a-half litres and put on the mask. It was the first time I had ever used supplementary oxygen, other than one or two puffs down at base camp to test the valve.

Here at 7,600 metres, the effect of the trickle of pure oxygen was immediately noticeable. Within three or four minutes my head was clearing of the throbbing headache which had been nagging all day. Within ten minutes, the ever-present feeling of slight nausea was also gone, and within fifteen minutes I was laughing out loud with the sheer joy of breathing oxygen-rich air. Whatever a medic might say, I could swear I could actually feel the oxygen coursing through my blood supply, bringing warmth to frozen fingers and toes.

'Al, you will not believe what happens when you put this on!'

Al was busy sorting out his pack and had not yet rigged his cylinder.

'Yeah?'

I knew Al was in two minds about using the oxygen. He had climbed K2 and all his other 8,000-metre peaks without it. I think in the back of his mind he felt that using it could compromise his reputation as Britain's most successful high-altitude mountaineer.

But he strapped the mask on nevertheless and within a short while he was smiling just as I had done.

'I see what you mean. Not bad stuff this, is it?'

We both experimented with the valve settings, getting used to the different levels of flow. It was difficult to tell much difference between one and one-and-a-half litres per minute, but knocking it down to half a litre was noticeably thin. Pumping it up above two litres a minute was a real treat – delivering an O_2 'high' which was sheer delight for our oxygen-starved bodies.

Al pointed out the useful fact that there would be three extra cylinders here for Brian, Barney and Kees. That meant we could use two bottles rather than one each for sleeping at night. The same would be true up at camp six. Simon had promised from the beginning that there would be sufficient supplies of oxygen for everyone to have an attempt, and the extra margin we now had might prove extremely useful if we were pinned down at camp six by a storm.

The oxygen had done more than eliminate my headache and depression. I suddenly realised that I was hungry and so was Al. We ate two Wayfarer meals each and some pistachio nuts I had brought up from advance base. Then we got the camera out and filmed a short sequence of cooking and eating in the tent. I filmed Al putting on the oxygen mask and bedding down in his sleeping bag. He filmed me eating from one of the ready-meal packs, complaining about the lack of calories whilst stuffing my face with beef and dumpling stew.

With very little daylight remaining, Al then took the camera outside and filmed the view across towards Pumori.

'Get a panning shot of the platform,' I yelled 'and make sure you can see all the shit and the ripped up tents.'

'Yeah.'

As the light fell, I began to search the rucksack for my headtorch. A first and second rummage failed to find it so I emptied every single item out on to the floor of the tent. No sign. I shifted position, and checked underneath and inside the sleeping bag. Still no sign of the torch. Then I checked every corner of the tent, inside my discarded clothing, and Al checked his side of the tent. Nothing.

I just couldn't understand it. I was absolutely certain that I had packed the torch in the rucksack that morning. I definitely remembered checking the two spare bulbs and batteries that were taped to it. But now it seemed to have vanished.

The seriousness of this was far greater than the inconvenience of having no torch inside the tent for the night hours. It ruled out my summit bid completely. Five or six hours of the summit day climb would be through darkness, and without a headtorch I was going nowhere.

I searched the pack again and again, increasingly desperate. Inwardly I cursed myself for this mistake. There would be no spares up here, and trying to borrow one from another expedition would merely put them in the same predicament. How could I have been so careless?

'Maybe it fell out of the pack at one of the filming stops.' Al was sounding sympathetic, but I knew he had every right to be angry. My stupidity could adversely affect his own summit bid as well.

I thought through the day. There had been one stop, in the rock section, when I had dug deep into the pack for a battery. Maybe the headtorch had fallen out then.

'The six o'clock radio call's coming up. I'll ask Simon if they've found it in your tent down at the Col.' Al picked up the walkie-talkie and radioed down.

As he talked to Simon, I chewed over the hard reality of the situation. Even if they found my torch, it could not get up to me until the 'B' team arrived the following afternoon. Then, unless I could make it through the night to six, there would be too little tent space for us all at five. I would have to go down. A wave of unbearable self-pity swept over me. To lose all this from one tiny mistake? I hated myself for being so fucking sloppy. Where was that torch?

Team 'B' had made it safely to the Col and were resting when we called. Simon was pleased to hear that camp five was in good shape but a search of the tent I had left that morning revealed no sign of the headtorch.

Al clicked off the radio.

'That's a bummer.'

'It has to be here.'

I began another search of the tent, shifting every single item down to the end and then sorting through the pile as methodically as I could in the cramped conditions. Nothing.

Then I noticed that the side wall of the tent was folded over. I ran my hand underneath the flap of fabric and brought out the torch. How I had missed it in the earlier searches was beyond belief. I can only assume that my brain was still running at half speed from the oxygen depletion of the climb.

'Panic over.' Al lit the stove for another brew.

'Thank God.' I was hugely relieved. My chance for the summit had just been reinstated.

We radioed down to Simon again to tell him the torch had been found, then spent the rest of the evening brewing tea and hot chocolate. By 9 p.m. we were preparing to bed down.

Sleeping in the mask was hard to get used to. The Russian apparatus was as uncomfortable as it was ugly, with the restraining straps always digging into some part of the face. The exhaust system was inefficient too, so that small pools of icy liquid collected periodically inside the flange of the mouthpiece. Shifting from side to side in the search for a comfortable sleeping position delivered a quantity of disgusting frigid spittle down our necks.

But no matter how difficult it was to sleep in the mask, the prospect of trying to sleep without it was worse. I passed a restless night, waking to readjust the mask every time it began to slip, and checking the cylinder was still delivering the flow.

The wind also conspired to make sleep elusive, dropping away to a whisper and then sweeping back against the walls of the tents with a huge crack as a new surge of energy ran across the Ridge.

At 5 a.m., I heard the Sherpas moving around outside, collecting snow for their morning tea. By 6 we had our own gas cookers burning. At first light, Al was already poking his head out of the tent to check on the weather.

'How's it look?'

'Mixed. There's a lot of cloud about.'

'Can we get up to six?'

'It's the wind that'll stop us if anything. We'll just have to see how it goes.'

Our preparations were carried out slowly and methodically, checking off each bit of gear as it went back into the rucksack. It is surprising how much mess a two-man tent can get into, and the last thing we could afford was to leave a vital piece of equipment behind. I made a special mental note to check the torch was in place. Then, critically aware of how even the smallest piece of missing equipment could bring us to a grinding halt, I checked it again.

Al gave the tent a last-minute tidy.

'No point in leaving it in a mess for the others.'

Then we rigged the oxygen cylinders in our packs and left for camp six, climbing with oxygen for the first time.

*

The first obstacle was a steep snowpatch directly behind the tent platform. Even with the trickle of oxygen flowing into the mask, this was a strenuous burst of activity to come so early in the day, frontpointing with the crampon spikes and pushing the ice-axe deep into the snow pack for stability.

Panting for breath at the top of the snowpatch, I checked the visual indicator on the oxygen line to confirm it was working. I was not at all convinced I was getting any air. But inside the clear plastic section of the tube, the indicator was clearly activated.

I had imagined that climbing with the supplementary oxygen would be like climbing at sea level, but this was another miscalculation. The gas definitely helped, but I still felt dizzy and breathless after any sudden moves.

It would have been useful to get into a plodding rhythm but one factor ruled this out: the wind. Within thirty minutes of leaving the tent we were lashed by the strongest winds we had yet experienced. As the North Ridge narrowed, sometimes becoming quite exposed with very long drops down to the East Rongbuk, we were increasingly brought to a complete halt to avoid being bowled over the edge. The power of the blasts was both terrifying and impressive.

On two occasions I was physically hurled off my feet, to crash on to my knees among the rocks, both hands clinging tightly to any holds I could find.

After an hour of this battering, the first doubts were playing through my head. How much longer could we continue in these conditions? A morbid fear struck me that Al, seeing me struggle, would decide the wind was too much and call the attempt off. Every time he stopped to clear his goggles or take a rest, he looked out towards the west – the direction the wind came from – appraising the situation. There was plenty of scattered cloud cover, but as yet there was no evidence of a large mass which could indicate a storm. We climbed on.

I was so wrapped up in the process of staying upright that I failed to notice the climber coming down until he was right upon us. It was John, the leader of the Norwegian expedition, on his way down from a disastrous stay at camp six. He was moving awkwardly, clutching his chest and grimacing with pain each time he coughed.

'What happened?' Al asked him.

'It's my throat. I've spent the whole night coughing and I think I've broken a rib.' Even as he spoke, a massive coughing fit overtook him, bending him double in agony. He looked utterly bereft. We all knew he was on his third attempt to climb Everest.

'What about the rest of your team?'

'They left camp six this morning . . . but the winds . . .' He turned his face up to the Ridge, where scudding clouds were racing past. He shrugged.

'How about the Austrian? Have you got any news on him?'

'Not good. He's in a coma. Cerebral and pulmomary oedema.'

'Shit.' We had heard that Reinhard was in trouble at camp six but this was exceptionally bad news.

We stood silently for a few moments as John's information seeped in.

'Anyhow. Good luck.' He picked up his ice-axe and continued his lonely trek down the mountain, the sound of his coughing quickly swallowed up in the wind.

By late morning we were approaching the point where the route leaves the North Ridge and begins to traverse across and up the North Face itself. Here we had to take special care not to miss the right line, as numerous old fixed ropes travel directly up the North Ridge. By the time we discovered the mistake we could be a long way off track and facing a lengthy detour to get to camp six.

Al made the decision on which route to take, and we began to traverse diagonally up a series of snowfields interspersed by bands of crumbling rock. In the post-monsoon period this part of the Face is a lethal avalanche slope, but in the pre-monsoon the snow is compacted and stable. The snow was a welcome change from the problems of picking a way up through the rock.

The wind dropped off rapidly from midday onwards and cloud swept up once more as it had done the previous day. Soon we were climbing in the same murky white-out we had encountered on the route to camp five.

To distract my mind from the effort needed for each step, my old mantra came back: 'every metre up is a metre less to go'. The words, recycled time after time, had a hypnotic effect, lulling my brain into a near trance as the day wore on. At the top of each snowfield I would stop and try to assess how many vertical metres it had won us. Because we were traversing, the height gain per hour was less than on the Ridge. Thirty minutes of hard progress might equal as little as fifteen or twenty vertical metres.

The steepness of the Face meant we could see no sign of camp six, and for much of the time the summit was also out of view. On the occasions when we were able to see the summit pyramid, my only thought was how distant it still seemed. The traverse was demonstrating in the plainest way possible the sheer immensity of the Face. Hours were passing and the summit was still kilometres of climbing away . . . and almost a vertical kilometre above us.

Somewhere during that long afternoon we passed the 8,000-metre mark. We were now firmly in the Death Zone, the place named by the Swiss physician in 1952 who described it thus:

Survival is the only term suitable for describing the behaviour of a man in that mortal zone which begins at about 25,500 feet. Life there is impossible and it requires the whole of a man's will to maintain himself there for a few days. Life hangs by a thread, to such a point that the organism, exhausted by the ascent, can pass in a few hours from a somnolent state to a white death. This depends first on the age of the subject, and then on his reserves of energy. It is now no longer a question of adaptation, but only of the number of days or hours allotted to the strongest persons.

Now the clock was ticking away. We had to move fast but the conditions remained uncertain.

By mid-afternoon a light fall of snow was dusting the North Face and the cloud had thickened above us to become a total cover. With it, my optimism plummeted rapidly. All our good progress would be for nothing if the cloud brought a heavier fall of snow.

But the snowfall vanished as rapidly as it had arrived and with it went the cloud. With just a short distance to go, the skies were clear and blue and the cloud had dropped to the level of the Col.

The problem of the previous day, when my body had switched off as soon as we reached the lowest tents, was uppermost in my mind as we came to the first tents of camp six. I was terrified of hitting another 'flat spot' and, even though I was physically exhausted by the day's efforts, I prepared myself mentally for the extra stage which would take us to our own tent.

I needn't have worried. The tent pitches of camp six are spread over a large area, but the vertical gain between the top and the bottom tents is not as great as at five. We reached our tents thirty minutes later.

The Sherpas had reached the camp two hours earlier and were already occupying one of the two tents which had been erected during the previous weeks. Like camp five, a stack of oxygen cylinders was arranged here in a neat pile.

Deeply relieved to have made it, I drank my last dribble of juice from the water bottle, took off my pack and lay down to rest. It took me quite a long time to get my breathing rate down, and even longer before my mind was alert enough to notice the incredible location we had reached.

Camp six, at 8,300 metres, is the highest camp in the world and it feels it. The extra 600 metres of elevation gave it a far loftier view than camp five, to the extent that it was possible to look right down the entire length of the Rongbuk glacier during the moments when the cloud wasn't obscuring it. If it hadn't been for a layer of haze sitting to the north we might even have been able to see the monastery.

The perspective on the Col was also far more impressive than from five. Because we had traversed quite a distance across the Face, we were now looking down at the western side of the wall, with the avalanche-swept South-Western Face of Changtse behind.

Somewhere at the bottom of that face was the Catalan camp. We had heard little of the Catalans beyond the news that one of their team members had returned to Kathmandu with a suspected heart condition. From our vantage point we could see the hanging glaciers of the western side were far more threatening than those on the east. Furthermore, their route was sitting in the full force of the prevailing westerly wind, whereas our route on the eastern side was to some extent protected.

I didn't envy the Catalans their task. Their chances of getting anywhere on the mountain were hampered by the western route to the Col and they had virtually no Sherpa support. By contrast we were in a very privileged position, with significant amounts of oxygen and food waiting for us here at camp six.

The two tents were set fifteen metres apart, with the Sherpa tent at the top of a snowfield and ours positioned on a very narrow platform midway down. Both had an awkward lean down the slope, being perched on areas which were not strictly big enough for the floor area of the nylon base. A cat's cradle of guy ropes pinned the tents down to snow stakes and nearby rocks to prevent storm damage.

Gyaltsen came over from the Sherpa tent to speak to Al.

At base camp I had noticed he was always on the move, with a spring in his step. Here he was walking in slow motion, and obviously very tired.

'What time do you want to leave tonight?'

Al pulled his oxygen mask aside to reply.

'Wake up midnight. Leave by two.'

'Fine.'

Gyaltsen showed us where the cooking gas cylinders had been cached in the snow and then plodded back up the snowfield to join Mingma and Lhakpa in their cramped dome tent.

Al and I sat, too tired to talk, watching the clouds gathering over the Rongbuk. To our right, on one of the rock areas, the ten or so dome tents of other expeditions were gathered. Looking over, there was no sign of life.

A nagging voice in my head was telling me we should get some shots of camp six before the cloud came up and obscured the view. When I asked him, Al dragged himself to his feet to do this without a complaint – which, if he was feeling as utterly drained as I was, showed an impressive level of commitment.

While Al was shooting, it was as much as I could manage to unstrap my crampons, pull off the snow gaiters and crawl into the tent. As soon as I was lying down, both legs suddenly locked again into the spasms of cramp which I had now virtually come to expect at the end of each climbing session. The culprit was my hamstring

– the largest muscle in the human body, which runs down the back of the leg from the buttocks to the ankle. Both hamstrings locked rigid until I managed to push back my toes and ease the pain.

In addition to the filming, Al cut some snow blocks for melting and arranged a small platform of flat rocks in the foyer of the tent for the gas cookers to stand on. After a few false starts with the burner, we had the first precious pans of snow melting slowly away shortly before dark.

The tent interior was stuffed with coils of rope and the prepacked food bags we had selected back at base camp. Ripping my own pack open, I could only wonder at the choice of foods I had made all those weeks before. The tin of tuna salad I had so confidently packed was now enough to make my stomach churn. Just looking at the picture of the fish on the label was enough to bring me out in a wave of nausea. Fish and altitude do not mix very well.

We ripped open Brian's, Al's and Barney's food parcels and found better fare. Best of all were the sachets of muesli, which I added to a mug of hot chocolate and ate warm. Then we heated up a couple of wayfarer meals and forced them down, taking breaths from the oxygen masks between mouthfuls.

Sunset must have been an incredible sight, but all I saw of it was a glimmer of red light reflected in the metal of an oxygen cylinder outside the tent. I was determined to conserve every single scrap of energy and getting out of the tent to take a still photograph was not a priority no matter how splendid it was.

Our main discussion was about the oxygen. With three members of our own team now definitely out of the equation, there was the possibility that we could take an extra cylinder each for the summit push. The pro was that we would be able to set the cylinders on a higher flow with the obvious advantages that would bring. The con was the weight, an extra six kilogrammes – a very serious consideration given the physical demands of what lay ahead. We talked round the issues and decided we would postpone a decision until we packed to leave in a few hours time. (In fact when it came to it Al decided he would take an extra cylinder and I decided against it.)

By 8 p.m., we were into the third round of melting snow, when footsteps approached from outside. A figure crouched down at the entrance to the tent, red-eyed and desperate. It was the Hungarian climber who, with Reinhard Wlasich, the Austrian, had been attempting the North Face without oxygen.

His first words were in French but when he saw our blank faces he changed to English.

'I need some . . . have you a way to help . . . some oxygen and some gas . . . please.' His speech was slurred and barely understandable. He sounded like he was suffering from the onset of high-altitude sickness.

'Take it easy and calm down a bit. Now what's the problem?' Al made some space for him to kneel in the front of the tent.

'My friend is dying. I want you to try and help me rescue him. We're in that tent over there.' He pointed out into the night.

'You're talking about Reinhard?'

'Yes. Reinhard. He's dying. If we don't get him down the mountain he'll be dead. You have to help me.'

'What about the Norwegian doctor – Morton. Has he seen him?'

'He did. This afternoon.'

'And what did he say?'

'He has Oedema – on the lungs and cerebral.'

'Is he conscious?'

'He's in a coma.'

'Well, if he's in a coma he *is* going to die. There's no way anyone can get him off the mountain. Have you got oxygen?'

'It's finished. Can I take a bottle?'

'You can take as much as you need. Have you got a regulator?'

'Yes. But if we go now we can rescue him.'

'How?' Al was icy calm.

'I don't know. We can carry him. I have to do something!' The Hungarian was distraught, and beginning to vent his frustration as anger on us.

'There's nothing we can do. No matter how many people we had up here, we still couldn't get him down to five. Think about the rocks, how are you going to lower him down?'

The Hungarian went quiet. In his heart he knew that Al was right. Even if Reinhard had been conscious, a rescue would have been impossible. The fact that he was in a coma was as good as a death sentence here at 8,300 metres.

'How much longer do you think he will live?'

'I don't know. He's hardly breathing.'

Al and I exchanged a glance. The same thought occurred to both of us at the same time: the Hungarian, determined to stay with his fellow climber right to the bitter end, was even now putting his own life in danger.

'Listen. Your friend is definitely going to die. You have to get off the mountain or you'll die too. Do you understand?' Al was speaking forcefully now, driving the news as hard as he could into the Hungarian's confused mind. He went quiet once more as this sank in.

'You'll be dead by tomorrow night if you stay here. So take two oxygen bottles now, get through the night, and come back at first light to take another bottle to get you back down to five. OK?'

The Hungarian nodded slowly.

'You're doing as much as you can by staying with him. But he can't be rescued. If you stay here now you'll be putting other lives in danger. Are you still fit enough to get down tomorrow on your own?'

'Yes.' His reply was barely audible.

He picked up the two oxygen bottles and walked off into the night, the very picture of a broken man. I wondered what kind of hell he was returning to: within a few hours Reinhard would be dead by his side.

'You know the strangest thing?' A chilling memory had come back to me.

'What?'

'When you and Barney decided to turn Brian back on the ridge you saw Reinhard and his mate carrying on and said he might die.'

'That's true. I could see by the speed they were moving that they were heading for trouble.'

Then another memory hit me – a recollection of a discussion I had with Al before leaving for Kathmandu.

'And do you remember the conversation we had when you came round for the meal?' Al had visited us in Hertfordshire a few weeks before the expedition left. 'You predicted this would happen. You said we'd get to camp six and find someone in exactly that state. In fact I think you specified it would be an Eastern European.'

'Yeah, I do remember.'

'Don't you think that's bizarre?'

Al thought for a moment. 'Not really. There's so many disorganised teams on Everest these days you're more likely than not to find someone in trouble here.'

And with that we resumed the cooking and the subject was closed for discussion. But in my mind the extraordinary conversation we had just had with the Hungarian was churning away. Why didn't I feel more compassion for him? Why hadn't we at least offered to go and check on Reinhard just in case he had miraculously recovered?

The truth was that the mountain had dehumanised me and hardened my emotional response. The news about Reinhard's impending death had neither surprised me nor shocked me. Instead it seemed normal. This is camp six – 8,300 metres, my mind was telling me, this is where people *do* die if something goes wrong. Reinhard was beyond help. We all were. To be prepared to go this high, we had all willingly made an unwritten pact with the mountain that says: 'I'm putting myself in a position where I know I can die.' Given that level of personal commitment, perhaps it is not surprising that luxuries like pity and compassion are often left behind at base camp along with other unnecessary baggage. If we had brought those emotions with us, perhaps we would be needing them now – for ourselves?

I was beginning to understand what the Death Zone really means.

IO

At 11.20 p.m. Al drifted off into a light sleep, his rhythmic breathing muffled by the oxygen mask. At midnight, summit day would begin.

Even though my body craved it, for me there was no question of sleep. Like a child lying wide-eyed in bed on Christmas Eve, expectation ran like an adrenalin shot through my body. I pulled the frozen fabric of the down sleeping bag as tight as I could around my head and lay perfectly still.

Staring into the dark confines of the tent, super-sensitive to the ghosts of wind playing around us, I found myself entering a state of Zen-like calm. During the long-haired phase of my teens, fuelled by a dangerous overconsumption of Carlos Castaneda and Aldous Huxley, I had often tried to meditate my way into an altered state of consciousness. How I had tried!

In a candlelit bedroom, filled with the aromatic smoke of joss-sticks and the trance-inducing pentatonic synthesiser cords of the psychedelic band 'Gong', I sat in a half-lotus position and waited to lock on to the astral plane. But no matter how long I spent in the ticket queue, my journey to Ixtlan never began. Perhaps Hemel Hempstead is not the best starting place when you're heading for Nirvana.

Now, zipped into that tiny plastic capsule 8,300 metres above the rest of the world I slipped effortlessly into a state of euphoric trance. The cramped Quasar mountain tent suddenly took on the dimensions of a cathedral, its domed roof becoming a series of soaring arches suspended hundreds of feet in the air. The soothing hiss of the oxygen feeding into my mask took on a musical quality, like pan-pipes, and the wind became a whispering voice murmuring encouraging words for the day to come.

The music faded and was replaced by the thudding beat of blood-rush echoing in the back of my skull. The fantasy changed. I imagined myself diving into the sea and letting my lungs fill with water.

Then I snapped back to consciousness with a horrible gasp, gulping frantically for air. That was why the music had faded: the oxygen cylinder was out of air. Confused and disorientated, I had trouble finding my headtorch and then struggled to unscrew the frozen regulator valve on the dead tank.

The interior of the tent was now encrusted with a thin hoar frost of frozen vapour. With every movement, irritating showers of tiny crystals fell, freezing any exposed skin.

Replacing the valve on to a fresh oxygen bottle, I set the gauge on one litre a minute and slumped exhausted back into the sleeping bag. Now the waking trance was anything but euphoric; the sweet dreams went distinctly sour. I suddenly remembered that not ten metres from our tent the Austrian, Reinhard, was dying, beyond help.

Camp six, which had seemed such a welcome refuge when we'd arrived some hours before, now became a place of overwhelming fear and anxiety. The fact that there was nothing we could do for Reinhard put everything into perspective; the mountain was in control. Altitude, with all its deadly effects, was snuffing the life out of a strong, healthy mountaineer, as if he was a sickly child. In the face of this invisible force, our own enterprise felt fragile and doomed to fail.

For the remaining twenty minutes before midnight I lay in a state of cold fear, praying that the weather would hold, that my body would be capable of meeting the challenge ahead, and – most important of all – that I would not make a mistake. My lack of confidence in my own mountaineering abilities had dogged me from the start of the expedition. Now the fear of a trip, of a sudden fall, of fumbling a piece of protection as I'd done with the figure-of-eight on the Col; those were mistakes which I had got away with in the early stages of the climb. On summit day, even the slightest mistake would be a potential killer.

Mallory and Irvine probably died that way . . .

Midnight. Al's digital watch bleeped a feeble alarm and I could hear muffled shouts from the Sherpas' tent. Al roused himself from sleep and we set about the tiresome task of lighting the gas cookers.

The cigarette lighters were now even more reluctant to ignite than at camp five. It took forty or fifty strokes with my thumb to coax a flame out of the frozen gas. By the time I succeeded, blood was flowing freely from the cracked skin.

The gas cooker burned fiercely for a few seconds then spluttered out.

'Bastard!' I was beginning to loathe the cookers.

Al patiently took over with the cigarette lighter and managed to relight it. This had been a regular pattern since camp five. The intense cold and thin air made the propane burners extremely fickle. They frequently flared out for no apparent reason, filling the tent with nauseating gas until they could be relit.

Once warmed up, the gas seemed to flow better, and after ten minutes of frustration, we had both cookers happily burning. Al busied himself cutting up blocks of snow into pieces small enough to fit into the pans while I tried to make some order out of my side of the tent.

Al, canny as ever, had bagged himself the flatter, uphill sleeping platform, leaving me to compete for space with the pile of equipment. Thanks to the precarious angle, leaning sharply down the snowfield, the interior, and my side in particular, had become a jumbled mess.

Used oxygen cylinders, food rations and climbing equipment formed a chaotic heap on the downward slope. The side wall of the tent was sagging alarmingly under the weight of the gear, and I imagined that the slightest tear could split the fabric like the belly of a whale, emptying the contents and me on to the ice slide outside, where a one-way trip down the North Face would rapidly ensue.

I tried to rearrange the heavier objects at the foot of the tent where they would be out of the way. Then I set about extracting the vital pieces of gear which would be needed for the day ahead: the lithium batteries for the video camera, the red wind suit, the outer shells of my plastic boots. Highlighted by the beam of the headtorch I saw the food packets which each of us had prepared with such optimism back at base camp seven weeks before.

Written in blue marker pen were the names of the owners: Tore, Simon, Sundeep, Barney, Brian . . . I ripped open Brian's pack and extracted the precious sachet of muesli. My appetite had become super-selective and this was one of the few foods I could face.

It took over an hour to melt the compacted snow down to boiling water. We shared a pack of pistachio nuts and drank mugs of tea and Bournvita before loading the pans with more snow for another meltdown . . . our drinking supply for the climb.

Gagged by the oxygen masks, we had little urge to talk, but concentrated on the vital task of forcing as much food and liquid down as we could.

Al's long years of Himalayan expeditions had taught him the enviable knack of pissing into a pee bottle whilst lying on his side. Lacking the confidence to risk a sleeping bag full of urine by getting this wrong, I relied on the surer but less energy-efficient technique of crouching on my knees to perform the act.

The minutes ticked by, and with them came another dreaded bodily demand.

'I need a crap.'

'Me too.' Al was in the same state.

The prospect of putting on the boots and going out into the freezing night wind was extremely depressing. Just the thought was exhausting and demoralising.

'Better do it,' Al advised. 'Nothing else for it. No point in taking any excess baggage up. Besides, if you're shitting yourself now, imagine what you'll be like on the second step.'

As an avid consumer of Himalayan climbing books, I had always been mystified by the high-altitude mountaineer's obsession with bodily functions. What, I had wondered, was the problem?

It took nearly fifteen minutes to prepare ourselves to exit the tent. Taking our oxygen cylinders with us was not a realistic option. Moving carefully to avoid the cookers, I crawled out of the front of the tent. Doing so, I nudged an empty cylinder which had been propped outside. It fell on to the ice slope and accelerated away quickly. There was a clanking sound as it hit rocks once – twice – and then cartwheeled out of sight down the North Face to land on the glacier some six thousand feet below.

Mistake.

Stumbling across the ice slope, I realised that what I was doing was extremely stupid. I should have crampons and an ice-axe. One slip and I would follow the oxygen cylinder down the Face. With a shudder I remembered that this was exactly how one of the Taiwanese climbers had fallen on the southern side just days before.

I found a narrow ledge and managed to pull down the down suit and thermal underclothes. Calf and thigh muscles protesting, I squatted for what seemed like an eternity, puffing and panting for air. A few metres away, Al was doing the same. There is no such thing as embarrassment at 8,300 metres.

At the Col and above I found myself experiencing acute pain

when going to the toilet. This time was by far the worst, bringing tears to my eyes. My whole system was completely dried up, and it felt like I was splitting inside.

'I'm having a baby here, Al.'

An answering grunt came in reply.

With the pain came blood – quite a substantial amount. I closed my mind to the implications of this, putting it down to that well-known climbers affliction, piles, even though I was pretty sure I didn't have them.

Collapsing back into the tent I strapped on the oxygen mask and gulped hungrily at the clean-tasting air. In the warmth of the sleeping bags I thrust my hands under my armpits to defrost, another surprisingly painful process.

Al came in. 'You all right?'

'Fine,' I replied, not wanting to let on how I really felt. Close to vomiting, with a skull-splitting headache, I now knew why a visit to the toilet above 8,000 metres inspires such dread amongst mountaineers.

Al added some more snow blocks to the pans of water and then curled up in his bag to try and regain some precious warmth. I could just make out his muffled words:

'My feet are frozen.'

Outside, I could hear the three Sherpas preparing their equipment. Gyaltsen made his way across the snowfield and shouted into the tent.

'Two o'clock. You ready?'

'We need another brew,' Al replied. 'Let's leave in half an hour.'

The two other Sherpas, Lhakpa and Mingma, came across to join Gyaltsen outside our tent. They began to sort out the oxygen cylinders which were stacked neatly there in a pile.

'There's no way we're leaving with fingers or toes frozen,' Al told me, 'they have to be perfectly warm when we set off or we'll end up losing them.'

I took my feet out of their inner boots and massaged them back to life. The smaller toes felt curiously waxy to the touch, as if the skin was thicker than it should be.

By 2.30 a.m., fortified by a last cup of Bournvita and a few lumps of chocolate, we were outside the tent with crampons and neoprene gaiters fitted. Over the 'Michelin man' down suits we wore the red Berghaus wind suits with harness fastened over the whole ensemble. Movement was severely restricted by the thickness of this specialist clothing and I had to get Al to tighten my harness buckle up so it fitted snugly around my waist.

We arranged the rucksacks to carry the oxygen cylinders. With this, as with every other tiny part of the high-altitude survival jigsaw, attention to detail is critical. The oxygen bottle must be carried upright. If it falls in the sack the oxygen feed pipe could crimp and cut off the supply. Having tested my system at base camp, I now rolled up my Karrimat and inserted it in the pack. Slid into the roll, the oxygen cylinder was held in place firmly by the foam with the valve clear of obstruction.

There was the added advantage that if we had to bivouac for whatever reason, the Karrimat would be a very valuable asset.

I ran through a mental check-list as we put the final touches to the equipment. Ski goggles ready in the pocket of the wind suit. Spare glacier goggles in another pocket. Headtorch ready with two spare bulbs and spare battery. Two one-litre water bottles filled with 'isotonic' high-energy glucose drink. Walkie-talkie checked. Food – chocolate and Christmas pudding – ready. Stills cameras loaded with fresh film. Crampon repair kit. Spare carabiner. Figure-of-eight descendeur. Jumar clamps.

'Where's your drink?' Al asked.

'In the rucksack.'

'You're better off putting them inside the down suit next to your skin.'

I did as Al said, zipping up one of the plastic nalgene bottles into the suit just above the harness. The Sherpas were clearly ready to go. My mind raced through the mental check-list searching for the one missed component, the one small forgotten item which would bring the summit bid to a grinding halt.

There wasn't one. We were ready.

Without a word, we turned away from the tents and started our climb up into the night. Lhakpa led, with Mingma and Gyaltsen behind, then Al and myself at the tail.

After the suspense and tension of the preparation it was a sheer relief to be moving. Those first few steps had, for me, a truly epic quality. I knew we were in an incredibly privileged position – a position thousands of mountaineers would give their eye-teeth (and perhaps a lot more) to share.

We were leaving camp six bang on schedule on as near as the North Face ever gets to a perfect night. We had liquid, food, an adequate supply of oxygen and the assistance of three very strong

Sherpas. Our equipment was tried and tested, we were as fit as one can be above 8,000 metres with no major sickness or injury to cope with.

It doesn't get much better than that. The 'window' was open. For the first time, I allowed myself the luxury of thinking that we might just make it. If our luck held.

In the precise minutes of our departure from camp six, as we later learned from the Hungarian climber who was with him in the tent, Reinhard died.

The Sherpas set a fast pace up the first of the snowfields lying above the camp. Al kept up easily but I found myself lagging behind. The thin beam of light from the headtorch, seemingly so bright when tested in the tent, now felt inadequate for the task, illuminating a pathetically small patch of snow.

Catching up, I concentrated on watching Al's cramponed feet as they bit into the snow. The conditions were variable with an unpredictable crust. Frequently it gave way, plunging us thigh deep into a hidden hole.

I quickly learned not to trust the headtorch with its tunnel vision effect. It confused the eye by casting shadows of unknown depth. Rocks could be bigger than they seemed. Holes in the snow lacked all perspective. Distances became hard to judge. Was Lhakpa's light ten metres in front of me . . . or fifty? I couldn't tell.

We crossed several old tent platforms, abandoned by previous expeditions. Each one was littered with the usual shredded fabric, splintered tent-poles and empty oxygen cylinders. A foil food sachet got spiked by one of my crampon teeth and dragged annoyingly until I could be bothered to remove it.

At each of these wrecked sites, Al, the mountain detective, would pause for a moment to cast his headtorch around the remains. Even now, on our summit bid, his fascination for them was as keen as ever.

The climb continued, step after step, up the snowfield towards the much more demanding terrain of the yellow band. Very conscious of our limited oxygen supply, I tried to concentrate on regulating my breathing; I knew from scuba-diving training how easy it is to waste air.

But the terrain of the North Face is mixed; both in steepness and in composition. Steep ice fields give way to shallower rock slabs. Demanding rock sections end in long traverses. Establishing a breathing pattern is virtually impossible. Mostly I found I was puffing and panting at a very fast rate and there was nothing I could do about it.

After an hour I found I was feeling better. The headache and nausea had faded away with the concentrated physical work of the climb. My feet and hands both felt warm, and the weight of the rucksack was not as bad as I had feared.

Reaching the end of the larger of the two snowfields, we encountered the first bare rock. I watched in horror as the three pinprick lights of the Sherpas began to rise up what seemed to be a vertical wall. Surely it was an optical illusion? I had never heard anyone talk about any actual climbing before the Ridge. But, standing at the foot of the rock section, my heart sank. It was steep. Very steep. I was completely inexperienced in night climbing, and fear formed an icy pool in the pit of my stomach.

We were about to tackle the yellow band.

Worse, we would have to climb on rock with our crampons on. This is like trying to climb stairs on stilts. The spiked fangs act like an unwanted platform sole, elevating the foot away from any real contact with the rock. Using crampons on rock greatly increases the risk of a misplaced foothold or a twisted ankle. In a tight spot, where the feet have to move in close proximity, they are even more deadly. A spike can snag in the neoprene gaiter of the other foot, a mistake which invariably leads to a heavy fall.

On other mountains we might have stopped to remove the crampons, but here that was not an option. On the North Face of Everest, removing crampons every time you made a transition from snow to rock would waste hours of precious time and risk almost certain frostbite to the hands.

I paused for a brief rest as the others made their way up into the rock band. Turning off my headtorch, I let my eyes adjust to the dark. The sky was mostly still clear of cloud but I could see no sign of the moon. The only illumination came from the stars, which were as dazzling as I have ever seen them. The towering mass of Changtse was now far below us, I could just see the sinuous curves of its fluted ridge.

Further down, thousands of metres further down, the great glaciers were just visible, reflecting the dull metallic grey of the starlight against the darker shadows of their deep valley walls. The whole of Tibet lay beneath us and there was not a single electric light to be seen.

Taking off my Gore-tex overmitts, I reached up to the oxygen mask. Ice was beginning to constrict the intake valve at the front. I carefully broke the chunk away.

Then, my crampons clanking and scraping with a jarring metallic ring against the rock, I began the climb up. The route took a line up a series of ledges, linked by narrow cracks. It was a nasty scramble, involving strenuous leg and arm work to lunge up steps which were often uncomfortably high. More than once I found myself jamming a knee into a crack for support, or squirming up on to a balcony on my stomach.

'This must be the first step,' I yelled up at Al. He didn't reply and hours later, when we reached the real first step, I realised how far out I had been.

We came to a platform and took a few minutes' rest before beginning the next section.

The climb was littered with tatty ropes. Some were frayed, some were kinked from unknown causes, others were bleached white from exposure to the intense ultraviolet radiation here above 8,000 metres. Al sorted through them with a professional's eye, muttering under his breath.

Selecting the best of a bad lot, Al attached his jumar clamp and started up, sliding the handgrip of the camming device with each move. I waited for him to gain some height and then followed on. The crampons made every move a nightmare, as they had to be jammed into crevices or rested on protrusions to gain a purchase. Often I found my feet scrabbling frantically for a hold, the metal spikes grinding the flaking rock into granules of grit.

A steady barrage of small stones, and the occasional fist-sized rock, came down from above where the Sherpas were climbing. Normally this is avoidable by all but the clumsiest climber, but here every foothold had the potential to dislodge debris. Our ears rapidly become adept at guessing the size of an approaching missile as it clattered down the rock-face.

'Below!' A flat, briefcase-sized rock slithered down the face and spun off into the dark depths.

After sixty or seventy metres of ascent I made my first mistake. Pushing down to lift my body weight up on a boulder foothold, my crampon slipped away with no warning, unbalancing me and crashing my knee into a sharp ledge. The down suit cushioned much of the blow but it still took me several minutes to regain my composure as a series of sparkling stars did cartoon laps of honour across my field of vision.

On that fall, as at many other times, my entire body weight was suspended on the rope.

Another twenty metres of ascent brought me to the anchor point of the rope I was climbing on. Shining the headtorch on to the fixing point, I could scarcely believe what I was seeing. My lifeline was attached to the face by a single, rusting metal piton which had been ineptly placed in a crack.

Out of curiosity I tested the solidity of the anchor point with my hand. It moved. With one gentle pull, the piton slid right out. I stared at it dumbly for a few seconds, incredulous that my recent fall had been held by this pathetic piece of protection.

Throughout the expedition the knowledge that fixed ropes existed on the more technical rock had been a reassuring notion. 'Get to camp six and then you're on the fixed ropes' was a much repeated mantra, implying that they were somehow safe. In that one heart-stopping moment as the piton slid out of its crack, my faith in the fixed ropes was destroyed. I resolved to rely on them as little as I could.

The incline eased off and I found Al and the three Sherpas waiting for me. As I arrived they continued onwards up a series of steps cut into wind-hardened snow. At the next steep section Lhakpa again led the way up the rocks. Climbing strongly and steadily, the light from his headtorch rapidly went out of view.

I had a favour to ask. 'Al, can you let me go in front? I'm not happy at the back.'

'No problem.' Al unclipped his sling from the rope and let me pass. It was a generous gesture which I greatly appreciated.

I started up the next rock section feeling a lot more confident with Al behind me at the tail-end of the rope. This was partly psychological, and partly from the practical help he could give by shining his headtorch on to holds. I found myself moving easier and with more certainty.

As everywhere on Everest, the rock was fragmented and unreliable. Apparently solid handholds came away easily in flakes, boulders trembled under the weight of a leg, and a flow of gravel-sized stones seemed to be perpetually on the move.

Just inches from my hand a stone the size of a telephone directory fell out of the night. Impacting hard, it shattered into hundreds of pieces, showering me with splinters of stone. Mingma's warning cry from above came simultaneously. I saw his headtorch flash down the face.

'You OK?'

'OK.' We carried on up.

By now I had no idea of our precise position on the Face. From the Rongbuk glacier the distance from camp six to the North-East Ridge does not look great. In fact, as I was discovering, it is a significant climb. It was now many hours since we had left the camp and my body was already feeling as if it had done a substantial day's work.

There was still not the slightest glimmer of dawn. I began to long for the first rays of light.

Now we started what I guessed was the final section of the yellow band; more steep slogging up an eroded fault in the rock strata. It began with a stretching high step of a metre or more up on to a ledge; another occasion when there was no choice but to rely on a fixed rope. Then, with the infernal crampons scraping horribly on the rock, we scrambled up for about thirty minutes, pausing every five minutes or so for breath.

Turning back for a moment, I saw that Al was free-climbing the section. He, like me, had no confidence in the fixed ropes, but, unlike me, had the experience to know he could climb the route without a fall.

As the ground evened off, we began another traverse to the right, across a field of dirty snow. A bright red rope had been laid across it – the newest protection we had seen so far. Clipping on, I wondered who had fixed it: the Indians, or perhaps the Japanese?

The line continued up through a crack and then on to a sloping rock plateau the size of a tennis court. Crossing it, I realised we had finished the first stage of the climb.

The horrors of the night climb ended as we took the final steps on to the North-East Ridge. The crumbling cliffs of the yellow band had been steeper, more complex and much more committing than I had imagined. Climbing them in the dark, with just the glow-worm light of the headtorch, had been a nightmare.

Now, with the first rays of dawn to light our route along the Ridge, I reached up and turned the headtorch off. If all went well now, we could be on the summit within the next six hours.

The three Sherpas stood hunched over their ice-axes, alien figures in their goggles and oxygen masks. They had set a blistering pace through the dark hours and now rested as we waited for Al to join us on the Ridge.

One of the Sherpas – Lhakpa – had climbed to the summit before, but I knew the others had never been this high. Each had stalactites of ice clinging to the bottom of their oxygen masks where exhaled vapour had frozen into spikes several inches long. Mingma was having trouble with his mask. I watched him take it off to unblock the frozen pipe and remembered the expedition doctors warning that we might be unconscious within thirty minutes if our oxygen supply failed.

My oxygen hadn't stopped yet, but the hard frozen shell of the mask was eroding a nagging sore where it rubbed at the bridge of my nose. I eased it away from my face for a moment to relieve the irritation. Then, sucking deep on the oxygen, I prayed it wouldn't let me down.

With the dawn came the wind, our greatest enemy. As Al picked his way carefully up to join us, the first few gusts of the day began to play along the North Face, sending up flurries of ice crystals. While we waited for Al to recover his breath, I moved carefully on to the crest and looked over the knife edge drop down the Kanshung – the Eastern – Face.

There can be few more terrifying sights anywhere on earth. Seen from my vantage point, the Kanshung Face was a sheer 10,000-foot wall of ice falling away beneath me, so steep it seemed almost vertical. Vast fields of ice – hanging glaciers – perch precariously on its walls. It is deeply etched with fragile fissures and crevasses. It wasn't hard to imagine the whole Face – all those billions of tons of ice – giving up its fight with gravity and peeling off in one monumental avalanche down into the valleys below.

When Mallory first saw the Kanshung Face during the British reconnaissance expedition of 1924, he pronounced it unclimbable. He would leave it, he decided, 'to others less wise'. Now, looking down the Face, I understood precisely what he meant. The fact that it has subsequently been climbed – and by several different routes – seems to me an incredible achievement.

The Kanshung Face is home to, and creator of, some curious winds. With day breaking, one of those winds was beginning. As I looked down the Face, a billowing cloud of ice crystals was moving vertically up towards me. It was like looking down directly into the gaping mouth of a power station cooling tower. This is the tail of the massive 'rotor' that Everest spins out of the constant north-westerly Tibetan gales. As the ice crystals come up to the Ridge, they are blown to the south-east in a deadly plume which can be thirty miles long.

Few people summit when Everest's plume is running.

Lhakpa shouted something to me which broke the spell and I turned back towards the group.

Now our climb along the Ridge itself was about to begin. From where we were standing, it looked incredibly complicated: a dragon's tail of switchbacks, dips and rocky steps. Two of these, the 'first step' and the second, are regarded as the most formidable of the obstacles on the North Face route, but it was the sheer length of the Ridge that most worried me.

Back in London, I had met Crag Jones, one of the four British climbers to have summitted via the North Face. We sat in a Soho coffee bar drinking cappuccino while Crag cracked his knuckles and rolled up his sleeves to reveal Popeye muscles and veins the thickness of climbing ropes.

'The first and second steps *are* problems,' he told me, 'but it's the size of the Ridge you want to think about. When you get on to the Ridge you have to realise there could be another twelve hours of climbing to get back to camp six via the summit. Twelve hours. It's a hell of a long day.'

From where I was standing, Crag was right. It was already looking like a hell of a long day and we'd only cracked a tiny proportion of the route. Lhakpa moved towards me and shouted, his voice muffled by the mask:

'We move fast. Move very fast. OK?'

He tapped his wrist to indicate that the clock was ticking away. At 8,600 metres we were the highest human beings on the planet; and we were dying a little more with every hour. In the Death Zone, you have to move fast to keep alive.

Now in full daylight, we set out along the lifeline of tattered ropes which snake along the Ridge, the legacy of previous ascents. With the night hours behind us, I felt a glimmer of optimism creep in. I was feeling strong.

Thirty minutes later we rounded a small cliff and found the first dead Indian climber. We knew that the three Indian bodies would still be there on the Ridge where they had died a few days earlier, but, ridiculously, I had completely forgotten about them.

Now, here was the first body, lying partly in the shelter of an overhanging rock and ringed by an almost perfect circle of wind-blown snow.

Al shouted through his mask, 'Must be one of the Indians.'

We would have to step over his outstretched legs to continue along the ridge.

The Sherpas stood side by side, seemingly rooted to the spot by the sight of the dead man. Their heads were bowed, as if in prayer; perhaps, it occurred to me later, they were praying.

I felt an almost irresistible urge to look at the dead climber's face. What expression would be fixed on it in those final moments of life? Terror? A smile? (They say that those who die of acute mountain sickness have a delusion of well-being in the final stages.)

But his head was thrust far into the overhang, the neck bent so his face rested against the rock. All I could see was the edge of his oxygen mask. From the mask ran that precious, life-giving tube to the oxygen cylinder which was standing upright against a rock. It was an orange cylinder, a Russian one like our own.

I bent down, using my ice-axe for support, to have a closer look at the gauge on the top of the cylinder. It read, of course, zero. Even if he had died before the cylinder ran out, it would have continued to spill its feeble trickle of oxygen into the atmosphere until it emptied.

He was wearing very few clothes, just a lightweight red fleece top, some blue Gore-tex climbing trousers and a pair of yellow plastic Koflach boots similar to our own. His rucksack lay nearby, flat and empty. I wondered about this mystery for a moment. What had happened to his high-altitude gear? His down suit? His Gore-tex mitts? We knew the Indian team had been well-equipped. That left only two possibilities: either he'd ripped them off in the final stages of delirium, or someone had stolen them from the corpse.

In a way I found the first scenario an easier one to imagine.

The tragedy of the Indian team was central to the film I was making. Seduced by Everest's siren call, they had pushed themselves well beyond their own limits of endurance and had failed to reserve enough strength to get down in the worsening conditions which preceded the big storm. Summit fever had killed them.

Yet, even though we had the video cameras with us to record the actuality of our climb, I could not bring myself to film the dead man lying so pathetically at our feet.

I knew that ITN and Channel 4 would want this most graphic illustration of Everest as killer but I couldn't bring myself to do it. Even the victims of war eventually find a grave – even if they are shoved into it by a bulldozer. This Indian climber would remain exactly where he lay now, frozen for eternity. His grave was the bleakest imaginable and to think that his family, his friends, would see the reality of that was too much to contemplate.

As we stepped over the legs of the corpse to continue along the Ridge, we crossed an invisible line in the snow . . . and an invisible line of commitment in our own minds. Altitude is an unseen killer. Human life, any life, does not belong in the Death Zone, and by stepping over the dead body we made the conscious decision to push further into it. The dead body had been the starkest reminder we could have that we were now reliant for our lives on our equipment, our own strength and our luck.

There was the irresistible feeling that it was the Indian who was perfectly in tune with this place, and that we, being alive, were the invaders. All places above 8,000 metres belong to the dead because up there human life cannot be sustained. Wrapped up like spacemen in our huge high-altitude suits, breathing through the mechanical hiss of the oxygen system, I felt for the first time in my life like an alien on my own planet.

Our assault on the Ridge continued.

By 7 a.m. we reached the first step. It was both higher, at about twenty metres, and more of a climb, than I had imagined. Overshadowed by the bigger cliff of the second step, it tends to get treated as an insignificant obstacle but, looking up at it with my ski goggles beginning to acquire a frozen internal layer, it looked daunting enough.

It was not possible to remove the crampons to cope with these changing conditions as unfixing and then refixing them would risk fingers to frostbite (it was about −35°F at that point), and also waste too much time.

The three Sherpas went up first and I followed. For three metres or so, the route led up an ice-filled crack on the left side of the cliff. Next came a traverse across to a rocky ledge and then a precarious scramble up between two rounded boulders. I jammed the front metal points of my crampons into a tiny rock crack and pushed up . . . all my weight relying on the insignificant hold.

I paused for some moments to gather breath after the strenuous move, and then tackled the crux.

The move required a delicate balancing act which I could have achieved easily at sea level. Up here in clothes which reduced all sense of being in touch with the rock, and with the added exposure of an 8,000-foot fall directly down the North Face as a penalty for a mistake, it felt epic enough.

I snapped my jumar clamp as high as I could on the best looking of the many ropes which were hanging beguilingly around the crux. It gave a sense of security to protect a fall but that was a psychological advantage rather than a real one. In fact, a fall would leave the unlucky climber swinging helplessly in open space underneath the overhanging section of the cliff. Assuming the rope held.

Moving out into the exposed position, I stuck a leg around the smooth edge of the ridge and planted it on to the foothold which, fortunately, waited on the other side. I had to sense its security rather than see it . . . the leg was out of my field of vision.

My left hand instinctively snaked up to try and find a handhold above. A tentative pull on a possible hold merely made it give way, and I threw the cigarette-packet-sized piece of rock down the North Face beneath me.

Not many people can imagine that Everest is a crumbling wreck of a mountain. It looks as if it should be made of granite, but in fact it is friable limestone . . . the worst of rocks to climb at any altitude.

Locking my fist on to a ledge above my head, I took a deep breath and shifted my entire weight on to the out-of-vision foot. Then I swung over and around the rock, to the safety of the other side.

Lhakpa was waiting there. He put his thumbs up and I replied with the same. Another obstacle over. Another step closer to the summit.

II

Now the wind was definitely picking up and we were still only half-way along the Ridge. We began to push harder. The plume of ice crystals from the Kanshung Face was now billowing up more strongly on our left, a sign we could not afford to ignore. Whenever we stopped to regain our breath, I looked away to the north, the direction a storm would come from. Plenty of clouds were moving rapidly towards us but nothing so far looked too threatening.

I had been so wrapped up in the climb, I had completely forgotten my stills camera. The tiny Olympus had a brand-new lithium battery and a full roll of transparency film. Squinting through the eyepiece, I took two pictures of the terrain ahead and one shot of Al. Then we pressed on.

At several points, the route took us right on to the very knife-edge crest of the Ridge itself. Then, we would time the dash along the ice to miss the blasts of wind. I had never been able to imagine how climbers could be blown off a ridge. Now, I was acutely aware of that possibility. One of the theoretical ends for Mallory and Irvine had them plummetting off the Ridge and down the Kanshung Face . . . perhaps their bodies, or their ghosts, were close by?

One particularly hair-raising section of the Ridge, only a few metres long, involved stepping down on to what seemed to be a corniced section of crumbling ice cross-sectioned by a crevasse. The Sherpas, lighter and more agile than we were, ran across easily. I took each step with my heart in my mouth, expecting at any moment that the cornice would give way and leave me dangling over the Kanshung Face.

The ice held.

By 8.30 a.m. we reached the second step. This step is another cliff, steeper and more than twice the height of the first. There is no way around it, it has to be tackled head-on.

Back in the 1980s, a Chinese expedition had fixed a lightweight climbing ladder to the most severe part of the cliff. It had been destroyed in a recent storm and the Indian climbers and their Sherpas had fixed another in its place. I had been greatly reassured by the notion of the ladder. Anyone could climb a ladder... couldn't they? In my mind it had lessened the severity of the second step.

In fact the ladder, which I had always thought of as a friendly aid, was about to prove a significant problem in its own right.

At the foot of the second step two unexpected things happened: the first was my discovery that both my litre bottles of juice, boiled down from snow so painfully slowly at camp six the previous night, were frozen solid. Even the bottle I had kept next to my skin inside the front of my down suit was a solid mass of ice. At the time it seemed like an inconvenience. Later on during the day I was to realise in the starkest way possible the seriousness of that event.

Al checked his bottles too. They were also frozen solid. Now neither of us would have a single drop of moisture through the whole day. Many experienced high-altitude mountaineers would have turned back at that point.

The other unexpected thing was that Al leaned towards me to speak.

'Open up my pack,' he said. 'Put the oxygen up to four litres a minute.'

He turned his back to me. Taking off my overmitts, and going down to the finger gloves, I undid the clips closing his pack and found the oxygen regulator valve inside. It was a difficult, fiddly job in the close confines of the rucksack. I clicked the regulator round to read four and closed the pack.

Now Al was pumping twice as much oxygen into his system as my rate of two litres a minute. I could understand his desire for more gas to tackle the second step, but even so his request surprised me. We both knew the risks of pumping up the oxygen too high. It runs out twice as fast and, with your body tuned in to operate at a higher level, you come down with a bigger crash when it ends.

'OK. It's on four,' I shouted to him. For a fleeting moment I thought I sensed something more than just tiredness in the way Al was moving. Was he having a harder time than he was revealing?

It was a measure of our increasing disorientation that neither of us thought at that stage of dumping the two litres of frozen liquid. Now we were climbing with two kilogrammes of superfluous weight on our backs up the hardest rock-climbing section of the North Face route.

The first six metres or so were simple enough. A tight squeeze through a chimney filled with ice led on to an easier graded ledge with a snow bank against the cliff. I used the jumar clamp to help my ascent, sliding the device up as high as my arms would stretch, then pulling up where it gripped against the rope. Someone had rigged a virtually new, 9mm rope on this lower part and that helped considerably.

The crampons scratched and bit into the rock steps like the claws of a cat trying, and failing to climb a tree. Then came a big step up. I tensioned my foot against a ripple of protruding rock to my right, and, cursing the crampons to hell, just managed to ease my body up on to the ledge which led to the ladder.

I paused for a long moment to catch my breath. The beat of my heart was sending a pounding rush of blood through my head. I was aware of my pulse-rate being higher than I have ever sensed it before. My breathing was wild and virtually out of control. For one panic-stricken moment I thought my oxygen had failed. Then I realised I could still hear the reassuring hiss of the gas and told myself to calm down.

I was standing more or less exactly in the place where Mallory and Irvine were last seen alive, spotted by telescope from the North Col camp. Their 1924 climb had been the hardest, and perhaps, the greatest, of the pre-war efforts on Everest.

There had been no ladder for them on the second step. If they'd tried it, one of them may well have fallen, taking his partner with him to certain death. The horror of imagining that final moment had always eluded me until now. Now I had no trouble in imagining a fatal fall from this spot. It was the most exposed and dangerous part of the climb.

My friend the ladder was the next obstacle. I put a hand on it and felt it sway and flap against the sheer face it was attached to. I had always imagined it to be solid. I began to climb.

The first problem was caused by the crampons. The metal spikes snagged against the rungs, or grated against the rock and prevented me from getting a proper footing on the ladder. Unable to look down, blinkered by the goggles into a front only view, I had to sense as best I could when my feet were in the right place.

My breathing rate went up again . . . the greater volume of escaping moisture running up through gaps in the mask and freezing inside my goggles. Halfway up the ladder I was almost blinded by this, and I ripped the goggles up on to my head to be able to see. We were all aware of the dangers of snow blindness but I felt I could take the risk for the next few crucial minutes.

The ladder had a distinct, drunken lean to the left. This, coupled with the fact that it was swaying alarmingly on the ragbag selection of pitons and ropes which held it, made it extremely physical to cling to.

My Gore-tex overmitts were hopelessly clumsy in this situation. I could barely cup them tight enough to cling to the rungs. But, having started with them on, I could hardly remove them now; and any lesser protection would almost certainly result in frostbite from contact with the frozen metal of the ladder.

The 'friendly' ladder was anything but. I resolved to move quickly to get off it, and off the second step, as soon as I could.

Reaching the top rung, I assessed the next move. It was a hard one: a tension traverse using only the strength of the arms. The objective was to swing up on to the ledge which marked the end of the second step. To do it, I would have to cling on to a collection of rotting ropes tied to a sling of dubious origin. Then, with no foothold, I would have to tension as many spikes of my crampons as I could push on to the Face, and then in one fluid motion swing chimpanzee-like up to the right.

Down at base camp I had talked about filming this stage of the climb when Brian got there. Six weeks later this now seemed a supreme joke. Firstly, there was never any chance of Brian getting here; secondly, the thought of filming in this most deadly of places was the last thing on my mind. This was a survival exercise pure and simple.

Trying the move, I realised that there was a critical moment of commitment when the body would be neither supported by the ladder, nor safely on the ledge. To complete the climb of the second step, I would be, albeit for a split second, hanging over the North Face by the strength of my arms alone.

I tried it . . . and failed. Clinging to the ladder, I retreated several rungs to get some rest while my breathing rate subsided. Without sufficient oxygen powering the muscle tissue in my arms, they were tiring extremely quickly. Instinctively I felt I would have one or perhaps two more tries in me before I weakened to the point where I would have to retreat.

It was several minutes before my runaway breathing came down to a controllable rate. I tried the move again, and this time succeeded. With both arms fading fast, I pulled up on to the ledge and then stumbled the few metres of rocky slope to the top.

From this new vantage point on the Ridge, the summit pyramid was for the first time fully in view. The four of us waited for Al to come up the second step and then continued.

For the next hour we continued to make good time, climbing up gradually on the mixed ground of snow and rock. I paused several times to take photographs but by the fifth or sixth shot the camera began to behave strangely, winding on erratically and failing to close the automatic lens cover. On the seventh shot the Olympus ground to a halt and gave up completely in the sub-zero temperatures. That left me with no SLR camera as my Nikon F3 had similarly succumbed to the cold down at camp four.

Cursing this piece of bad luck, I unzipped my down suit and put the camera against my thermal layer beneath the fleece in the hope the body warmth might revive it (it never did). Then I took out that eight-dollar plastic 'fun' camera I had bought in Kathmandu, and realised that this recreational toy was now my only means of taking stills. On the cardboard cover was a picture of a bronzed woman in her bikini playing with a beach-ball. Feeling utterly ridiculous, I stared through the 'eyefinder' (basically just a hole in the plastic) and clicked the first of the twelve shots available.

The camera breakdown brought back the old nightmare; would the video cameras work in the −40 degree winds? The thought of them giving up now was too much to contemplate.

Once or twice I looked back down the ridge we had come up. The figure of Al, bright red in his Berghaus wind suit, was dropping further behind. Somewhere in my oxygen-starved brain a few connections were still working. Al had not asked me to click his regulator back down to two litres.

He was still climbing on four litres a minute . . . and he was dropping further and further behind. On two occasions we waited for Al to catch us up, and then we reached the third step, where we stopped ourselves for a rest.

The third step is nothing like as demanding as the previous two, but it comes higher into the climb. Beyond it is the steep avalanche-prone ice-field of the final summit pyramid, the rock traverse, and then the summit ridge.

Grateful for the rest, I took off my pack and sat down, my heels digging into the ice to prevent a slide. Sensing the pressing need to drink, I pulled out the water bottle from where I had left it inside my down suit, half expecting it to have magically defrosted. Of course it was still frozen; what else could I expect in these temperatures?

Realising finally, and much too late, how stupid I had been, I took both bottles of ice and put them at the foot of the third step next to some abandoned oxygen cylinders. Two kilogrammes less weight to carry.

Al was resting further down the Ridge where it had flattened out into a broad expanse. I pulled out my camera and took a shot of him lying down on his back. Not far away was the second of the Indian bodies, lying with his face towards us and with no sign of pain or distress on his frozen features. Unlike the first of the bodies, which had shocked me when we came across it, I now felt no sense of surprise at the presence of the corpse – a sure indicator that my mind was occupied with other thoughts.

After a while Al joined us, and we were now contemplating the final stages of the climb. Lhakpa was increasingly agitated about the weather. The wind was now stronger than before, and the spindrift from the summit ridge was filling virtually the whole of our view to the south. The plume was starting to run in earnest, and the sinister howl of a strong wind at high altitude was beginning to fill the air.

I followed the Sherpas up the third step and we gained the steep ice of the summit pyramid. If all went well now we could be on the summit within the next two hours.

After one rope's length on the ice, Lhakpa tugged my arm and yelled above the wind:

'Where's Alan? No Alan.'

Looking back down the ice-field, I could see he was right. Al had not appeared at the top of the third step.

Every minute we waited now was putting our summit attempt in jeopardy. The weather was increasingly threatening. The Sherpas were looking to me for a decision. Should we leave Al where he was and hope his oxygen held out? Should we go back down and see if he had fallen and was lying injured at the bottom of the third step?

Of all the scenarios, the trial runs that had run like fast-forward movie previews through my mind, the possibility that Al would have a problem had never occurred to me. I was confused and shocked.

For what seemed like an age, but probably was no more than three or four minutes we looked back down at the windblown lump which marked the top of the third step. The wind played strongly across the snowslope ... causing the four of us to turn our faces away from the blast.

My brain was struggling to come to terms with the situation and, luckily, a few synapses were still connecting. I ran through the options and realised that it was very unlikely Al had fallen: he was far too good for that. Also, he had the extra oxygen bottle, so there was no danger he would run out of air. Probably he was just resting or sorting out his gear.

That was the logical response. I convinced myself that he would follow us up in his own time. The pause gave my feet a chance to go numb; wriggling them inside the plastic boot, I could sense them freezing up. My hands were also, for the first time, beginning to freeze.

Something inside me made the decision.

'Let's go,' I told Lhakpa. The words were whipped away by a sudden gust. He stepped down the slope next to me to hear better. I didn't bother shouting again but just pointed up towards the summit. He nodded and tapped his wrist to indicate we were running out of time.

I tightened the wrist strap of my ice-axe, and followed the three Sherpas up the steepening ice.

Inside me a tiny voice was making a faint protest, posing a few uncomfortable questions: shouldn't you go back to check? Shouldn't you consider the possibility that here nothing is certain – anything can happen? Some accident might have befallen Al, his oxygen valve might have frozen, he might have broken a crampon, he might have pulled out a rope anchor on the third step.

Pausing for breath, I looked back again at bottom of the snowface. Still no sign of Al. I carried on climbing.

Back came the soothing logic, extinguishing those glowing embers of doubt. Relax. He'll be fine. He's always run his own agenda. He's climbed K2. He's probably stopped for a call of nature. Perhaps he just doesn't want to summit with us ... preferring to reach the top alone?

Three rope lengths up the ice-field. I looked back again. Nothing. I carried on climbing towards the rock which marked the end of the triangle. And this time I didn't look back.

I had crossed another of those invisible lines in the snow. That same force – the one which had been unlocked from its cage inside me back at the Col – had now taken complete control. I wanted the summit so much that I was turning my back on Al whatever had happened to him.

In that final hour there was really only one single focus in my entire being; the desire to reach the top of the world had become all consuming. It had extinguished my concern for my fellow climber, blocked my capacity for questioning my own actions, and turned me into little more than a robot . . . placing one foot in front of the other like a pre-programmed machine.

Summit fever had me body and soul, and now a new wave of strength seemed to flood power into me. I suddenly felt myself driving upwards almost effortlessly, and only having to stop because the Sherpas in front of me were moving more slowly. Even in my disorientated state it occurred to my mind to wonder where this new surge had come from. I was sure that by now my body should have been running close to the point of exhaustion.

What exactly was it that was propelling me up to the highest point in the world?

Now the Sherpas were tired. Lhakpa's lightning pace had run down like a discharged battery. At the start of the snow pyramid they were resting every five or six steps. At the top of the four-rope-length pitch, they were managing only one or two steps between rests.

8,750 metres. Just under 100 metres of vertical ascent to go.

The snowfield arched up, ever steeper, in a soaring curve towards what I imagined was the summit. But instead of continuing up the ice as I had hoped, Lhakpa led the way back into another of the rock cliffs which flank this final buttress.

My heart sank. More rock . . . again with the crampons.

In fact, as I saw when I examined the ice route in more detail, the top section was obviously prone to avalanche. Fresh avalanche debris, blocks the size of cars, lay scattered not far away. The way up the rock cliff was the safer of the two, if safe is the right word.

First came a traverse along another tiny ledge, eroded into a fault in the rock. Clipping on to a rope which looked like it had been there for decades, I carefully made my way along, swinging my right foot far out to avoid snagging the left. Midway – about fifty metres – along the ledge, an outcrop forced a fine balancing manoeuvre to ease the body around a bulge and back on to the ledge on the other side. At that point, the rope was forced to rest against the rock. The wind had beaten it down to just one single frayed strand, about the width and strength of a piece of knitting wool. And about as much use in stopping a fall.

I found myself laughing as I shifted my cramponed feet into position to make the move.

The drop falling away beneath us here was the most sheer yet. We had made our way across the Face and were now positioned almost exactly below the summit, far to the right of the great couloir. The small stones and flakes of rock which we all unavoidably kicked loose, didn't bounce their way down as they had before . . . they just fell out of sight into the abyss.

My face sliding against the rock to press as much of my weight away from the fall, I inched nervously around the obstacle and then rested, gasping for breath. Only then did I realise that I had held my breath during the move . . . a wave of blackness, a desire to faint, swept over me as I struggled to get oxygen into my body. Regaining my composure, I carried on along the decaying ledge. I had thought I was moving faster than the Sherpas, but they had already rounded the corner and were out of sight.

At the end of the traverse, the route stepped up abruptly in a series of ledges similar to those we had encountered on some of the night stages. I used my arms to pull myself up wherever possible, still stubbornly reluctant to trust my weight to the crampon points.

On one of the steps my safety sling got snagged into an old piece of rope and caught me in mid-move. I had to fall back on to the ledge and regain my balance before clearing the snag and continuing on.

After perhaps twenty minutes of climbing, we emerged on to the upper slopes of the summit pyramid snowfield, having effectively bypassed the more avalanche-prone section and gained about fifty metres of height.

During the detour, the wind had increased again. Now the snow ridge, and the skyline above us were cloaked in snarling clouds of airborne ice. The wind was fickle, blowing with unpredictable violent blasts. The upward view was the most intimidating, with a huge circulating mass of ice particles twisting like a miniature tornado above what I presumed to be the summit, just twenty metres of steep ice above us.

We found some shelter in the lee of a rock outcrop and waited there to gain our breath for the final push. So close to the summit, I found myself barely able to wait. An irrational wave of paranoia swept over me; we were just minutes away . . . what if it was snatched away from us at the final moment?

Lhakpa looked at his watch again and then spoke to Gyaltsen. I couldn't hear their words but, in my paranoid state, I imagined them discussing how dangerous the wind would be on the top . . . agreeing that we should turn back. . . .

Then my senses snapped into gear, and I recognised my paranoia for what it was: the insidious beginnings of high altitude sickness where irrational thoughts are often the first stage. Since leaving the tent eight hours before, I had not drunk a single drop of fluid. My body was dehydrating dangerously.

Lhakpa led the way up painfully slowly into the cloud of spindrift, with Gyaltsen and Mingma behind him and myself at the back. There were no ropes here and I took care to dig as many crampon spikes as I could into the ice. Halfway up, I took out the plastic camera and framed it vertically for a shot of the three Sherpas as they rested.

I hadn't thought that it might be a false summit. But it was. Reaching the crest of the snowfield, I was taken completely by surprise by what lay before us. Instead of the short final stage I had imagined, we were now standing at the beginning of the final ridge; with the great bulging cornice of the true summit waiting at the far end. Between our position and the top lay a series of switchback ice waves, blown into shape by the wind, and overhanging the Kanshung Face.

By some trick of perpective, or perhaps another irrational side effect of oxygen starvation, the ridge looked huge, and the summit seemed kilometres away. For another of those bizarre moments of doubt, I thought Lhakpa and the others would pull the plug and decide not to continue. The wind was blowing hard now, and more consistently. The plume was running and we were about to walk right into it.

Then I noticed the clue which revealed the true perspective of the ridge; a string or prayer flags which had been fixed to the summit was now hanging sadly down the side. I could clearly make out the individual pennants of coloured silk. That visual reference pulled the ridge back down to scale and I realised it was much smaller than I had at first thought.

The summit was just a few hundred metres away.

I moved into position behind Lhakpa and we began to negotiate the undulating waves of fluted ice. It was as dramatic an approach to a summit as one could have wished. To the right, the mountain fell sheer away for 10,000 vertical feet, leaving unrestricted views across to the fairy-tale peak of Pumori, 7165 metres, and the other northern sentinels of the Himalayas. Beyond them lay the arid brown plateau of Tibet with the curvature of the earth clearly discernible.

To the left, down the Kanshung side, nothing was visible at all . . . just the white mass of the plume as it swirled off the ridge. There were no footprints or crampon marks to be seen. We favoured the right-hand side of the approach, where rock was still visible, to avoid stepping out on to one of the overhanging cornices.

Taking out the plastic camera once more, I took a shot of Lhakpa in front of me as he continued, head down, with the great bulging nose of the summit itself framed in front of him.

Hearing the successful click of the plastic camera set my mind off again on another worry: would the video camera work when we got to the summit? To get the summit pictures was the only way to resolve the film. I had had camera failures before at critical moments. I breathed a silent prayer that everything was going to work.

Then it occurred to me that, without Al, I would have no meaningful summit sequence anyway. The film had shifted sharply away from Brian after his decision to turn back, and was now firmly focussed on Al and the Dalai Lama's scarf which he had promised to take to the top.

I looked back along the ridge, hoping against hope to see Al following us. Nothing. I told myself to take things one step at a time, get to the summit first and then worry about how to film it.

Strangely, the nearer we got to the summit, the more the wind seemed to drop, even though the plume was still blowing as hard as ever. At the beginning of the ridge we were buffeted strongly by each blast, enough to have to lean into the wind to avoid being bowled over. But, now, as we took the final few steps on to the summit of Mount Everest, the wind magically dropped away.

I placed my hand on the summit pole and pulled myself up on to the top of the world. To my surprise I found I was in tears, the first time I had cried since childhood.

I looked behind me on the ridge. Mingma and Gyaltsen were following up, but I could still see no sign of Al. With four of us on the summit, there was not much room to spare. Shaped by the prevailing westerly wind, the very top is about the size of a billiard table, sloping steeply away to the north and south, and jutting out in a bulbous overhanging cornice to the east.

Lhakpa took off his overmitts and pumped my hand up and down in joy. We all shook hands in turn and shouted muffled congratulations.

My overwhelming impression was of stupendous height. Even though it is surrounded by other gigantic 8,000-metre peaks like Lhotse and Nuptse, Everest does not compete with them once you are on its peak . . . it dominates them completely. Everest does not jostle for position in the heart of the Himalayas, it presides over its lowlier cousins with effortless majesty.

But the view was not complete. To the east, almost one-third of our horizon was blocked by the soaring cloud of ice crystals forming the plume. Seen this close, the plume has a hypnotic quality which is quite mesmerising. I watched the clouds of ice for a few moments and then realised why the summit was so calm. The wind was striking the North Face and then curling above our heads in a great 'rotor' before doubling back and biting into the Kanshung Face.

Planting one leg on the south-facing slope, and one on the north, I sat down astride the summit crest and pushed my ice-axe as far as I could into the crust. Technically I was straddled on the precise borderline between China and Nepal.

In front of me was the alloy summit pole, festooned with a colourful collection of prayer flags and scarves. Leaning against it were some curious alloy panels – perhaps a reflecting device for a past height survey – and two empty orange-coloured oxygen cylinders.

Conscious that our oxygen supply was diminishing with every minute, I retrieved the video camera body from Mingma and dug one of the lithium batteries from my pack. There was work to do. I had to remove my overmitts to complete the fiddly task of connecting up the battery. Then, with bated breath, I clicked on the switch. Pushing the ski goggles up onto my forehead, I looked through the tiny postage stamp-sized viewfinder and there – just as it should be – was the picture I desperately needed to see.

The camera was working perfectly. I pressed the record switch and watched the red REC light flash on. Eureka! Filming on the top of the world.

Still sitting, I started with two long sweeping panoramic shots which began at the cloud-covered mass of Lhotse and ended on the three Sherpas. Lhakpa was trying to get base camp on the walkie-talkie so I zoomed in on the end of the lens to get a close-up.

When Lhakpa finished his conversation he handed me the set. Placing the camera down to take the walkie-talkie, I heard an exclamation from Gyaltsen. Following his outstretched arm, I saw Al working his way along the final ridge towards us.

I had a few words with Barney and then Brian's ecstatic voice came out of the set.

'Matt? We're all thrilled down here! Don't forget to say a few words for the Dalai Lama!'

A sudden thought occurred to me.

'Make sure Kees films all this at your end.'

'Kees is right here now, he's filming now.'

'OK. Over and out.'

I returned the walkie-talkie to Lhakpa and picked up the camera once more. This was perfect. I could cover Al's arrival at the summit, and then shoot him having a radio conversation with Brian. Down at base camp, Kees would film the other half of the conversation and we could intercut the two to form a unique summit sequence.

Holding the camera as steady as I could, I framed up on Al and filmed him as he slowly plodded towards us. Every few steps, he would pause for breath as we had done. He looked like he was having a hard time. My heart was racing, and not just from the lack of oxygen; those few moments of filming were exquisitely exciting . . . the most thrilling of my life. Here I was, sitting on the summit of Everest filming one of the world's great mountaineers as he fought his way up the final snowfield to that sacred place.

This was no re-enactment, no set up scene, this was the shot that was going to make this Everest film – my Everest film – special . . . the shot that would take the viewer up there with us.

Realising I couldn't stay on the wide shot indefinitely, I zoomed in to Al's feet and held for a few seconds as he kicked up the slope. Then I panned up his body and got a close-up on his face, the icicles clearly visible on the oxygen mask.

As he stepped up the final few metres I pulled back wide again and held the shot as the Sherpas let out a cheer.

'Well done, Al. We've made it.'

'Finally made it. On top of the world!'

Al paused for a long breather. His shoulders were slumped and he seemed pretty exhausted but he was speaking coherently. Lhakpa handed him the radio set.

'Brian! Can you hear me? I'm on the summit. I'm on the summit and I've got the Dalai Lama's scarf here with me!'

'Is that that Yorkshire lad? How's tha'doing?' Brian's booming voice resonated through the airwaves. 'I'm down at base camp. Can you see me? I'm waving at you!'

Al turned his head around and looked back down the Rongbuk glacier. The scale of the landscape was so huge that we couldn't even make out the monastery, let alone the tiny tents of our camp which was a good sixteen miles away!

'Well not quite, but I can imagine I can.'

'We're all very proud! You're both great heroes, and the Sherpas too. Just get back safe and say a prayer for world peace for the Dalai Lama! Don't forget, *Om mane padme hum.*'

Al gave the handset back to Lhakpa and unravelled the scarf from his neck. There was a muffled exclamation of delight from the Sherpas as they realised what he was going to do. Taking the length of white silk, Al tied it to the summit pole and let the ends fly free in the wind.

He said a brief prayer for peace as Brian had asked.

I held on the scarf for as long as I could, and then gave the camera to Al to film me as I had a few brief words with Brian on the radio. I thanked him for being the impetus behind the expedition . . . and the film. After all, it was Brian's genuine passion for Everest which had brought us all here in the first place and I didn't want him to think I had forgotten that.

The one shot we didn't have was a wide establishing shot of us all on the summit. Al took the camera back ten metres down the ridge and framed it up. When the camera was running, we cheered and waved our ice-axes in the air. And that was it. Job done.

'We'd better get out of here.'

Oxygen was now running low, we had been on the summit for far longer than any of us had anticipated. Almost fifty minutes had elapsed.

Hurriedly, we took our stills, mine with the plastic camera which was still happily clicking away. The temperature seemed to be dropping drastically, or perhaps it was just the amount of time we had been motionless on the summit. My hands and feet were both freezing up and becoming numb. It was time to go.

Then I remembered the Christmas pudding – a gift cooked with love by my mother and which I had saved for this precise occasion. It took a few moments to find it at the bottom of the rucksack. The bacofoil had ripped a little in transit, but it was otherwise in good condition. I peeled back the top section of foil and took a large bite.

It was as hard as granite, frozen solid. Furious at the thought that I had carried this half-kilogramme load up the highest mountain in the world for nothing, I very nearly tossed it down the Kanshung Face in disgust.

But how would I explain that to my mother?

Risking serious damage to upper and lower incisors, I managed to nibble off a symbolic raisin then replaced the offending pudding back in the pack to be consumed at a later date.

Then, taking a last long look into Nepal, we began the journey back down to camp six.

*

For me, the descent was the most nerve jangling part of the nightmare. Having had just five extremely cold and restless hours of sleep out of the last fifty (and no sleep at all in the last thirty), I found myself fighting an overwhelming fatigue. The demands of the climb were more physically draining by far than anything I had ever done, and the fact that we had had no fluid for the entire fourteen climbing hours of summit day meant that both Al and I were right on the edge of acute mountain sickness with chronic dehydration threatening pulmonary or cerebral odeoma; and for me some kind of frostbite was now virtually inevitable.

Downclimbing is always more dangerous than going up. The body is facing away from the face, so that the chances of an accidental slip become much more likely than they are on the ascent. Shod in the infernal crampons, skittering and clattering across the loose, frozen slabby rock of the North Face, I several times felt myself close to plummeting down the 10,000-foot precipice.

As the hours went by, we negotiated the third and second steps, passed the bodies of the Indian climbers, and then abseiled down the first step. The traversing along crumbling ledges seemed to go on for ever. The Face feels bloody big on the way up, but on the way down it is absolutely huge, impossibly so. Concentrating on getting the figure-of-eight descendeur into the rope and clipped on to my harness at one of the vertical rock climbs, I managed to lose my balance. I swung round in an arc and smashed my knee hard against the rock. For a couple of seconds I thought I was going to faint.

The three Sherpas watched from below, unable to help, as I

dangled clumsily on the lifeline, swearing with the pain of the
impact. My fall had been held by an ice stake driven into the snow
above the cliff. I don't know who put it there but whoever did made
a good job. It took me several minutes to get myself disentangled
and sorted out before I could continue the descent.

Rest stops became more frequent. Every time I sat down, my eyes
would spontaneously close and my mind drift off into the beckoning
darkness of sleep. Then the red warning light would snap on and I
would force my body to rise and carry on. Increasingly my mind
was wandering into strange corners of imagination and I do not
remember Al passing me on the Ridge and going ahead.

The Sherpas were much faster than us now, and they reached
camp six at least an hour before we did. The last section, down the
evil gulleys of the yellow band, took me beyond the physical limits
of my own endurance, I think it was gravity alone that was pulling
me down. Al stayed with me more or less the whole way, waiting
for me at the end of each rope length.

The last 100 metres down to the sanctuary of camp six took me
at least an hour to complete. Somewhere during the descent my
oxygen cylinder had run out but I was too fazed to have noticed it.

By the time we got there, all the warning sirens in my body were
wailing for attention. A pulsating throb inside my skull was bleeping
an emergency signal which told me that if I didn't get some fluid
inside me soon then I was likely to lapse into unconsciousness and
enter a coma. The problem was that my body was so absolutely
shattered that I knew there was no way I would be able to co-
ordinate myself to get the cooker going.

Simon had just arrived at the camp on his way up from camp
five. He had no fluid on him and he looked extremely tired himself.
He weakly shook Al's hand then sat down in a heap. I asked him if
the Sherpas had prepared any tea but he didn't know. Al shouted
over to the Sherpa tent but there was no reply. Somehow I got my
pack off and wormed my way into the squalid interior of the tent.
Al wasn't far behind. I can faintly remember babbling for fluid.

'You've got to help me, Al, I'm going down here. I can feel myself
blacking out. You've got to get the fucking stove on, man, or I'm
going to have a serious fucking problem.'

Al, himself dazed and moving in slow motion, began the ever-
lasting process. I could feel the waves of black overwhelming me
but I fought back as hard as I could to stay conscious. Then we
heard footsteps outside the tent. It was Sundeep, also arrived up

from five, looking every bit as knackered as Simon, and swaying slightly as he leaned forward on his ice-axe.

'Have you got any juice?' I asked him.

He pulled his oxygen mask aside and mumbled something. I saw the padded water bottle strapped to his belt and pointed to it. My brain had just enough power to utter one more sentence.

'I have to have some liquid, Sundeep. I won't take it all but I need something or I'm going to collapse.'

That was what I was trying to say but all that came out was an unintelligible stream of gibberish. But Sundeep understood and passed the bottle in. I drank one-third of the contents then passed it to Al who also drank.

Half an hour later we drank the first tepid cup of liquid from the melted pan of snow. That was when I finally let myself believe that I was going to survive.

12

At 2.30 the following morning, Simon, Sundeep and two Sherpas set out for their own summit bid. The noise of their preparations woke me up but I was too fatigued to put my head out of the tent and wish them good luck. They climbed up the cliffs of the yellow band making slower progress than we had the day before and reached the Ridge one hour after sunrise. There, in a rising wind, they reluctantly conceded defeat. It was clear to them both that they would not make it to the summit.

Roger and Tore also did not realise their dream of making it to the top of Everest. Roger had turned back from a position just above camp five after realising that, although he felt he could reach camp six, he was absolutely sure he would not get any higher. Tore, who had had a bad day climbing up to the Col on 17 May, turned back in the high winds midway up the North Ridge on the following day.

Al and I left camp six in the early morning of the 20th for our ten-hour descent to advance base camp. As we passed Reinhard's tent I suddenly realised that I had completely forgotten about the Austrian climber who now lay dead inside. I hurried past – if hurried is the right word to describe my hobbling progress – closing my mind to the awful temptation to look inside.

The next day, in a radio call, Reinhard's distraught wife asked Simon and Sundeep to bury her husband as best they could. Exhausted after their own aborted summit attempt, they did not have the strength to scrape even the slightest hollow in the iron hard, frozen, ground. With the help of Ang Chuldim, the best they could do was to collapse the tent over the body, wrapping it like a shroud and placing a few rocks and empty oxygen cylinders on top. It took them several hours. Simon made a simple cross out of a couple of shattered tent-poles he found lying around, and the three climbers stood with their heads bowed in the biting wind around the grave.

Simon said a brief, dignified prayer for Reinhard which moved them all to tears. Then, with hands and feet already dangerously frozen, they began their descent to the Col which they reached on the evening of 21 May. They made it safely down to advance base the following day.

Simon remained at advance base camp to supervise the clearing of the mountain while the rest of us descended to base camp and began to pack. By the 24th, all tents and refuse had been removed by the Sherpas from camps four and five, and a train of yaks carried the gear back down to the Rongbuk glacier.

Three days later we left in a convoy of Jeeps for Nepal, each of us wrapped up in our own thoughts as the vehicles sped down the dusty track past the Rongbuk monastery. At the top of the Pang La pass the vehicles paused and we climbed out and looked back at Everest for the last time. The plume was running, just as it had been when we saw the mountain from the same position on our way into base camp. Standing apart from the others I found myself searching for words to offer a mountain that I was pretty sure I would never set eyes on again.

In the end a whispered 'thank you' was all I could manage before we climbed back into the Toyotas and set off across the rolling Tibetan plateau.

*

Kathmandu was a shock after the arid months in Tibet. The teeming traffic and crowded alleyways of Tamel seemed impossibly colourful and exploding with life compared to the monochrome, brutal mountain environment we had come to accept as home.

Craving fats and protein, I immediately set about trying to restore some of the eleven kilogrammes I had lost. In our first day back in Kathmandu I ate several fried breakfasts, pancakes and cream, chocolate cakes, banana cakes, fruit and ice-cream and a huge sizzling steak and chips. That night I was voluptuously sick for my gluttony. Kees was worse; his eating session put him in bed for three days with a gastric fever which was a bit rough when his wedding was just a week away.

For the first time we had a chance to see how sharply the world's press had focused on the Everest disaster. Isolated from all but radio reports on the mountain, we had seen none of the sensational newspaper and magazine articles which had followed the event. Now in the bookshops of Kathmandu we found out just how big an impact the storm and the fatalities had made. The front covers of *Time* and *Newsweek* were both devoted to the disaster and friends and family faxed us other articles from the UK.

The reports differed hugely in the quality of research which had gone into them and certain aspects of the stories – enduring controversies both from the south and north sides – did not always tally with our own opinions – or what we had seen on the mountain.

The tragedy of the Indian climbers – and the perceived failure of the Japanese team to attempt a rescue was one example.

The widely accepted story had it that the lowest of the dead Indian climbers was found just 100 metres from safety above the top camp. This information – also used by Richard Cowper in his *Financial Times* article of 18 May entitled 'The climbers left to die in the storms of Everest' filtered down from climbers at the high camp on the northern side in the days following the storm. The fact that Cowper ran the information is not a negative reflection in any way – he was writing in good faith with the best information he could get his hands on at the time.

Nevertheless, the '100 metres' figure added fuel to the fire – and made the Japanese actions seem even more heartless. If the Indian climber was '100 metres from safety' then the Japanese failure to rescue him on the 11th was completely indefensible. The figure makes it sound like he was almost within reach.

In fact, having seen the precise position of the lowest of the Indian bodies (i.e., the one nearest to camp six), the figure of 100 metres is way off the mark. As Al, the Sherpas and myself found, the climber was on the Ridge, at least 300 *vertical* metres above camp six – and perhaps as much as 500 metres in actual climbing distance from safety. It had taken us at least four-and-a-half hours of hard, continuous, climbing from camp six to get to the position of the Indian body.

But even those figures do not reveal the true nature of the Indian's position. To have got him down to camp six, any rescuers would have had to have negotiated his semi-conscious body down the yellow band – the massive strata of rock which creates the barrier of crumbling cliffs we had climbed through the night.

The terrain is extremely steep, with several small cliffs which have to be downclimbed with extreme care even by a fit climber. There are few if any secure belay points in the rotten rock, and the snow gulleys – the natural cracks and fissures – which are used for the descent are barely narrow enough to allow a standing climber to pass, let alone big enough for a comatose body to be lowered down.

In short, I do not believe that a rescue attempt was ever a real possibility even if a stretcher was available (it wasn't), and it is my opinion that any climber arriving on the stricken Indians in the position (and condition) they were in on the mountain would immediately conclude, as the Japanese did, that they were beyond rescue.

Why the Japanese climbers did not seek to alleviate the last hours of suffering for the Indians by giving them fluid or oxygen is a separate question and one which only they can answer.

The other debate which our team, like every other, endlessly discussed amongst ourselves was also the subject of intense speculation in the media: why did Rob Hall and Scott Fischer summit so late when they were both known to favour the 'turn-around' tactic of setting a time when team members would be turned back regardless of where they were? What were the turn-around times and why didn't the two teams stick by them?

In his book *Into Thin Air*, journalist Jon Krakauer (a member of Hall's team) writes:

At base camp before our summit bid, Hall had contemplated two possible turn-around times – either 1 p.m. or 2 p.m. He never declared which of these times we were to abide by, however – which was curious, considering how much he'd talked about the importance of designating a hard deadline and sticking to it no matter what. We were simply left with a vaguely articulated understanding that Hall would withhold making a final decision until summit day, after assessing the weather and other factors, and would then personally take responsibility for turning everyone around at the proper hour.

Fischer's group were also not made aware in advance of a specific turn-around time which would be applied although, again, both 1 p.m. and 2 p.m. had been mentioned. In fact, come summit day, both guides were relying on their own experience to decide on the point at which their groups should go no further. This would depend on a complicated set of factors including the speed of the group and the condition of the weather.

On 10 May, by 2 p.m. just six of the climbers had made it to the summit so why weren't the remainder told to retreat? Perhaps one answer is that *most* of them were *extremely* close to the summit at that precise point. Close enough to arrive there in a line of eight climbers from 2.10 onwards. It was over the deadline, yes, but at the moment the deadline had expired, the main group had been perhaps less than fifty metres from the summit and within sight of it. In that situation, it is extremely unlikely that any of the clients would have obeyed the orders of their leaders to retreat, effectively negating the whole point of the turn-around – which requires total discipline by the leader. To turn someone around at the bottom of the Hillary step is one thing, but to try and turn them around as they climbed the final summit ridge would be nigh on inconceivable.

The flaw was that whilst most of the climbers were on the summit on or before 2.30 p.m., two key climbers were not. As the main body of climbers began their descent, Doug Hansen – Hall's client – and Scott Fischer, who was having an extremely hard time on his ascent, were both still battling up. Fischer summitted at 3.40 p.m. and left fifteen minutes later.

Why did Fischer continue to climb up? He'd been to the summit before of course, and all of his clients had summitted and gone down. But Fischer knew that Rob Hall and Lopsang, Fischer's right-hand man and strongest Sherpa, were both on the summit waiting. That knowledge, along with his high level of personal motivation, must have encouraged him to continue. To have turned around himself just under the nose of his friend and competitor would have been a difficult thing to live with. They were both members of the mountaineering élite, and it can be imagined that Fischer would have lost a lot of face if – for whatever reason – he hadn't followed his clients up.

For Hall, too, the presence of Lopsang and Fischer must have been an additional inducement to let Hansen continue. With three (normally) strong guides in place, Hall must have reckoned they would have a fighting chance of getting Hansen down. Three of the strongest guides in the world had lulled themselves into a false sense of security. But by the time Hansen arrived, the exhausted Fischer and Lopsang had already gone.

Rob Hall waited until 4 p.m. for Doug Hansen to reach the summit, a full two hours after his latest announced turn-around time. Why did he allow himself to be trapped into what was (with the benefit of hindsight) clearly a dangerously late summit scenario?

For the probable answer we have to turn back the clock one year, to the Adventure Consultants' summit bid of May 1995. On that expedition, Rob Hall had turned back Doug Hansen at the south summit at about 2 p.m. Hansen had wrestled with the bitter frustration of that 'so near but so far' decision and then decided with Hall's enthusiastic support to give it another go in 1996. Hansen was no millionaire; he had a modest salary as a postal worker and had taken extra work to pay to join the expedition. It was very unlikely that Hansen would ever be able to afford to come again.

The two men were close friends and Hall had a special commitment to get Hansen to the top. As he waited on the summit for his client to appear, Hall must have been fighting a titanic struggle within himself. Turning Hansen around again, this time even closer to the summit than the previous year, would have been an unbearably difficult thing to do.

In the end, the desire for his client to reach the top clouded Hall's judgement sufficiently for him to wait.

And wait.

As Hansen came up, the clouds came with him, and then so did the wind. Fischer and Lopsang were already out of sight. Hall was left on his own with his exhausted client as the storm swept in.

True to the highest principles of his profession, Hall stayed with his client until the end.

*

By 6 June, all members of the Himalayan Kingdoms 1996 North Ridge expedition had returned to their 'normal' lives.

Simon, the expedition leader, returned to the Himalayan Kingdoms office in Sheffield and resumed his duties as operations manager. He plans to return to Everest in 1999 on the southern side, and this will be his fourth attempt at the mountain.

Barney was back in the Himalayas within a few months, guiding a small group of five clients for Himalayan Kingdoms on Cho Oyu (8,201 metres) to the west of Everest. As on our Everest expedition, Barney did not reach the summit, having turned back again with a client. Since then he has been working partly on guiding contracts and partly on petroleum surveys in countries such as Pakistan.

Kees made it back to Toronto for his wedding with forty-eight hours to spare. On the great day his face still bore the ravages of radiation burns from the expedition and he was as thin as a strand of spaghetti. His son, Cornelius Alexander 't Hooft, was born on 19 November. After the birth Katie went back to her work teaching political science at the University of Toronto with Kees fulfilling the duty of house-husband and shooting the occasional film. Kees still makes the odd Club Class journey back to Britain where, for some whimsical reason of his own, he has commissioned a narrow boat to be built to his own exacting specification. Being a lover of fine things, Kees has instructed his boatbuilders to install a floor of solid oak in the five-star canal barge.

'It wasn't quite right,' he told me forlornly, 'so I had them remove it and replace it with teak.'

He watches my incredulous face for a moment then bursts into laughter, seeing I have fallen for it.

Brian returned to the UK sixteen kilogrammes lighter than when he left and gave a press conference in which he told newsmen that he *had* torn the Japanese expedition's flag from its pole and pissed on it – just one of numerous juicy quotes which the conscientious journalists duly reported verbatim. While the Press were taking pictures of Brian in the street outside ITN's Headquarters, a bus driver, distracted by the clamouring hordes, pranged his double decker into a plane tree with a resounding crunch, ending the session – perhaps appropriately – on a note of high farce.

Scarcely pausing to recover from the rigours of the expedition, Brian launched back into the frantic merry-go-round that is his working life. Voice-over sessions, a tour to promote his new Everest book, a season in pantomime in Tunbridge Wells, putting together the new feature film of *Macbeth* that he is to direct.

And of Everest – how did Brian feel about our expedition?

'I feel ashamed of my performance on Everest this year', Brian told me, 'I didn't have the nerve to carry on. But I'll be back in 1999 – to the southern side. Have another go.'

The passion still burns in Brian – that is what makes him special.

Al was not back for long before he was packing his barrels and heading out to Pakistan on a successful summer expedition to climb Gasherbrum 1 and 2 in the Karakorum. That brought his total of 8,000-metre-plus peaks to eight, a world class achievement in its own right. How he found the energy to turn around within a few weeks after the Everest expedition and tackle another mountain is beyond my comprehension. It took me and most of the other members of the expedition months to recover fully.

After Pakistan Al then returned to his Newcastle haunts and resumed his promotional work for the outdoors equipment company Berghaus, doing the rounds of the trade shows and lectures and putting the final touches to a master plan which – if it works – will launch him into the super-élite of high-altitude mountaineering. Under the title 'Challenge 8,000', Al has set himself the target of climbing the remaining six of the fourteen mountains of the world which are higher than 8,000 metres. If he succeeds, he will be the first Briton to have completed the challenge and only the fifth person ever.

The six mountains facing him are Lhotse (8,516 metres), Makalu (8,481 metres), Kanchenjunga (8,586 metres), Nanga Parbat (8,125 metres), Dhaulagiri (8,167 metres) and Annapurna (8,091 metres). As this book goes to press I have had the good news that Al summitted Lhotse on 23 May 1997.

The project is a high risk one: mountain statisticians have calculated that to climb all fourteen of the world's 8,000-metre peaks carries with it a 40% chance of fatality.

Al and I have never spoken about the events of summit day on Everest and my irrational fear that he wasn't going to make it. We don't need to. I realise now that it was the onset of altitude sickness eating into my brain which caused me to become increasingly convinced that he had dropped out of the attempt. The delay when I waited with the three Sherpas for Al to come up the third step, which to me had seemed like an age had in reality probably been just a few minutes while he sorted out his frozen goggles which had caused him trouble all morning. My brain was operating on the paranoid assumption that *something* had to go wrong – and I seized on the slightest evidence to build a theory that it had gone wrong for Al. In fact Al reached the summit not much more than ten or fifteen minutes after the rest of us.

To my surprise, a few of Al's old rivals, scenting perhaps that a flaw had been revealed in his otherwise untouchable 'hard man' image, called me at home after the expedition to relish the details of how I had 'beaten' him to the top; but if they thought I was going to dish the dirt they were disappointed. Al arrived at the summit in immaculate style and when he was there he was lucid enough to hold a long radio conversation with Brian and then put the flag on the summit pole. He also made sure he stayed with me all the way down to camp six, when I am sure he could have moved faster if he had chosen.

Sundeep came home to a £20,000 mountain of debts and the news that he was shortly to be sent to Bosnia with his unit. This was later called off and he went on to attempt the course which would qualify him for P Coy – the selection for British airborne forces. Sadly, a serious shin complaint – perhaps a legacy from the Everest expedition – ruled out his chances. Sundeep resumed his duties as an army medic, trying like crazy to lock away the frustration of having got so close on Everest to his dream of completing the seven summits.

'I was offered a place for £10,000 on an expedition going out in spring '97, but with all the debts from this one to pay off, I just couldn't afford it,' he told me.

Hearing that Sundeep had found this opportunity, Roger quietly offered to lend Sundeep the money; an act of extraordinary generosity which touched me greatly when I heard of it. But other commitments made it impossible for Sundeep to go. At the time of my finishing this book he is with a British Army non-combatant evacuation force in Zaire.

Sundeep can still be the youngest person to complete the challenge of standing on the highest points of each continent – but only if he summits Everest in 1998.

'I will go back,' he told me, 'if I can find the money!'

Roger Portch shaved off his beard, and climbed back into the hot seat of a British Airways 747 ferrying passengers around the world. Madras . . . Muscat . . . Johannesburg . . . Mexico City – his average working month contains a lifetime of travel, but the memories of the Everest expedition will never be eclipsed for Roger no matter how many take-offs and landings he performs.

'I'm learning to live with it – the fact that I didn't make it to the summit – but coming to terms with it is going to take a long time,' he told me. 'But I won't go back. That was my one and only chance. I'm too old to have another try and it really wouldn't be fair on Muriel and the girls. I can't put them through that again.'

There is one particular moment for Roger when thoughts of what might have been are almost too much to bear, and unfortunately it is a moment he goes through every day of his working life. It comes when he is flying, as the digital read-out on the cockpit facia of his Boeing 747 reaches 8,848 metres . . . 29,029 feet. That is when he looks out into the deep lapis blue of the earth's upper atmosphere, savouring the elevation, enjoying the curvature of the earth, wondering . . . dreaming . . . imagining what it might have been like to have taken those final few steps on to the very summit of the world. It is the infinite sadness of a dream that was never quite realised.

Roger still wears the red thread around his neck from our pujah ceremony.

As for me? I returned with my two frostbitten fingers to be told that I was the twenty-seventh Briton to have climbed Everest, and the fifth to have climbed it via the North Face. Quite a few curious friends asked me, 'What *happens* when you climb Everest?'

'What do you mean?'

'You know – invitations to Buckingham Palace for a quiet sherry – toasted tea and crumpets with Lord Hunt at the Royal Geographical Society mulling over the finer points of the route. Medals . . . that sort of thing.'

In fact nothing happens at all, which I find extremely refreshing. The nearest I got to a fanfare was a poster my son Alistair painted in crayon daubed with the legend 'Ruddy Well Done Dad!'. That was tribute enough.

For some weeks I paraded my fingers in front of various specialists. Between them they decided the best thing to do was wait, so I did. After two weeks the blistered skin went green, then black, then as hard as cardboard. Then the frostbitten caps fell off completely revealing, eight weeks later, two more or less perfect fingers underneath. The ends of those fingers will always be ultra-sensitive to heat and cold – and more susceptible to frostbite – but I am lucky to have them at all.

'Another three to four minutes of exposure,' one of the specialists told me, 'and you would have lost both fingers. Another ten minutes and you would have lost a lot more.'

Compared to the frostbite of 'Makalu' Gau and Beck Weathers (both of whom had major amputations) it was nothing at all.

During June and July, I worked on the film, reliving the expedition all over again in a cutting-room at ITN, and finishing the production in just six weeks. It was broadcast on Channel 4 on 26 August. Since then I have made films in Malaysia, Thailand, Yemen, Malawi and Oman, in addition to writing this book. The fact that I have filmed on the summit of Everest does not seem to have made much difference so far to my career. I am still writing movies in my spare time hoping to break out of adventure films.

As a person, I don't think that Everest really changed me at all – a fact which irritates Fiona somewhat as I think she was hoping a perfect butterfly of a husband would somehow emerge from the skeletal, frostbitten pupa that she picked up at Heathrow after the expedition. In fact I am still the same selfish, stubbornly nomadic creature I ever was. I still can't last more than a few days at home before I am pacing the floor thinking about where I am going next. I still lie awake in the early hours of the morning tracing journeys in my mind through the places I haven't yet been. We still share a great many dreams – but the ones we don't share haven't magically disappeared just because I climbed a mountain.

Whether I will ever climb another big mountain is a question I often wonder about. Several people have been kind enough to tell me that the determination I showed on Everest could get me to the top of other peaks. But I am not so sure. The reasons I climbed Everest are, I am now convinced, rooted as much in my mind and my heart as in the pump action of muscle and sinew. I climbed Everest in a moment of my life when a whole internal geyser of frustrations was building up to a pressure-blast of energy. If the chance had come to me some years earlier or some years later, I am not so sure I would have reached the top.

So the conclusion? It's all the same. Everything is the same. Everest is big but it wasn't big enough to change the patterns of a lifetime. The red final-demand bills are still stacked up against the telephone. The mortgage company is still calling to get the back payments we owe them. Our marriage is still locked into the same pattern it ever was . . . of the joy of being together and the pain of being apart. Luckily we can still laugh together, and neither of us can see any way the relationship is really going to change now it has survived Everest.

A part of me is still waiting for the bolt from the blue, the great celestial neon arrow that I didn't see on the summit. Perhaps it is Fiona who should go out and climb a mountain – maybe she *would* see the great celestial arrow when she dragged herself to the top. Perhaps I should suggest it.

But, thinking about it, I'm not so sure that is a good idea. The logistics of hauling all that gin and tonic up the mountain would defeat even the most brilliant leader.

Meanwhile, I am still making adventure films. I have to, to make a living, but my heart has already moved on. I see myself in ten years' time writing and directing movies in Hollywood . . . a noble vision until you realise that everyone who works in television has the same desire. So, I'm doing the only thing I can, letting my imagination fly and writing stories that come from some strange corner of my mind, hoping against hope that I can sell one of my movie scripts and launch myself into a new career before someone calls me up and asks me if I am interested in making a film about an expedition to K2.